John Man is a historian and travel writer with a special interest in Mongolia and the history of written communication. His *Gobi: Tracking the Desert* was the first book on the subject in English since the 1920s. He is also the author of *The Atlas of the Year 1000*, *Alpha Beta*, on the roots of the Roman alphabet, and *The Gutenberg Revolution*, on the origins and impact of printing. His books *Genghis Khan: Life, Death and Resurrection* and *Attila the Hun: A Barbarian King and the fall of Rome* are both published by Bantam Books. His latest book, *The Great Wall*, will be published by Bantam Press later in the year.

Praise for *Attila the Hun*:
'Shatters the clichés . . . As one's guide into this mysterious world, one could not wish for a better storyteller or analyst than John Man . . . His Attila is superb, as compellingly readable as it is impressive in its scholarship: with his light touch, the Huns and their King live as never before. There is something fascinating and new on every page'
Simon Sebag Montefiore

'Attila is known as a savage but there was much more to this great warrior. Man takes his readers on a thrilling ride alongside the man who marauded across Europe, striking terror into the hearts of entire nations' *The Good Book Guide*

'Racy and imaginative . . . sympathetically and readably puts flesh and bones on one of history's most turbulent characters' *Sunday Telegraph*

'There are moments when this book reads a little like a real-life Lord of the Rings . . . Meteoric and momentous . . . fascinating reading' *Guardian*

'The warlord's thunderous rise to infamy is enlivened by Man's constant asides, comments and comparisons. His obvious flair for conversational history and clear ability to get the most from well-informed modern sources drive the narrative along at a pace Attila himself would have been happy with. Man is a one man Time Team' *Western Daily Press*

'More like a piece of travel writing than history, as the author shares his imagination and enthusiasm for what he has found in modern day Hungary . . . the powerful heart of this study is Man's fine reconstruction of the battle on the Catalaunian Plains' *Newdirections*

Also by John Man

Gobi: Tracking the Desert
Atlas of the Year 1000
Alpha Beta
The Gutenberg Revolution
Genghis Khan: Life, Death and Resurrection
Attila the Hun: A Barbarian King and the fall of Rome
The Great Wall

KUBLAI KHAN

From Xanadu to Superpower

John Man

BANTAM BOOKS

LONDON • TORONTO • SYDNEY • AUCKLAND • JOHANNESBURG

KUBLAI KHAN
A BANTAM BOOK : 9780553817188

Originally published in Great Britain by Bantam Press,
a division of Transworld Publishers

PRINTING HISTORY
Bantam Press edition published 2006
Bantam edition published 2007

1 3 5 7 9 10 8 6 4 2

Copyright © John Man 2006
Maps © Malcolm Swanston, Red Lion

Set in 11/13pt Sabon by
Falcon Oast Graphic Art Ltd.

Bantam Books are published by Transworld Publishers,
61–63 Uxbridge Road, London W5 5SA,
a division of The Random House Group Ltd,
in Australia by Random House Australia (Pty) Ltd,
20 Alfred Street, Milsons Point, Sydney, NSW 2061, Australia,
in New Zealand by Random House New Zealand Ltd,
18 Poland Road, Glenfield, Auckland 10, New Zealand,
in South Africa by Random House (Pty) Ltd,
Isle of Houghton, Corner of Boundary Road & Carse O'Gowrie,
Houghton, 2198, South Africa
and in India by Random House Publishers India Private Limited,
301 World Trade Tower, Hotel Intercontinental Grand Complex,
Barakhamba Lane, New Delhi 110 001, India

Printed and bound in Great Britain by
Cox & Wyman Ltd, Reading, Berkshire.

Papers used by Transworld Publishers are natural, recyclable
products made from wood grown in sustainable forests. The
manufacturing processes conform to the environmental
regulations of the country of origin

CONTENTS

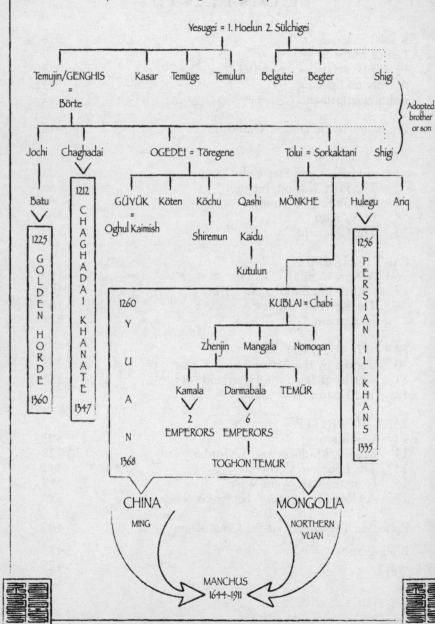

KUBLAI IN CONTEXT

This diagram shows, in simplified form, the main characters mentioned in this book, their relationships, their domains and a rough chronological sequence (GREAT KHANS in CAPITALS).

Yesugei = 1. Hoelun 2. Sülchigei

Temujin/GENGHIS   Kasar   Temüge   Temulun   Belgutei   Begter   Shigi
=
Börte

Adopted brother or son

Jochi   Chaghadai   OGEDEI = Töregene   Tolui = Sorkaktani   Shigi

Batu   1212 CHAGHADAI KHANATE   GÜYÜK = Oghul Kaimish   Köten   Köchu   Qashi   MÖNKHE   Hulegu   Ariq

Shiremun   Kaidu

Kutulun

1225 GOLDEN HORDE 1360   1347

1256 PERSIAN IL-KHANS 1335

1260 YUAN 1368   KUBLAI = Chabi

Zhenjin   Mangala   Nomoqan

Kamala   Darmabala   TEMÜR

2 EMPERORS   6 EMPERORS

TOGHON TEMUR

CHINA   MONGOLIA

MING   NORTHERN YUAN

MANCHUS 1644-1911

MAPS

ILLUSTRATIONS

Pages with no images credited are all © John Man.

FIRST SECTION
Page 1
Tolui and his family, from *Jami al-Tawarikh* by Rashid al-Din, fourteenth-century, Ms sup. pers. 1113 f. 164v, Bibliothèque Nationale, Paris; Karakorum, © Dean Conger/Corbis.

Pages 2 and 3
Alamut: Simon Richmond/Lonely Planet Images; Hassan i Sabbah leading the initiations at Alamut, manuscript illumination by the Boucicaut Master (*fl.*1390–1430): Bibliothèque Nationale, Paris/Bridgeman Art Library; Mongols storming and capturing Baghdad in 1288, from *Jami al-Tawarikh* by Rashid al-Din, fourteenth-century, Ms sup. pers. 1113 f. 180v-181, Bibliothèque Nationale, Paris/Bridgeman Art Library; Mönkhe Khan holds a feast at Karakorum: sixteenth-century illustration of a fourteenth-century Persian history of the Mongols, Werner Forman Archive/Gulistan Library, Teheran.

SECOND SECTION
Pages 2 and 3
Kublai Khan's armies lay siege to the Chinese fortress of O-Chou across a pontoon over the Yangtse River: sixteenth-century illustration of a fourteenth-century Persian history of the Mongols, Werner Forman Archive/Gulistan Library, Teheran; *A Mongol Siege*, detail from a manuscript of Rashid al-Din, Or. MS20 f. 124v, Edinburgh University Library;

modern trebuchet, Caerphilly Castle, Wales: general view and detail, © John Man; plan of Hangzhou from Henry Yule, *The Book of Ser Marco Polo*, volume II, 1903.

Pages 4 and 5
Street theatre, Guyuan, Gansu province, 2002, photo © John Man; *The Student Chang Bidding Farewell to his lover Ying Ying at the Rest Pavilion*, detail of an illustration of 'The Romance of the Western Chamber' by Wen Zhengming (1470–1559) and Qiu Ying (c.1494–1552), private collection/© Christie's Images/Bridgeman Art Library; Yuan dynasty terracotta figurine of an actor whistling, from Jiaozuo, Henan: Lauros/Giraudon/Bridgeman Art Library; *Sheep and Goat* by Zhao Mengfu (c.1254–1322), Smithsonian Institution, Freer Gallery of Art, Washington, D.C./© Photo Scala, Florence; Yuan dynasty Qingbai vase, with the distinctive *qingbai* (greenish-blue) glaze from Jingdezhen in Jiangxi Province in southern China, © Royal Ontario Museum/CORBIS.

Pages 6 and 7
White Pagoda, Beihai Park, Beijing, Panorama Media (Beijing) Ltd/Alamy; Kublai Khan in council with his courtiers and scribes: sixteenth-century illumination of a fourteenth-century Persian history of the Mongols, Werner Forman Archive/Gulistan Library, Teheran; manuscript illumination by the Boucicaut Master (fl.1390–1430): how the Great Khan used tree bark as currency, Bibliothèque Nationale, Paris/Archives Charmet/Bridgeman Art Library; bank note from Henry Yule, *The Book of Ser Marco Polo*, volume II, 1903.

Page 8
Mongol Rider with Administrator, Yuan dynasty, The Art and History Trust, Courtesy of the Arthur M. Sackler Gallery, Smithsonian Institution, Washington, D.C. LTS 1995.2.7.

THIRD SECTION
Page 1
Inset, explosive shell, © John Man; Japanese Invasion Scroll: both courtesy The Art Archive.

Pages 2 and 3
Japanese Invasion Scroll: courtesy The Art Archive; all other photos © John Man.

Pages 4 and 5
Kublai Khan hunting and portrait of Chabi, National Palace Museum, Taipei; portrait of Kublai Khan: courtesy The Art Archive.

Pages 6 and 7
Kublai Khan and the Polo brothers from an illuminated manuscript of 1375, Bibliothèque Nationale, Paris (MS 2810)/akg-images; paiza, © John Man; illumination from the *Chronica Major* of Matthew Paris, Corpus Christi College, Cambridge, MS 16 f. 166v; details from Giotto's *Resurrection*, *c*.1305, Arena Chapel, Padua, © Photo Scala, Florence; autograph manuscript of Samuel Taylor Coleridge, *Kubla Khan*, 1798, © The British Library Add. Mss. 50847/Heritage Image Partnership; illustration to *Kubla Khan* from A. C. Michael, *A Day With Samuel Taylor Coleridge*, 1912, Mary Evans Picture Library; other photos © John Man.

A NOTE ON SPELLING

The two main systems of transliterating Chinese, Wade–Giles and pinyin, still overlap. Although pinyin is now standard usage, I have used whichever seems more appropriate in each case, keeping the older spelling for names that have become most familiar to western readers in that form as well as for those that appear in a more remote historical context.

Spellings of personal names vary widely. For ease of reading, I have in this book used the more familiar form 'Kublai' rather than, for example, 'Khubilai', 'Qubilai' or 'Kubla'.

'Genghis' is still the most common spelling in English, though the more correct 'Chingis' is coming up fast.

ACKNOWLEDGEMENTS

With thanks to: Charles Bawden, who started it all; Anne Cullen, who introduced me to Zhao Mengfu; Chuluun Dalai, Mongolian Academy of Sciences; Paul Denney and Julie Douglass, for opening the world of trebuchets; Yuefan Deng, Stonybrook University, NY; Luc Kwanten and Lilly Chen, Big Apple-Tuttle Mori, Shanghai; Shizuya Nishimura, Professor Emeritus, Hosei University, Tokyo; Benjamin Ren, for hospitality at Shang-du (Xanadu); Professor Yao Dali, History Department, Fudan University, Shanghai; Yuan-chu Ruby Lam, Department of Chinese, Wellesley College, MA; Igor de Rachewiltz, School of Pacific and Asian Studies, Australian National University, for vital and unstinting guidance through the fog of ignorance; Randall Sasaki, Texas A&M University, for an initial introduction to Kublai's lost fleet, and Kenzo Hayashida, who generously showed me the remains of the Japanese wall in Fukuoka and the finds made by him and his colleagues off Takashima; 'William' Shou (Wei Zhong) and Shijun Cheng, for the Xanadu trip; Helen Tang, the best of Chinese teachers; Jack Weatherford, Macalester College, Minnesota; Doug Young, Simon Thorogood and all at Transworld; Gillian Somerscales, for brilliant editing; and as ever, Felicity Bryan, Michelle Topham *et al.*

KUBLAI KHAN

PROLOGUE:
TO GENGHIS, A GRANDSON

IN 1215, THE WORLD WAS NOT A JOINED-UP PLACE. PEOPLE and animals alike travelled at an amble. It took days to reach the next town, weeks to cross a country. The great continental land masses were island universes, knowing next to nothing of each other. No-one went from Asia to Australia, except a few inhabitants of Sulawesi, who crossed the Timor Sea to collect sea-cucumbers, then as now a delicacy much in demand in China. No-one from Eurasia visited the Americas, except a few Inuit paddling back and forth across the Bering Strait. In Greenland, communities of Norwegians were thriving in a long warm spell that kept their seas ice-free for a few crucial months, but these hardy voyagers had never been tempted to repeat their forefathers' brief attempt at colonizing the American mainland two centuries before. Ships hugged shorelines; with the remarkable exception of Polynesian canoes island-hopping the Pacific, few yet tackled the open oceans.

But there were signs, if not of globalization, then at least of regionalization. Europe and Asia had a head start, because they were two continents in one. The links between them had once been forged by great empires and cultures: Rome, Persia, China. Now they were forged by religion.

In Europe, Christian scholars from Ireland (and even Iceland) chatted in Latin to their counterparts in Rome, and architects from Assisi to York vied for glory with flying buttresses and tracery; in Reims, they were five years into the creation of one of France's greatest Gothic cathedrals. The church had found new muscle, having ruined much of southern France in a vicious crusade to wipe out the heretical Albigensians. That year the pope condemned them at the 4th Lateran Council (which also, by the way, excommunicated the English barons who had just forced King John to sign away some of his divine right in the Magna Carta).

Europe was reaching outwards as well: a certain Albert, from Buxtehude in north Germany, pushing Christianity into the Baltic regions, had just founded Riga, where he put on a biblical play with the aim of converting the locals. It was the first play the Latvians had ever seen. When Gideon attacked the Philistines on stage, they thought it was for real, and fled for their lives. The same church council that castigated the Albigensians also looked south-east beyond the borders of European Christendom, where there lay a constant affront to Christian sensibilities: Islamic control of what Christians called the Holy Land. There would have to be yet another crusade.

Crusaders had been forging rather unwelcome links between Christian Europe and the Islamic Middle East for over a century, building Christian enclaves in present-day Syria, Lebanon and Israel. Nor was all the hostility directed against the 'heathen'. Nine years earlier, soldiers of the Fourth Crusade, supposedly on their way to Egypt, had shown themselves to be particularly cynical by seizing Constantinople from its Orthodox rulers. In 1215 they held it still, steadily undermining all hopes of a unified Christendom.

Islam, though, was now more than a match for Christianity. Scholars and traders could travel from Spain, across north Africa and the Middle East to Central Asia, and find common roots in Islam's 500-year-old religious community, in 'God's tongue' (Arabic), in the Qur'an and in trade – in slaves, for instance, and gold, both of which flowed from sub-Saharan Africa. A Muslim merchant could travel from Timbuktu to Delhi and be sure of finding some like-minded trader there; and if he went via Baghdad, as he would because it was the heart of Islam, he would mix with Jews, Zoroastrians, Manicheans and Christians of many sects – Nestorians, Monophysites, Gnostics and the Greek Orthodox. Arab captains found it worthwhile to sail the coasts for a year or two all the way to southern China to load up with silks and porcelain.

As for overland links between west and east, they had once been much stronger, thanks to the trade routes known as the Silk Road. Now fewer camel trains made the six-month haul between the world of Islam and China. The Mongols under Genghis Khan had recently assaulted the key Buddhist state of Xi Xia, north of Tibet, in present-day Xinjiang, and few had faith that camel caravans would get through unscathed.

The connections were all very tenuous. But these places and cultures, so distant from each other in time and space, were about to be jolted together, thanks to two events occurring that very year.

The first was a great assault against the major city of north China, today's Beijing. The besiegers were the Mongols, led by Genghis Khan. Genghis had risen from nowhere and nothing – a down-and-out fugitive, in fact – to found a nation, and was now seeking to fulfil his destiny. Having survived many a close call in his youth, he had realized, much to his surprise, that he had been chosen by Heaven to rule. To rule what and whom, exactly? Certainly, his own Mongols. But then, as conquest followed conquest, he saw that the domain accorded him by his divine brief was wider. How wide? North China? Probably. *All* China, although no nomad power had ever managed it? Possibly.

North China, the source of wealth and power, had always lured warrior nomads from beyond the Gobi desert, and had always done its best to defend itself – with walls, armies, bribery, diplomacy and marriages. North China was the traditional enemy, the key to wider empire, and Beijing, the seat of the region's Jin rulers, was the key to north China. It should have fallen the previous year, after a series of long campaigns during which Genghis had neutralized the Tangut empire of Xi Xia and invaded, devastating much of the country north of the Yellow River and besieging Beijing until the Jin emperor capitulated. In 1214 Genghis had left Beijing untaken and unpillaged, thinking that he had a new vassal – only to discover, when the Mongol armies withdrew to the grasslands, that the Jin emperor had decamped, with 3,000 camels and 30,000 cartloads of possessions, to the ancient Chinese capital of Kaifeng, well south of the Yellow River.

Genghis was furious. 'The Jin Emperor mistrusts my word!' he stormed. 'He has used the peace to deceive me!'

Now the Mongols were back, and this time there would be no let-up until Beijing fell, and the whole empire of Jin was Mongol. All through the winter of 1214–15 the Mongol army blockaded the city. There would be no outright assault, for Beijing was too formidable, with 15 kilometres of walls, 900 guard-towers, catapults that could throw boulders and fire-bombs, and vast siege bows that could fire arrows the size of telegraph poles. No: Beijing would be starved into surrender.

So it happened. On 31 May Beijing opened its gates. In the subsequent onslaught, many thousands died; fires burned for a month. A year later, there were still bodies lying about, and disease ran wild. A Muslim envoy reported that the ground remained greasy with human fat.

The fall of Beijing in 1215 unlocked a series of events that changed the course of Eurasian history. It was not yet the end for north China, because Genghis was distracted from his assault by events further west. Four years later a trade delegation to the new Islamic state of Khwarezm was slaughtered in its entirety. With north China neutralized, Genghis was free to turn on his western neighbours in swift vengeance, unleashing devastation on an unprecedented scale and razing the old Silk Road cities of Bukhara, Samarkand, Merv and Urgench. Then he sanctioned an extraordinary campaign of reconnaissance across Georgia and Ukraine, the opening phase of 200 years of Mongol rule in southern Russia. Only when his men returned from this great adventure did Genghis turn once again to the lands across the Gobi. In the summer of 1227, extending his campaign into mountains south of the Yellow River, he died.

His great task remained unfinished. Much of the Islamic world, including Baghdad itself, was still unconquered, as were the Russian steppes, and the remaining pockets of north China, and all of south China – a separate state ruled by the Song dynasty – and beyond that the outlying peoples who must, inevitably, acknowledge the overlordship of Genghis: those on the eastern rim of the Mongol empire (Korea and Japan) and those to the south (present-day Cambodia, Vietnam and Burma) and all those beyond across the rich islands of Indonesia, while way to the west, the Hungarian grasslands would surely be a highway into Christian Europe.

This was the Mongols' Heaven-ordained destiny. Why this should be, Genghis never fathomed, nor did his heirs; they simply accepted that it was so.

Much unfinished business, then: but already on his death Genghis had transformed his world. Never before had East and West been so tightly linked. Mongolian generals now had intimate knowledge of the rivalries of Russian princes, and how to divide them further when the time came. Express riders galloping some 150 kilometres a day, with numerous changes of mount, could deliver a message over the 4,000 kilometres from Beijing to Afghanistan in six weeks, an operation made possible by Mongol control of all the land in between.

What, then, might not be achieved, given an extension of this empire? Traders would bring the wealth of East and West, artists would flock to serve the World-Conqueror, clerics of every religion would bring their insights, scholars would collect and translate books from the greatest libraries, embassies would arrive from rulers of East and West to offer their submissions. The world would be one under Heaven, and at peace. Such was the vision that filled the minds of Genghis's heirs.

It was, of course, a hopeless dream, as time would show. Like all empires, this one would reach limits, divide against itself, and dissolve.

But on 23 September 1215, almost four months after Beijing fell, back in the Mongolian heartland, a royal child was born who, as khan of khans, the Great Khan, would accept the challenge of Genghis's impossible vision and do more than any other leader to make it a reality. With an authority that reached, albeit shakily, from the Pacific to southern Russia, he would become the most powerful man who had ever lived – who *would* ever live until the emergence of the modern superpowers. He would hold nominal sway over one-fifth of the world's populated land masses, perhaps half of all humanity. His name would spread far beyond the areas he conquered, to Europe, to Japan, to Vietnam, to Indonesia: those sea-cucumber gatherers, harvesting their delicacies off northern Australia, would perhaps hear of his attempt to invade Java in 1292. It was the legend of his wealth that, two centuries after his death, would inspire Columbus to head westward on a voyage that ended, not in a new route to an ancient land, but in the chance rediscovery of one long forgotten. Had he not existed, had there been no Mongol empire in China, who, I wonder, would have rediscovered America?

The Great Khan's legacy was an enlarged and unified China, with its present-day borders, give or take a few bits and pieces round the edge. By a strange irony, one of those bits is Mongolia itself, the Great Khan's country of birth. It is a truth only grudgingly acknowledged in China that today's superpower owes its self-image as a geographical entity – the dusty north, the lush south, the huge western deserts, the high fastness of Tibet – to the Mongolian baby born in the year of Beijing's destruction.

The boy was Genghis's grandson, Kublai.

I

SPRING

1

A LIONESS AND HER CUBS

ONE THING YOU NOTICE IN MONGOLIA: THE WOMEN command attention. In the countryside, crones with walnut faces skewer you with direct, self-confident eyes; tough, red-cheeked girls ride like master-horsemen. In Ulaanbaatar, the capital, you cannot walk from the main square to the department store (there is only one) without passing a beauty radiating elegance, and proud of it. They have a bearing, an assurance, that is more New York than Beijing. Not all, of course, because Mongolia has its share of poverty. But for centuries Mongolia's nomadic, herding traditions ensured that women matched their men in self-reliance. Even today, country women not only cook and mend and raise the children – they hunt and herd if they have to. One of Genghis Khan's decrees reflected an every-day reality: 'Women accompanying the troops carry out the work and duties of the men when these go to war.' They fought as well. In 1220, Genghis's daughter led the final assault on the Persian town of Nishapur, slaying 'all the survivors save only 400 persons who were selected for their craftsmanship'.[1] In family life and in politics alike women have always been a force. Inheritance was through the male line, but widows – upper-class widows, that is – could take over their late husbands' estates, which made some of them rich, powerful and fiercely independent. It is a strange fact that the world's greatest land empire, the very image of masculine dominance, owed its existence and growth to extraordinary women.

As a child, young Genghis was a down-and-out, cared for by his widowed mother Hoelun, who was rejected by her clan and reduced to scrabbling on mountain flanks for juniper berries. It was Hoelun who showed him what it took to survive; how to rebuild family links, call upon traditional friendships, create new ones, forge alliances and reward loyalty, never seeking personal gain, always looking out for ordinary people and their families. If he went wrong, she would rant at him until he saw the error of his ways. When as a teenager he killed his own half-brother, thus ensuring that he would become the unchallenged head of the family, she gave him hell. The Mongols' foundation document, *The Secret History of the Mongols*, records her words in verse. 'You who have destroyed life!' she yells, and compares him to many sorts of animal in acts of viciousness and stupidity. How could he do such a thing when they had nothing going for them except their own unity as a family, at a time when—

---

[1] Ata-Malik Juvaini, *Genghis Khan: The History of the World Conqueror*, trans. and ed. J. A. Boyle.

We have no friend but our shadow,
We have no whip but our horse's tail?

Genghis learned his lesson, and was keen for others to learn it too, because it was surely he who, in his maturity, encouraged his bards to turn this story into song. As emperor, Genghis honoured – some say feared – his mother all her long life.

The wife Genghis gave to his son Tolui was another one in the same mould. Her name was Sorkaktani, and she is the focus of this chapter, because in 1215, although she could not have had an inkling of the fact, she held the future in her hands – and not just because of the new-born Kublai. Of her five children, two became emperors and a third ruled Persia. Had it not been for her ambition, foresight, good sense and a couple of interventions at crucial moments, Genghis's empire might have dissipated in family squabbles 20-odd years after it was created, and Kublai would never have come into his inheritance.

Sorkaktani was not even a Mongol. She was a Kerait; and her upbringing in this Turkish-speaking group that dominated central Mongolia when Genghis was born provided good training in the politics of Inner Asia. The Kerait king, Toghrul – 'falcon' in Turkish – was Sorkaktani's uncle. He was the alpha ruler among the many heads of the clans that grazed the grasslands beyond the Great Wall, with good contacts to the west and south. Toghrul's people had been converted to a form of Christianity by Nestorian missionaries, followers of the heretic Nestorius who had claimed that Christ was both God and man equally, two persons in one, not the single, indivisible Word-Made-Flesh of mainstream Christianity. But Toghrul also had relations with north China, in later life being awarded the title of prince (*wang*), becoming better known to historians as Wang Khan, 'Prince King'. He had been crucial in the fortunes of Genghis's father, who had come to Toghrul's aid on several occasions and become his 'sworn brother'. Under Genghis, the relationship had started well, but it went sour, and the two ended up fighting a war from which Genghis emerged as victor.

Toghrul had a younger brother, Jakha, whose story reflects the complexities and dangers of the shifting alliances among the steppe tribes of Inner Asia. Jakha had been raised among the Tangut people of Xi Xia, the Buddhist state of present-day Xinjiang, and rose among them to the rank of commander – *gambu* in Tangut, which became part of his name: Jakha Gambu. As a warlord with his own small army he returned to Mongolia, joining Genghis at a time when Mongols and Keraits were still friends – and, unlike Toghrul, remaining true to him when things went wrong between the Mongols and Keraits. In the decade-long inter-tribal war for national unity, Keraits fought on both sides. When the main body of Keraits was beaten in about 1200, Genghis forged the tribes together with marriages. Jakha had two daughters. The elder, Ibaqa, Genghis took as one of his own wives – quite an honour for her proud and loyal father – though he later handed her on to one of his generals. The younger one, Sorkaktani, he gave to his youngest son, the teenage Tolui, right at the start of his distinguished military career. Over the following years of a marriage punctuated by her husband's long absences on campaigns in China and Muslim lands she produced four sons, so gaining both a motive and a means to win friends and influence people.

Among them, her four boys would dominate much of Asia for 50 years, and redefine the course of its history.

But she had a long wait for time's whirligig to spin in her favour.

Sorkaktani's first lucky break, if you can call it that, came when Genghis died in 1227. Genghis had decreed that his third son Ogedei would be his heir as emperor, with all four sons exercising personal authority over their own areas. Jochi, the eldest, had received what is today Russia, from half way across Siberia to the Black Sea; but he had died shortly before Genghis, and the area was inherited by his sons, Orda and Batu. Central Asia from the Aral Sea to Tibet went to Chaghadai. Ogedei's personal estate was Xi Xia (basically, most of western China) and north China. Tolui, the youngest, as tradition demanded, inherited the lands of his father's 'hearth', which in this case meant the whole of Mongolia. This was what would, in due course, give Sorkaktani her power base.

The division involved much wishful thinking, because the borderlands were rather vague and still much disputed by locals. North China was only half conquered; Khwarezm still needed pacifying; Russian princes, though beaten once, would not stay beaten. The strongest position was Tolui's, because he had authority over the heartland with a ready-made corps of civil servants. In addition – since herdsmen were also soldiers – he could in theory have exercised some control over the army. This, though, was a possibility he would not exploit, being not only subject to Ogedei but happily so: the two brothers were very fond of each other. There would be no challenge from Tolui, and thus no reason yet for Sorkaktani to dream of glory for her sons.

Ogedei began his reign with a flurry of martial activity

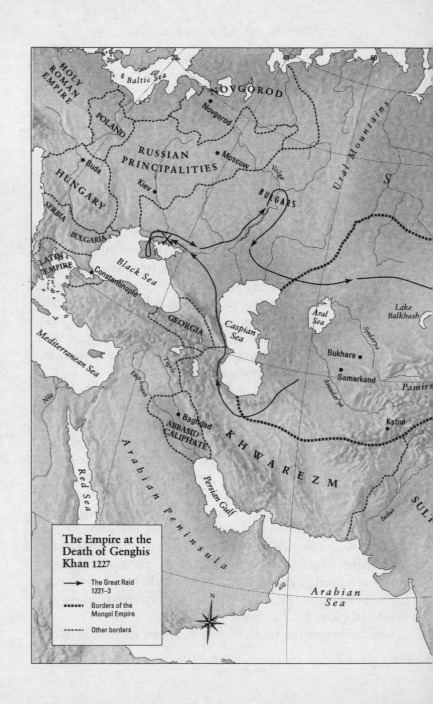

The Empire at the
Death of Genghis
Khan 1227

→ The Great Raid
1221–3

▪▪▪▪▪ Borders of the
Mongol Empire

----- Other borders

100

120

140

S i b e r i a

Altai Mtns.

Lake
Baikal

Burkhan Khaldun

Avraga

Kherlen

40

Sea of
Japan

M O N G O L   E M P I R E

Gobi Desert

Yellow River

Ordos
Desert

Beijing
(Zhongdu)

KOREA

JAPAN

Shan

Makan
Desert

Kunlun Mountains

JIN

Kaifeng

Yellow
Sea

East
China
Sea

Hangzhou
(Linan)

TIBET

Lhasa

Yangtze

SONG

20

alayas

Dali

F DELHI

Bay of
Bengal

South
China
Sea

0   1000 km

0   1000 miles

in pursuit of his father's vision, in four huge and independent campaigns. One re-established the Mongols in Iran, seizing it from its Seljuk rulers. An invasion of Korea began a conquest that would not be finalized until 1260. And in 1231 came the return to north China, which had been Genghis's immediate aim when he died. The Mongol forces advanced in three wings, commanded respectively by the greatest of Genghis's generals, the one-eyed Subedei; Ogedei himself; and Tolui, who had conquered several towns on the first invasion 20 years previously.

Sorkaktani's next stroke of luck was that, early in the campaign into north China, her husband Tolui died. *The Secret History* tells of his death in a well-spun account intended to dramatize the loyalty of a younger brother towards his elder, of a general towards his emperor. Soon after the start of the campaign in 1231, Ogedei falls ill. Land and water spirits rage within him – delirium tremens probably, the result of a lifetime of alcohol abuse. Shamans go into a huddle to divine the cause. After examining the entrails of slaughtered animals, they state that a sacrifice is needed. But no sooner have the shamans gathered captives, gold, silver, cattle and food for the offering than Ogedei becomes worse. What now? A question arises: Could a member of the khan's family serve as a substitute? Tolui is in attendance, and volunteers to take on Ogedei's illness. But how? Another shamanistic huddle, more advice. Tolui will have to drink an alcoholic potion of some kind, which will attract Ogedei's illness to him. Tolui agrees: 'Shamans, cast your spells and make your incantations!' What he does not know is that Ogedei is suffering not simply an illness but death-pangs. That's the burden he unwittingly assumes. Tolui drinks. The potion works fast. He just has time to consign his family to Ogedei's care before words fail him. 'I have said all I have to say,' he slurs. 'I have become drunk.' On that he passes out, never to regain consciousness. In *The Secret History*'s abrupt words, 'Such was the manner in which he died.' Well, perhaps; or perhaps he just died from drinking too much. Ogedei, distraught at the loss of his brother, never recovered his health. Grief became an excuse for yet more drinking, which he would somehow survive for another ten years.

Tolui's death opened a new chapter for Sorkaktani, as his widow, at the heart of an expanding empire. It was traditional in Mongol society for the widow of a wealthy man to administer her husband's estates until her eldest son was of an age to do so. As it happened, her eldest Mönkhe was already 21, but still Ogedei gave Sorkaktani enduring authority to handle Tolui's estates: her family, an army of her own, a secretariat and the local population, 'all should be under the control of her command and prohibition, her loosening and binding, and should not turn their heads from her commandment'. In essence, Sorkaktani became the queen of Mongolia, though subject to her emperor.

Fate had made her independent, and she, in her forties, was shrewd and ambitious enough to stay that way. When Ogedei proposed that she marry his son (and her nephew) Güyük – an alliance that would have linked the two main family lines – she courteously declined, saying that her prime responsibility was to her own sons. She never did remarry. She ruled well for the next 15 years, earning herself an unrivalled reputation for wisdom and firmness. Reports by outsiders all concurred. 'Among the Tartars this lady is the most renowned, with the exception of the emperor's mother,' wrote one of the pope's envoys, John of Plano Carpini.[2] 'Extremely intelligent and able,' said Rashid ad-Din, going on to praise her 'great ability, perfect wisdom and shrewdness and consideration of the latter end of things'. 'All the princes marvelled at her power of administration,' said a Hebrew physician, Bar Hebraeus, and added a verse quotation: 'If I were to see among the race of women another woman like this, I should say that the race of women was far superior to men.'

Her good sense was apparent in the way she raised her four boys. She made sure they were well educated in traditional Mongol ways and knew all about Genghis's law codes. But the empire was wide, and had many faiths. She knew from her own experience – a Kerait and a Christian married to a Mongol shamanist – how important it was not to alienate allies and subjects. So there were tutors in Buddhism, Nestorianism and Confucianism, and, later, wives who were chosen in Sorkaktani's own image – assertive, dynamic, intelligent, undogmatic and highly independent, thus carrying on the tolerance that had been one of Genghis's more surprising traits. Mönkhe, the eldest son, chose to remain a shamanist, but was married to a Nestorian; Hulegu, later ruler of Islamic Persia, also married a Nestorian. Kublai would marry several times, but his lifelong companion was his second wife Chabi, a famous beauty and an ardent Buddhist.

Meanwhile, the empire grew, and wealth flowed in. Kaifeng, the Jin capital, fell in May 1233, forcing the Jin emperor to flee (he was surrounded near the Song border and committed suicide). Twenty years after Genghis's first

[2] He is referring to Güyük's mother, Töregene, of whom more shortly.

invasion, all north China was in Mongol hands. Between 1236 and 1242, a western campaign extended Mongol control across the Russian steppes into Poland and Hungary. At home, Ogedei continued the process started by Genghis of building a sound base for imperial administration, with written laws and censuses and a flow of tax revenue.

Ogedei now saw what Genghis had seen: that an empire of this complexity could not be ruled from a campsite. He needed a capital, a replacement for the old Mongol base of Avraga on the Kherlen river. This place, which still awaits a detailed archaeological survey, stands on the southern edge of the original Mongol heartland, where the Khenti mountains give way to grasslands. To the north lie mountains, forests and safety; to the south, pastures and Gobi and China, the source of trade and booty. For a clan it was a perfect HQ; but not for an empire. Genghis knew the best place from which to rule his newly founded nation. It lay further west, in the valley of the Orkhon river, where previous Turkish empires had ruled. Turks called it Khara Khorum, 'Black Boulder'. Genghis had chosen it as his new capital in 1220, but had done nothing much about it. Ogedei launched his reign in 1228 with a huge gathering in Avraga, where in all probability he supervised the gathering of the tales and information that went into *The Secret History of the Mongols*, but already he had grander plans. It was he, once again, who fulfilled his father's dream, starting to turn Karakorum into a permanent settlement in 1235, just after the conquest of north China, just before the next push westward.

Earthen walls with four gates surrounded a small town, including a palace, with wooden floors, wooden pillars, a tiled roof and nearby cellars for the storage of treasures –

recent digs found several statues and some terracotta heads of Buddha. Attached were private apartments, while in front stood a giant stone tortoise bearing an engraved pillar, like those that commonly guard Chinese temples – the very tortoise, perhaps, that still holds a lonely vigil beside Karakorum's replacement, the monastery of Erdene Zuu. Inside, a central aisle led to steps, on which stood Ogedei's throne. Of course, Mongols never did cities – and still don't: as any visitor to Ulaanbaatar will tell you, the zest of the place comes from the people, not the buildings. So it must have been in Karakorum. Soon, one-third of the town was taken up with government departments controlling sacrifices, shamans, merchants, the postal relay system, treasuries and arsenals. But even when Muslim merchants and Chinese craftsmen began to crowd inside the walls, it wasn't much of a town. Friar William of Rubrouck saw it in 1253–4, and was not impressed: 'You should know that discounting the Khan's palace, it is not as fine as the town of St Denis, and the monastery of St Denis is worth ten times that palace.'

Never mind: it was a centre, where previously there had been no centre; and here gathered felt tents (*gers*, as Mongolians call them) by the hundred, wagons by the thousand and animals by the ten thousand. Rich Mongols, of whom by now there were hundreds, each had anything up to 200 ox-drawn wagons, which would be linked into huge trains of 20–30 teams-and-wagons, all strung together lumbering slowly across the open steppe driven by one woman in the lead wagon. Perhaps a visitor would have seen a huge cart, 10 metres across, with axles like masts, drawn by 22 oxen, on which stood the imperial tent. Some doubt that such a vehicle existed, but there are at least three replicas in Ulaanbaatar today, and one of them lumbers round the stadium every July during the National Day celebrations. No-one knows how or where such a monstrosity was used, but in the 1230s it could have creaked its way back and forth between old Avraga and new Karakorum.

Such was Ogedei's headquarters for his newly formed administration.[3] In this his main guide was Genghis's Chinese adviser, an extremely tall (6 feet 8 inches) Khitan from the aristocratic Yeh-lü family, Chu-tsai (Chuzai in pinyin) by name. The Khitans had once ruled north China, until conquered by the Jin in 1125. Chu-tsai's father had chosen to serve the new regime, and in due course Chu-tsai followed, rising to become vice-prefect of Beijing. Although only in his early twenties, he was a famous figure, noted for his brilliance, his height, his sonorous voice and his waist-length beard. He had endured the city's sack in 1215, retired to a monastery for three years to regain his peace of mind, then – such was his reputation – been summoned to meet Genghis in Mongolia. Genghis offered him the job of head of the newly formed chancery, responsible for the scribes who recorded laws and taxes. It was an offer Chu-tsai was not expected to refuse, because, as Genghis said, the Khitans and the Jin had been enemies, and 'I have avenged you.' Chu-tsai had the nerve to point out that he and his father had been loyal servants of the Jin. Did Genghis really

[3] And for this reason it may be resurrected as the seat of Mongolia's government. In 2005, top officials were discussing a startling proposal, backed by the Prime Minister, to build a totally new capital in Karakorum. A decision is supposed to be made in 2006, the 800th anniversary of the founding of the nation by Genghis Khan.

expect him to regard his father and his ex-employers as enemies? Genghis took the point, offered him the job anyway, and always thereafter had the greatest respect for 'Long Beard', as he called him. Chu-tsai travelled with Genghis into Muslim lands in 1219 and on his master's final campaign in China in 1226–7. In 1229 Ogedei made him the provisional head of the new secretariat – in effect, governor – for those parts of north China that had already been conquered, the first civilian official to hold such wide responsibilities. In the same year, Ogedei appointed a foreigner of equal eminence as governor of his Muslim lands. His name was Mahmud, known as Yalavach (Turkish for 'the envoy', because that had been his first job under Genghis).

It was Chu-tsai who did his best to guide Ogedei away from a life of drinking and hunting and towards fiscal prudence. This was a political as well as a personal struggle, because traditionalists at court considered horses and cattle as the only true wealth, despised the land-grubbing Chinese and seriously suggested that the best use for north China was to depopulate all the farms and turn them over to pasture. Who cared what happened to the millions of peasants? They were worthless anyway. Chu-tsai pointed out that such callousness was self-destructive. Better to nurture the peasants and tax them, through officials who would collect silk, grain and silver. In 1230 Chu-tsai proved the system worked: he delivered 10,000 silver ingots. The following year, he was confirmed in his post.

Naturally, his Mongol colleagues were left seething. They saw Chu-tsai's proposals as a plot to deprive them of their just rewards and divert cash from their own pockets into the emperor's coffers. Ogedei didn't help because his response to this sudden influx of cash was simply to become doubly profligate, demanding money both for his military campaigns and to invest in Muslim businessmen, who promised high returns. Chu-tsai's reforms hit a dead end when Ogedei handed over tax collection to a Muslim 'tax farmer' called Abd al-Rahman. His cronies would buy the right to tax, with the freedom to impose whatever interest they wanted – up to 100 per cent per annum (Ogedei considerately banned higher rates). They became the Mongols' loan sharks, setting in motion a vicious circle of scams. The Muslim businessmen would lend Ogedei's money at exorbitant rates of interest to the unfortunate peasants, who needed the loans to make good what had been lost in taxes. The result was predictable: people fled their homes to avoid the tax collectors and their strong-arm gangs. According to one estimate, 50 per cent of the population were either of no fixed abode or enslaved by Mongol officials. Chu-tsai was effectively sidelined, and died three years after Ogedei, a broken man.

Sorkaktani, already a power in the Mongol heartland, benefited from these upheavals, and learned from them. In 1236, two years after Ogedei completed the conquest of north China, she asked for part of Hebei province as her appanage, her personal estate. Ogedei hesitated, but not for long. As Rashid ad-Din said, he 'used to consult her on all affairs of state and would never disregard her advice'. She quickly shamed him into compliance by pointing out that the place was hers by right anyway, because her husband had conquered it.

Travelling to it, she and her family – including the

21-year-old Kublai – would have seen the terrible destruction caused by the Mongol war machine: abandoned farms, overgrown fields, empty villages, refugees. There had been two other barbarian invasions in the past three centuries, but nothing like this. By 1234 the population of the north, perhaps 40 million people in the early thirteenth century, had dropped by three-quarters from 7.6 million households down to 1.7 million. This figure is so astonishing that many scholars simply don't believe it. There must be something wrong with the way the statistics were gathered, but no-one knows what. Perhaps households were broken up. Perhaps millions fled south. In any event, even if the drop was 'only' by a half or two-thirds, the social consequences were catastrophic.

Zhengding (Chen-ting), about 200 kilometres south-west of present-day Beijing, had escaped more lightly than most settled areas because it had been granted to a local warlord who had surrendered to Genghis. He had organized a self-defence force of peasant farmers, who preserved the area as an enclave of peace and stability, providing his son, Shi Tianze, with some good admin-istrative experience. Even so, it was not a place many Mongols would have bothered with. It was famed for its Buddhist temples, pagodas and statues; it still is, and some of them are the same ones that Sorkaktani knew, like the vast 22-metre-high bronze figure of the many-eyed and many-armed Buddhist deity Avalokiteshvara, who waves her 42 arms at tourists in the main temple complex. The area is on the western rim of the great north China plain, where rich farmland gives way to low hills rolling between river valleys. Its 80,000 households, probably over half a million people, would have been totally uninteresting to more traditional Mongols, who saw farmers as dross and farms as potential pastures. Not Sorkaktani. Thanks to Genghis's foresight and Chu-tsai's example, she spotted a chance to build up her personal wealth well away from the city areas ruined by the Mongol invasions. She would nurture her estates and their peasant farmers, flatter the local population by hiring Chinese tutors for her children, and woo them by patronizing Buddhism and Taoism (local rumour even claimed she had abandoned Nestorianism) – and wealth would flow to her and her family in the form of taxes.

The same year, she forged another link in this sensible scheme. Kublai received an estate of his own 100 kilometres south of his mother's, a region of some 10,000 households. Too young to be interested in good government, at first he allowed local officials free rein, with predictable consequences: more oppressive taxation, corruption, protests unheard, the flight of those fit and strong enough to set up house elsewhere, and a dramatic decline in both tax base and tax revenues. Shocked by this turn of events – or perhaps by his mother's reaction to it – Kublai ordered reforms. New officials were drafted (among them, Shi Tianze from his mother's appanage); tax laws were revised. A decade later, people had returned to their old homes. Kublai had learned an important lesson about business management.

From the mid-1230s, Ogedei drank himself steadily towards death. Wine was his tipple, not the traditional Mongolian mares'-milk *airag*. A special official was appointed by his staff to count the number of goblets he imbibed, in a vain attempt to control his consumption. The number went down, apparently, but only because he got himself a bigger goblet.

With a drunkard in charge, princes squabbled. One row

involved Ogedei's eldest son Güyük and his cousin Batu, khan of the Golden Horde, the steppe region of what is now Russia from the Caucasus to the Urals. During the 1236–41 invasion of Russia, Poland and Hungary, there was a feast at which both men were present. *The Secret History* quotes Batu's version of what happened, which he sent off across Asia at a gallop. Generally acknowledged as the senior, Batu naturally drank first. Güyük and two other princes took offence and rode away in a huff, throwing insults. They should all be equal! Batu shouldn't be claiming seniority! He was just an old woman with a beard . . . deserved to have his bosom struck with a stick of burning wood . . . have a wooden tail tied to him. Back home, Ogedei backed Batu and blamed his son: 'May he and he alone rot like an egg! He has turned against the bosom of a person who is senior to him!' What was Güyük thinking of, acting so high and mighty as if he had conquered the Muslims all by himself? In his anger, Ogedei disowned Güyük as heir and nominated a grandson, Shiremun, in his place.

In December 1241 the emperor took part in the annual winter hunt, a huge event for which he had had built a fence two days' journey in length to gather wild animals, mainly white-tailed deer and wolves. Then he started a night of heavy drinking, in the company of his favourite Muslim tax farmer, Abd al-Rahman. He died at dawn on 11 December, aged 55. The author of *The Secret History* sums up Ogedei's reign by putting a self-condemnation into his mouth: 'I was at fault to let myself be vanquished by wine. This was indeed one fault of mine.' It was an ignominious end, which was perhaps why he was not buried with his father on the Mongols' sacred mountain, Burkhan Khaldun in northern Mongolia, but on his own private estate in Jungaria, Mongolia's far west.

His widow, Töregene, took over the empire, ignored her husband's will and set about getting the throne for her eldest, Güyük, now aged 35. He couldn't have done it alone, because he was a sickly creature as dedicated to drink as his father. Töregene was one tough lady, the only woman who outranked Sorkaktani, according to John of Plano Carpini. She was, says Rashid, 'no great beauty, but of a very masterful nature', and a nasty piece of work by all accounts (though those accounts were written after she had been consigned to the dustbin of history, so perhaps she was not quite so bad as she is painted). She won over most of the family with arguments and gifts, but Batu she could not persuade. He refused to come to a *kuriltai*, the great assembly of princes which would elect the next khan, claiming he was suffering from gout. Delays continued for five years, with Töregene constantly shoring up support for her son through intrigue and bribery.

Realizing that Töregene was in a virtually unassailable position, Sorkaktani played a waiting game, remaining quietly supportive of Ogedei's family through the turbulent four-year interregnum. The dispute almost tore the empire apart, with every prince making his own laws for his own entourage, changing what had been written on the orders of Genghis himself. Genghis Khan's youngest brother, Temüge, now well into his seventies, even dared suggest that he, as elder statesman, should be nominated khan without calling an assembly, a claim for which he would pay in due course. Chaos threatened, until Sorkaktani – who had scrupulously refrained from issuing edicts of her own – came out in support of Güyük, giving Töregene a slight but significant majority among the princes. Töregene at last arranged the assembly, which convened in the spring of 1246.

This *kuriltai* was the grandest imperial affair yet, described by Juvaini in his usual flowery style. With the snow gone, the pasture renewed, ring-doves dallying with turtle-doves and melodious nightingales singing, Karakorum became a stage for the display of new-found power and wealth. Nobles by the hundred gathered from every corner of the empire: all of Genghis's scattered descendants, sons and grandsons, cousins and nephews, joined over the course of several weeks by subservient leaders from north China, Korea, Russia, Hungary, Turkestan, Azerbaijan, Turkey, Georgia, Syria, even Baghdad, though it was as yet unconquered, arriving to create a satellite city of 2,000 tents. It was a scene 'such as no man had ever seen nor has the like thereof been read of in the annals of history'. Juvaini's words were confirmed by the Italian monk John of Plano Carpini, who had just arrived and was busy gathering inside information from Russians and Hungarians, long-term residents who spoke Latin and French.

The feasting and drinking went on for a week, during which the princes grudgingly offered the throne to Güyük, who, after three routine refusals, accepted. His coronation took place that August at a second tented site in a river valley a few kilometres from Karakorum. Here the tribute was brought, in 500 cartloads of silks, velvet, brocade, gold, silver and furs, displayed in and around Güyük's coronation *ordo*, a huge tent-palace of yellow felt supported by gilded wooden columns. The ceremony – delayed for a few days by a vicious hailstorm – had Güyük crowned on an ivory throne inlaid with gold, made by a Russian goldsmith. It was Sorkaktani who oversaw a gigantic payoff, the tribute being redistributed among everyone, from grizzled companions of Genghis himself down through commanders of a battalion 10,000 strong to platoon chiefs in charge of ten men, from sultans to humble officials, as well as all their dependants.

Together, Güyük and Töregene wrung from the assembled princes a pledge that the throne would remain in Ogedei's direct family. This in effect counteracted Genghis's own will, which specified what should happen if Ogedei's direct descendants were unfit to rule. *The Secret History* underlines the point with a verse: if they prove so worthless that

> Even if one wrapped them in fresh grass,
> They would not be eaten by an ox.
> Even if one wrapped them in fat,
> They would not be eaten by a dog

> – is it possible that among my [other] descendants not even a single one will be born who is good?

So it would have been perfectly acceptable for the princes to look for a khan from another branch of the family – from Tolui's line, for instance. Might not Sorkaktani have pushed Mönkhe forward? He was already 36. But she was not yet ready to enter the fray. It would only further threaten the unity of the empire, and probably endanger her own position. So she held her peace, and went along with those princes who were strong-armed into pledging that the succession would always remain with Ogedei's line, swearing to Güyük that this would hold 'as long as there remains of thy race a piece of flesh such as an ox or dog would not accept wrapped in fat or grass'. It was a pledge that deliberately subverted words attributed to their lord and master, Genghis – a pledge, moreover, with immediate and shocking impact: Genghis's ageing brother Temüge, who had claimed the throne for himself, was put to death. Genghis's *brother*! Executed! There must have been much unhappiness among some of the princes.

Unhappiest of all was Batu. He had, reluctantly, been on his way to the assembly, but too late: Töregene managed to tie up the succession before he arrived, when he and his army were still over 1,000 kilometres away.

But mutterings of discontent persisted. Güyük was never a good choice. He was always in poor health, made worse by drink. He was moody, suspicious, unsmiling. His mother had foisted him upon unwilling relatives and subordinates, and the gifts with which she had bought their acquiescence would not be enough to keep it; indeed, Töregene herself continued to alienate family and officials, notably with her choice of a confidante.

It makes a lurid tale, which started some time before the coronation. Töregene had employed a Muslim woman called Fatima, who had been brought as a captive to Karakorum, where she set up trade managing the local prostitutes. Somehow she wormed her way into Töregene's household and became the queen's close friend and adviser – a sort of female Rasputin. Knowledge of the queen's secret views and court intrigues gave Fatima far too much influence. No minister could do his job without her say-so. She even began issuing her own decrees. Top people had to grovel their way into her good books. Inevitably, they resented her, praying for a come-uppance. It came soon after Güyük succeeded, when his brother fell ill. Someone suggested that Fatima must have bewitched him. To his credit, Güyük tried to reverse the damage. He prised her out of his mother's control, had her accused and tortured until she confessed, and then consigned her to a dreadful death, which graciously conferred upon her the upper-class honour of dying without shedding blood. 'Her upper and lower orifices were sewn up, and she was rolled up in a sheet of felt and thrown into the river.' No doubt most breathed a sigh of relief, but such a conflict between son and mother was no basis for sound rule.

What, meanwhile, of Batu? Still advancing slowly. Güyük suspected rebellion. He mustered his own army and marched westward, ostensibly to check on his estates on the Kazakh–Mongol borders. Once there, he set about preparing a counter-invasion. All this took months, opening a window of opportunity for one of Sorkaktani's most crucial interventions. It was a difficult decision, fraught with danger. If she was discovered, all would be lost – her years of waiting, her careful networking, her hopes for her sons. She would be seen as a traitor and executed, along with her family. This is what she did: recalling the ties of brotherhood between her late husband and Batu's father, she sent a secret message to Batu warning him, in the words of Rashid ad-Din, that Güyük's advance 'was not devoid of some treachery'. Taking advantage of this advance notice, Batu prepared himself for action – unnecessarily, as it turned out, because in April 1248 the two armies were virtually squaring up along the shores of Lake Balkhash when Güyük, always sick and now worn out by travel, died: possibly poisoned, possibly in a fight, but most probably from disease.

Batu, who was content with his own empire in southern Russia, had no interest in promoting himself as the new khan. And he owed Sorkaktani a favour. So he instantly turned his army into a princely assembly and proposed that Sorkaktani's eldest, Mönkhe, should succeed.

Back home, of course, Güyük's sons, under their mother's aegis, demurred, and all set up their own courts, as did Ogedei's favoured grandson Shiremun. Again, the empire was in tatters. Local rulers looked after themselves, wringing whatever they could out of their subjects. Princes used the postal relay system, set up to speed imperial communication, for their own ends, rather like officials of some failing dictatorship using ministerial limos for their own businesses on the side. No-one knew who was going to rule; everyone scrabbled for influence; many sent messages saying they would not even come to a meeting to elect a new khan.

Güyük's widow, Oghul Kaimish, would by tradition have acted as regent until her eldest was fit to rule. But her sons – Ogedei's grandsons – were too young. Besides, she was overwhelmed by events, closeting herself with shamans, trying to achieve her ends by witchcraft. People remembered Genghis's words: that if Ogedei's descendants were unsuitable, then the new khan should be chosen from other lines, that is, from the offspring of Genghis's other three sons. Two of them (Jochi and Chaghadai) had estates so distant that their heirs were out of contention. That left Sorkaktani's children, the offspring of Genghis's youngest son, Tolui, inheritor of the Mongol heartland.

Now at last Sorkaktani went into battle on her own account. She was about 60, and it was her last chance. She had a lot going for her: her own power base, money, respect, influence. The court was torn apart over the Fatima affair. And she had an advantage in that Güyük's offspring were Genghis's great-grandchildren, whereas her own were his grandchildren, a generation closer to the great man. Mönkhe, almost 40, was a good choice, and well qualified. He too had led a Mongol army westwards into Europe in 1238–41, burning Kiev and destroying the Hungarians at the battle of Mohi. Moreover, he had two younger brothers who were also experienced generals, and they would be vital when the empire resumed its Heaven-ordained task of imposing Mongol rule on the world.

The dispute was almost ended in 1250, when the rivals came together at Batu's camp and heard Batu again demand that Mönkhe be elected. But this assembly was not in the Mongol heartland, and carried little weight. The next year, a second assembly, this one in the traditional area near Avraga, confirmed the choice. As if concluding a presidential election, Mönkhe was all generosity, appeasing and befriending his former opponents and their families. It almost worked, except that Shiremun still had other ideas.

Juvaini picks up the story.

The scene is the princely assembly at Avraga. Imagine a few stone buildings and the surrounding masses of tents and wagons and herds. Everyone is happy that the succession is decided. A falconer named Keshik (*keshig* just means 'guard', but let's follow Juvaini) loses a favourite female camel. He sets out to find it, riding for two or three days here and there. He comes across an army. Who on earth are they? Oh, comes the reply, we are coming to offer Mönkhe our congratulations and obeisance. Reassured, Keshik continues his search. Seeing a broken-down wagon, being mended by a young man, he stops to offer help. Then he notices that the wagon is full of bundles of weapons.

'What are all these arms?' he asks.

'Same as all the other wagons,' the lad replies.

At last Keshik starts to wonder. He strikes up other conversations. Bit by bit, he pieces the story together. These are people 'meditating treason and duplicity and treachery and discord', aiming to launch an attack on Mönkhe while everyone is feasting. Finding his camel, he covers three days' journey in one, barges in on the new emperor and spills the beans. The company is aghast. They don't believe him. He tells his story again, and again. Mönkhe will still not take the threat seriously. His officers remonstrate. At last, it is agreed that Mengeser, chief judge and head of the emperor's guard, will take 3,000 men and investigate. They reach the army, find it to be Shiremun's, and confront him. Shiremun and his officers are flabbergasted: 'The tongue of excuse having turned mute and the leg of advance and withdrawal lame, they saw no hope of departing and no prospect of remaining behind.' Under guard, the leaders troop into Mönkhe's presence, in groups of nine. After three days of interrogations, Mönkhe comes to his conclusion. It's incredible, inconceivable, cannot be heard by the ear of intelligence nor accepted by the soul of wisdom, but still it is true: they are traitors. Arrests follow, and confessions, and – once Mönkhe has overcome his natural generosity and his urge to forgive – executions. This prisoner is beheaded, that one trampled to death, while others commit suicide with a sword in the stomach.

Purges followed, reaching as far afield as Afghanistan and Iraq. Among the victims was Güyük's widow, Oghul Kaimish, condemned by Mönkhe as viler than a dog, the worst kind of witch; Shiremun's mother; and, in due course, Shiremun himself. It was a terrible blood-letting. Mengeser himself claimed to have tried and executed 77 leaders of the opposition. Many hundreds of others must also have died. The grim episode marked the beginning of a regime more sternly dedicated to Genghis's vision, the new ideology being backed by the official worship of Genghis Khan (the birth of a cult that continues to this day).

And that was how Mönkhe came to absolute power, and how, thanks to Sorkaktani and a good deal of luck, Tolui's line took over from Ogedei's – meaning that, should anything happen to Mönkhe, there was a good chance of the succession passing to Kublai.

Mönkhe brought new vigour to the sacred trust imposed by Genghis, the task of striving for universal domination. He started with a flurry of reforms and plans for expansion. The two went together: renewed conquests would unite his divided people, but only if they stopped working for themselves and worked together; this required the exercise of authority, on the basis of an accurate account of available resources. So there would be a census (actually several censuses) covering the whole empire. This vast project was undertaken through the 1250s, generating a sort of Mongol Domesday Book, enumerating peoples, towns, animals, fields and raw materials from the Pacific coast to the Baltic. There would be no more self-seeking, no more using the postal relay system as a perk of high office. There would be a head tax (based on individuals in Islamic lands and on households in China) paid in cash, an agricultural tax paid in kind and a commercial tax on all businesses. The census also told Mönkhe's secretariat the potential size of his armed forces, and identified in every region households with young men available for military service.

On this basis there would be a push outwards such as the empire had never seen before. Mönkhe put his younger brothers and other relatives in executive charge of the campaigns. Hulegu would move westward, deeper into the Islamic world. Mönkhe himself and Kublai would undertake the final conquest of the Chinese south, the kingdom of Song. The third advance, a minor one by comparison, would be into Korea, under Genghis's nephew, Jochi Khasar. At the heart of this expansion was the triad of brothers – Mönkhe, Hulegu and Kublai – with Mönkhe at the tip, and his two brothers as his right and left wings, west and east, charged with tasks that were mirror images of each other: to extend the power of the empire and of their family, one in the world of Islam, the other in China.

In the meantime, Kublai, having learned from his mother how to take good care of his Chinese estate, had hired a brains trust of half a dozen Chinese advisers, most of whom shared religious and intellectual interests, all of whom were prepared to work with their new overlord, offering guidance in finding his way among China's three great religious traditions – Buddhism, Taoism and Confucianism – and hoping to mould the Mongol leaders into good Chinese rulers. This was quite a remarkable step by Kublai, because it was conducted across a linguistic and cultural gulf. He did not speak Chinese, and very few Chinese spoke Mongol. All communication was through interpreters.

Among the advisers, three were of particular significance.

The first was a brilliant Buddhist monk, Haiyun, who

was so clever as a child that he found Confucianism too easy. On the question of happiness and sorrow, he said at the age of seven, he had read Confucius and found him unhelpful. So he turned to Buddhism, and was ordained at the age of nine. When in 1219 the Mongols seized Liangzhou, today's Wuwei in central Gansu province, Haiyun, now aged 16, was found wandering with his master amid the devastation and looting, quite unconcerned. A general asked if they were not afraid of being killed by the troops. On the contrary, Haiyun replied calmly, they relied on their protection. Impressed, the commandant of north China, Muqali, brought the pair to the attention of Genghis, who ordered them to be clothed, fed and exempted from taxation. The master died soon afterwards, and the pupil went searching for a religious base, during which he attained enlightenment, expressing his sense of revelation in one of those enigmatic statements that in Buddhism are treated as evidence of wisdom: 'Today for the first time I realize that eyebrows run horizontally while the nose is set vertically.' He rose to become head of several temples, was further promoted by Yeh-lü Chu-tsai, and did a good deal to mitigate Mongol excesses in north China. Once, when asked for advice on hunting by a high official, Haiyun replied sharply that the urgent task of officials was to preserve life, not play games. Later, when the Mongols were debating whether to brand their Chinese subjects on the arm so that they could be identified when they fled, Haiyun again reprimanded his overlords: men were not cattle, he said; and besides, where could they flee, since the Mongols claimed the whole world? The idea was dropped. When Kublai met Haiyun in Karakorum in 1242, he asked the monk whether Buddhism offered a way to world peace. Haiyun replied that it did, but that understanding was required: Kublai should surround himself with scholars. But the prince was impatient for short cuts. Which of the Three Teachings – Buddhism, Taoism, Confucianism – was the highest? Haiyun replied that in wisdom and sincerity Buddhism was supreme, providing the best guidance for a prince wishing to promote virtue, relieve suffering, resist delusions, accept good advice, shun extravagance, and distinguish right from wrong. Kublai was impressed. When his second son was born in 1243, it was Haiyun who named him: Zhenjin, 'True Gold' – or Jingim, as the Mongols called him.

It was Haiyun, too, who introduced Kublai to another monk: Liu Bingzhong, a painter, calligrapher, poet, mathematician – the multi-talented product of a famous Taoist sect, the Complete Perfection, whose patriarch Ch'ang-ch'un Genghis had summoned all the way to Afghanistan. He later converted to Buddhism, without losing interest in Taoism and Confucianism. While Haiyun eventually returned to run his temple in Beijing, Liu remained on Kublai's staff, devoting his life (in the words of his biographer Hok-Lam Chan) 'to the ideal of modifying Mongol institutions according to Confucian principles'.

The third adviser, Yao Shu, had joined Ogedei's staff in 1235, being sent with raiding forces across the Song frontier, during which he too did his best to restrain Mongol brutality. He later helped found a Confucian academy in Beijing but then, resenting the Mongol administration, retreated to the country for ten years, until Kublai head-hunted him and invited him to Karakorum in 1251. There he became tutor to little Jingim, now eight, Kublai's favourite and his future heir.

Kublai employed other nationalities as well, for he was keen to balance his past and future, local interests and imperial ones, Mongol and Chinese and Turkish. For advice on government, he had his Chinese team; for military matters, he relied on Mongols; for translators and secretaries, Turks. It was a surprisingly large and varied group – some two dozen in all, a shadow cabinet carefully chosen for its political balance, almost as if Kublai were preparing himself for the administration of much more than his own estate.

He was thus well qualified when he asked Mönkhe for an extension of his responsibilities in north China. There was a good strategic reason for such a request – to ensure a reliable flow of supplies for the occupying troops. He had his eye on the rich farmlands along the Yellow River and its tributaries, in today's Shaanxi and Henan provinces, roughly between the ancient capital of Xian and the newer and recently conquered one of Kaifeng. Mönkhe was wary of handing over so much territory all at once, and gave Kublai a choice. His Chinese advisers told him that the land downriver was liable to flooding and saltiness, so he chose an upstream area on the Wei river, an irregular blob almost half the size of England running from the Wei valley southward across mountains to the Song border. Mönkhe was impressed by his reasoning – fewer people, many of them non-Chinese, and tricky to govern, but with greater potential – so he gave him some of Henan as well. In governing these areas, Kublai followed Yeh-lü Chu-tsai's advice, his mother's shrewd practices and Mönkhe's imperial strategy. He allowed the peasants to work, taxed them fairly, and also established 'military farms': colonies dedicated to supplying the troops. It worked. He had his power base – a

Chinese one, fanning suspicions among traditionalists back on the grasslands that he was going native.

He was, in a sense. But he could not afford to go the whole way. His mother would have advised him to remain in touch with everything Mongol in its latest imperial manifestation. There was, for instance, its western wing, which in 1251 consisted of present-day eastern Iran and Uzbekistan. For 30 years these regions, with their great Silk Road cities, remained in ruins, while western Islam, and its great capital Baghdad, was still untouched. Sorkaktani herself had kept links with the area, financing the building of mosques and *madrasas* or Islamic colleges – including one in Bukhara with 1,000 students – which, as Muslims noted, was a remarkable thing for a Christian queen to do.

In early 1252 Sorkaktani, now over 70, died. She was buried far to the west in Gansu province, in Zhangye, an ancient garrison town guarding the Silk Road and thus a staging post for Nestorian missionaries. Sorkaktani must have had some early and abiding connection with the town, for her final resting place was said to be the Giant Buddha Temple, famous then and now not only for the size and age of its statue – 34 metres, eleventh century – but for the fact that it is lying down. When I was there in 2005, the statue was undergoing restoration to scrape off 1,000 years of grime. Alone, in gloom, unaware of what to look for, I wandered right around the network of scaffolding, thinking it concealed a decorated wall. I realized only when I glanced up, and saw a huge beatific smile vanishing into darkness above me.

No hint of anything Christian. I began to wonder if I was dealing with a myth. I buttonholed the director, Wu Zhen Ke, who was between meetings to do with the restoration. A dynamic 40-something with a crewcut, he was just the man to ask, because he had written a book about the temple. He was also an enthusiast; information came fizzing out from behind his rimless glasses like shaken champagne. 'In the thirteenth century, this place was maybe five times the size. It contained elements that were both Christian and Buddhist. There is no doubt that Bie Ji [he used a Chinese 'respect name' I had never heard before] was buried here.' Indeed, so close was her connection that some believe she was pregnant with Kublai when she first arrived here, and that he was actually born in the temple. 'Local people, from generation to generation, have always said this.' But Wu, signing a copy of his book, was too careful a scholar to support such a claim. 'We do not have the evidence. Perhaps one day we will unearth some historical relic to prove what they say.' No rituals link the temple with Sorkaktani today, but elsewhere she became a cult figure, and is one of those remembered in the Genghis Khan Mausoleum, Edsen Khoroo – the Lord's Enclosure – the temple in Inner Mongolia where Genghis and his family are worshipped.

Sorkaktani must have approached the end of her days secure in the knowledge that her great work had been accomplished. Her eldest son was khan, the empire re-unified, Genghis's dream of world conquest once again becoming more of a reality by the year. Before her death, she would have heard reports of the beginning of Mönkhe's campaign to extend the empire further into Muslim lands, and known that Kublai was due to advance further into China.

She might have guessed, given the character of her boys, that this was a mere beginning. She could not possibly have guessed, however, that Kublai would one day inherit the lot.

2

THE FIRST WAR ON TERROR

HERE ARE CIRCUMSTANCES WHICH MAY SEEM ODDLY familiar. The leader of a great power needs to unite his people after a divisive election and makes plans for war. Suddenly, by curious chance, a fanatical sect of Muslims with a track record of extreme violence embarks on an underhand assault. Appalled, he turns on the terrorists with overwhelming force. This happened on 9/11/2001; but it *first* happened in the 1250s, when Mönkhe, the newly installed Mongol emperor, heard that a small army of assassins – 40 or 400 of them, the number varying with the source – had been despatched in disguise to kill him. These were killers of a very peculiar and dedicated nature. Like those who flew into the World Trade Center towers, they were quite prepared to die themselves. The threat, the outraged leaders' responses and the consequences were remarkably similar, and the parallels go further: the region at the heart of the conflict, the real danger posed by suicidal Islamic extremists, the vagueness of the current threat, the determination to extend the bounds of empire, the gathering of a massive army, a coalition of allies, overwhelming force, invasion, the fall of Baghdad, much collateral damage, and occupation.

One should not push the comparison too far. The Americans fell upon Iraq after Afghanistan, the Mongols came via Persia and would have come anyway, to fulfil the destiny inherited from Genghis; the Mongol conquest was achieved with a brutality vastly exceeding that of the Bush coalition; and the Mongols intended eternal occupation, whereas America intended regime change and a quick exit. But the echoes are resonant nevertheless, especially to Muslims, many of whom see the Americans as the 'new Mongols'. It is an easy comparison – perhaps too easy, as we see if we take a closer look at the events that added a huge new slab of territory to the empire that would eventually fall to Mönkhe's younger brother, Kublai.

The Mongols knew what they were doing, because they had done it all before, under Genghis Khan, 30 years previously. The army that prepared for the invasion from summer 1252 was formidable, and very well organized. Headed by the emperor's brother Hulegu, it included the best in siege weapons that north China had to offer, including 1,000 mangonel teams, experts in operating these massive catapults which could lob rocks and exploding 'thundercrash' iron bombs 100 metres or more.[1]

---

[1] These were almost certainly man-powered 'traction trebuchets', not counterpoise trebuchets, which the Mongols would soon acquire from Muslim engineers, with interesting consequences to be examined in chapter 8.

Governors and secretaries were appointed to administer the newly conquered lands. Vanguards rode off ahead to reserve pastures, places forbidden to non-Mongols and their animals until the army had passed. Herds of mares were gathered along the line of march to provide the troops with their habitual drink of fermented mares' milk. The invasion force would travel on the same road taken by Genghis, but after 30 years it would have needed a lot of attention. When the army finally left a year later, teams ranged ahead to repair bridges and build ferries – for the leaders and their families, at least: ordinary folk would have made their own way across the rivers, fording, swimming and using animal-skin floats.

This immense operation was greater even than that undertaken by the Mongols in their first move westward under Genghis Khan. Many books for and by non-specialists suggest that any Mongol advance was a storm, a whirlwind, as if it were a new force of nature. In fact, this was as much a migration as a military invasion, a population shift comparable to those that had been regular features of Central Asia for a millennium. The whole mass had to be self-supporting, which was possible because the way westward was across the vast pasturelands that make an irregular corridor for nomads between Manchuria and the Hungarian plain. As John Masson Smith has pointed out, 'The far-flung campaigns of the Mongols and the extraordinary extent of their empire were to a considerable degree the products of this great logistical boon.'[2]

This particular force (according to Rashid ad-Din) had 15 commanders, each with his battalion; as a battalion

[2] John Masson Smith, 'Ayn Jalut: Mamluk Success or Mongol Failure?'

was supposedly 10,000-strong, though in practice usually much less, this made something like 100,000–150,000 men in all, probably closer to 100,000. That was just the start. Every man, as usual, had at least five horses, sometimes more, to provide remounts and food – 120 kilos of meat from a butchered horse could feed 100 hungry men. But what set this enterprise apart was that the men had their families along, and each family would also have had some 30 sheep, on average. This was a nation on the move, occupiers and colonists: perhaps 150,000 people, with 300,000 horses and 1.8 million sheep, all widely dispersed to avoid overgrazing. Horses are usually moved in the morning, grazed in the afternoon and rested at night. The only way to travel really fast was to have fresh mounts ready in advance. This was how the pony express was run in occupied lands. But it could not be done during conquest and occupation. Hulegu's force would have been moving westward a few kilometres a day for a year: not so much a storm, more like a tide, bits of which would flow where required by the demands of conquest and occupation.

The cutting edge, of course, was the cavalry. It was the horses that gave the Mongols their superiority, not because of their strength or endurance, but because of the speed conferred by a regular supply of new mounts. These mounted forces could outflank, outpace, flee, gallop in close to fire their bows point-blank, avoid charges, and harry retreating foes until, like jackals on a buffalo, they would worry their foes to death.

But only if the horses had enough good grazing and enough water; and, though those could be taken for granted on the grasslands that stretched for hundreds of kilometres, it was a big *if* once their edge was reached. The average Mongolian horse needs about 14 kilos of grass a day, an intake that requires some 10.5 hours of grazing, whether or not they are being ridden. Now multiply this by 300,000. A horde of 250,000, with their horses and sheep, would cover 7,000 hectares a day – that's 70 square kilometres; and every day a new 70 square kilometres. This drifting horde of horses, wagons and sheep would be at least 8 kilometres across. Then think of the water needed: over a million gallons a day. Easily supplied by a large river in flood; but once out of the grassland zone, especially in the searing heat of the Middle Eastern summer, pastures dry up and rivers shrink.

The Mongols were about to discover that their reach had rather sharp ecological limits.

Whether the plot to murder Mönkhe was real or not is an open question. No-one recorded finding any assassins. But there was good reason to take the threat seriously, because these were not simply assassins, with a lower-case *a*; they were the original Assassins, capitalized: a long-established and notorious menace in the Islamic world, who gave their name to the very idea of murder for political and religious ends.

The story is rooted deep in Islamic sectarianism. Islam, like all the major religions, sowed sub-groups like dragon's teeth, each claiming that it alone was the true heir to the Prophet. All, of course, revered the Qur'an. But doctrinal disputes, political conflict and murder marred Islam from two decades after the Prophet Mohammed died, one of the victims being Mohammed's son-in-law Ali, husband of the Prophet's daughter Fatima. From these seventh-century beginnings grew hideous complexities, with dynasties, races, regions and sects rivalling each other for 500 years, through which we must now weave to trace the origins of the Assassins.

In the early days of Islam, rival leaders evolved a second doctrinal source, the Sunna, or deeds and sayings of both the Prophet and his successors, including some who were not his relatives. Its adherents, the Sunnis, were then opposed by the Shi'ites, the Shi'at Ali ('party of Ali'), who claimed that political authority derived only from Ali, from whose descendants a divinely appointed imam (spiritual leader) would emerge as the Mahdi, 'the guided one'. Since there was no obvious Mahdi, the Shi'ites came to believe that he was being hidden by God. The notion of the 'Hidden Imam' became a central tenet of Shi'ism, one that inspired numerous pretenders and some very strange sub-sects. From the Shi'ites, for instance, arose in the late eighth century the Ismailis, who claimed that Ismail, the disinherited son of the Sixth Imam, represented the true line of authority from Mohammed. Ismail died young, after which his followers claimed that he had been succeeded by 'hidden imams'. This became the creed of a dynasty who claimed descent from Ali's wife, Mohammed's daughter Fatima. The Fatimids, with Ismailism as their faith, built a kingdom in north Africa, then took over Egypt, planning to use this as a base for an anti-caliphate that would seize all Islam. It didn't happen. Fatimid power declined. But Ismaili missionaries, preaching their secretive mystical teachings, remained as active as ever. The sect appealed powerfully to the poor and oppressed, one group becoming notorious for their brutality against mainstream Muslims and established dynasties.

The Ismailis' next transformation was triggered by the

Turks, who swept into the Islamic world from the Asian heartland around the year 1000. As the Turks, headed by their rulers the Seljuks, struck westward from their power base in what is now Uzbekistan and Iran, they adopted the orthodox Sunni form of Islam, and turned on the Shi'ites, including the Ismailis, who responded by forming a network of underground cells.

In the second half of the eleventh century, there lived in Rayy (today's Tehran) a man named Hasan i-Sabbah. This Hasan (there are several other unrelated Hasans to come) had friends in high places, including the poet Omar Khayyam. He met one of the secretive Ismaili propagandists, converted, fell foul of the authorities – in the form of Tehran's vizier, Nizam al-Mulk – and fled to Egypt. There he found that Egypt's Fatimid/Ismaili rulers were mere shadows of their former selves, and decided to wage his own war for Ismailism and its Fatimid imam in the heart of Seljuk territory. He and his followers spotted the perfect base: a formidable castle, Alamut, almost 2,000 metres up in the Elburz mountains south of the Caspian Sea. Unfortunately, it was occupied.

Hasan acquired Alamut by converting some of the garrison, then slipping inside in disguise. Conversions continued. When he was discovered, it was too late. The garrison was his, and so was the castle. The owner received an offer he couldn't refuse – eviction, plus a cheque for 3,000 gold dinars (about £75,000). To his astonishment, the draft was honoured, by a local banker who was one of Hasan's converts.

This, then, is what the Mongols would be up against:

Alamut was a fortress within a natural fortress, the perfect heart for Hasan's intended Ismaili state. Tradition claims that it derives from a local phrase meaning 'eagle's nest' – a good name, if true, because it stood on a peak hundreds of feet above a single approach path, which itself could be entered only from either end of a narrow ravine through which the Alamut river flowed. The rock, in Juvaini's words, 'resembles a kneeling camel with its neck resting on the ground', the castle itself towering up like the load on the camel's hump. Its plastered walls and lead-covered ramparts concealed store cellars cut from the solid rock. A conduit from a stream led water into 'ocean-like tanks', which still gather rainwater today. The castle was some 140 metres long by 10–40 metres wide, over-looking precipitous slopes, steep paths and stairways guarded by lower defence works, with no cover at all for an assault force.

The traveller and writer Freya Stark went there by mule in the 1930s. Starting from Qazvin, she and her guides approached the hills over 30 kilometres of scorching plain, then up shale-covered slopes until, over a ridge, she saw the valley of the Alamut river leading into the Elburz mountains. 'Higher than all, uplifted as an altar with black ridges rising to it through snowfields, Takht-i-Suleiman, Solomon's Throne, looked like a throne indeed in the great circle of its lesser peers. Its white drapery shone with the starched and flattened look of melting snow in the distance.' In a village of mud houses, her host and his sons talked of the snowbound winter, 'when wolves in packs fight the village dogs; of bears and foxes and hunting; and of the mountain streams that swell in spring and wash away the small precipitous fields'. Upstream, a narrow path wound along a canyon wall, through two oases with grey-leafed trees and vines and corn and walnuts. Northwards up a side valley stood the Rock itself, like a ship, broadside on.

The great Rock looks a grim place. Mount Haudegan (*c*.15,000 feet) behind it rises in shaly slopes with granite precipices above . . . East and west of the rock, far below, run the two streams that form the Qasir Rud (river); they eat their way through scored and naked beds. There is no green of grass until, beyond a neck that joins the castle to this desolate background, one climbs under its eastern lee, reaches the level by old obliterated steps, and from the southern end looks down nearly a thousand feet of stone to the fields and trees of Qasir Khan, the sunny shallow slopes of the northern bank, and beyond the Alamut river, to the glaciers of Elburz.

Further up the Alamut was a cleft in an immense precipice, to which the only approach was through the forests of Mazanderan, up over the 3,500-metre Tundurkhan Pass. It was a perfect hole-in-the-wall sanctuary.

From here, Hasan, the first of the seven lords of Alamut, determined to assert his own peculiar version of Ismailism. He was a formidable leader, self-assured, learned, ascetic, severe, dictatorial and utterly ruthless – he had his two sons executed, one for drinking wine, the other for supposedly plotting to murder an Ismaili missionary. These were desperate times, with Islam corrupted by heresy, and in Hasan's view all means were justified in fighting his cause, which soon acquired a political cutting edge. In 1094, back in Egypt, an army strongman ousted the Fatimid heir, Nizar, had him murdered in prison and installed his own puppet. Hasan believed that Nizar's heirs would produce the Mahdi who would magically reappear to save Islam from impurity and the Turkish invaders. The fact that Nizar *had* no designated heir was only a temporary problem. The line was 'hidden' and would reappear in due course. Meanwhile, Hasan named himself Nizar's deputy and champion. His followers were formally called Nizaris, an offshoot of the Ismaili Shi'ite Muslims, a sect of a sect of a sect of Islam. This 'New Preaching' (as Hasan called it) appealed strongly to countryfolk, who, like today's suicide bombers, were desperate to escape war, poverty and uncertainty by devoting themselves to a cause in absolute and unthinking obedience. The world soon knew Hasan's young fanatics as Assassins.

It is a puzzling term. The European word in various spellings derives from the Arabic *hashish*, from which comes the English word for good old Indian hemp, *cannabis sativa*. Some people referred to the Nizaris as *hashishiyya* (or a Persian equivalent) – hashish-users – and that was the term picked up by the Crusaders in the twelfth century when they heard of them in Syria. So everyone assumed that's what they were: killers who took hashish as their secret drug of choice to relax them before going off to stab some high official, and perhaps meet their own deaths. The idea was reinforced in 1818 in the first serious study of the Assassins, written by the Professor of Arabic in Paris's School of Oriental Languages and later Professor of Persian at the Collège de France, Baron Antoine Silvestre de Sacy. After that, it became a conventional wisdom. But it was not so. Hashish was widely known, not a Nizari secret; and no Nizari source mentions it. More likely, the term was an insult applied to this despised and feared group, much as suicide bombers might be referred to as crazies or pot-heads, simply as a put-down for behaviour that struck outsiders as both appalling and irrational.

Other hilltop castles fell to Hasan – Girdkuh, dominating the main road from Khurasan; Shadiz, to the south near Isfahan; Lamasar; Tabas, near today's Iran–Afghan border. These strongholds, along with several dozen others, gave him an impregnable power base from which to launch his malign campaign. He himself never again left Alamut, where for 35 years he instructed, inspired and organized followers whose obedience extended to the grave. Like those who join Al-Qaeda today, they welcomed death as martyrdom, confident they would be rewarded by an afterlife in paradise.

Later, Hasan's techniques of persuasion became the stuff of legend, as Marco Polo heard when he came by some 20 years after the Assassins had vanished, on his way to China and to fame as the most vivid (if erratic) source on Kublai and his court. In his version, Alamut's stark valley has now become the most beautiful garden ever seen, filled with gilded pavilions and painted palaces, where honey, wine, milk and water flowed in conduits. Damsels played and sang. It was indeed paradise as conjured up in the Qur'an. Here the imam kept a group of lusty teenagers, whom he groomed to become Assassins. He would have them drugged, carried into the garden and, when they awoke, pampered in every way. 'The ladies and damsels dallied with them to their hearts' content, so that they had what young men would have.' Another draught of the sleep-inducing drug, and the young men found themselves back in the real world, bereft, and willing to do anything to regain the joys of paradise. 'Go thou and slay So and So,' the imam told them, 'And when thou returnest my Angels shall bear thee into Paradise. And shouldst thou die, natheless even so will I send my Angels to carry thee back into Paradise.'

Well, there was no garden, and no drug. Hasan did not need either. His first victim was the vizier Nizam al-Mulk, from whom he had fled years before, followed later by his two sons. Dozens more went the same way: the mufti of Isfahan (slain in the mosque), the qadi of Nishapur, the prefect of Bayhaq, the chief of an anti-Ismaili sect: and more, 50 officials being listed as victims in the Assassins' roll of honour. The area was in the throes of civil war, and Ismailism, with its promise of an Islamic renaissance, found many converts. Commanders and officers went out only with armed guards and wearing armour under their clothes. Terror spawned counter-terror, an official persecution of Ismailis with harbingers of modernity – random accusations, round-ups, imprisonments and deaths in custody. Nothing worked. 'Very well, you have killed me,' said one prominent victim to his gaolers. 'But can you kill those in castles?'

A good point. Some castles fell, but Alamut, even after an eight-year siege, remained impregnable. The result: compromise, and a live-and-let-live arrangement, with occasional assassinations – a prefect here, a governor there, and in 1131 the caliph himself in Baghdad – and occasional unsuccessful reprisals. So it remained after Hasan's death in 1124, with the Assassins slowly gaining more than they lost.

It was another Hasan who injected a further element of revolutionary zeal, which cast the Assassins into outer darkness. During the fast of Ramadan in 1164 he gathered his followers and addressed them, placing his pulpit so that no-one faced Mecca. The time had come, he announced: the Hidden Imam had spoken to him and named him, Hasan, as his representative. Thenceforth, the only rules were his. 'The Imam has freed you from the burden of the rules of Holy Law, and has brought you to the Resurrection.' No need for law, for they would be face to face with God through Hasan, who was in spirit the Imam himself, and the true descendant of Nizar. And his first command was that they break the sacred fast by joining him in a banquet, complete with music and wine. Hasan did not enjoy his new status for long. Two years later, his more orthodox brother-in-law stabbed him to death. But the doctrine of the Resurrection, with this Hasan as its messianic leader, became part of Assassin lore.

Not that this should be revealed to the world: it remained an Ismaili secret, protected by the principle that anything – even a lack of principle – was allowed, if it preserved core Ismaili beliefs. Therefore it was perfectly OK to pretend to other, more mainstream beliefs, if that's what it took to survive. Outward law of any kind, even Ismaili law, was mere 'occultation', under which the truth lay covered. Law, indeed all morality as understood by the outside world, was nothing compared to the inner truth; therein lay the *qiyama*, the Resurrection. It was perhaps this duplicity that explained a sudden, if brief, change of heart expounded in 1210 by the current imam, Jalal al-Din. To the astonishment of his followers and the Islamic world, he announced that it was time for a new conversion, back to old-fashioned Islam. He approached all other Islamic leaders so convincingly that they believed him, until his death allowed a reversion to assassination and brigandry.

There was more, however, to the Assassins than duplicity and violence. They were, after all, asserting what they believed was a truth about God's will. Truth can always do with extra help in the form of reason and science; and so, surprisingly, Ismaili imams were lovers of objective as well as esoteric knowledge. They built a famous library. Scholars were welcomed, one being the famous astronomer and theologian Nasir al-Din Tusi, who lived in Alamut for many years.

They were still there, assassinating now and then, when in 1219 the Mongols attacked their new neighbour to the east, the sultanate of Khwarezm, whose upstart shah had chased out the Seljuks in 1194. In the cataclysm of 1219–22 over a million died, great cities were destroyed, the kingdom shattered. Great turmoil usually favoured the Assassins – more castles to be seized, more converts made with visions of an Islamic renaissance. So it was no wonder that Mönkhe feared for his life, and made the Assassins his first target when he decided to extend the empire westward under Hulegu.

This was a challenge which called for spirited leadership. But the Assassins got nothing of the kind. The incumbent imam, Ala ad-Din, still only in his thirties, was driven crazy by isolation, drink and the uncritical obedience of all around him. It was well known that his mistress was the wife of a good-looking young man named (yes) Hasan, who had been captured by the Mongols during their first incursion, escaped, joined the Assassins, and become a sort of lap-dog for the unstable Ala ad-Din, now favoured, now abused. Made to wear tattered clothing like his eccentric boss, Hasan had most of his teeth broken by blows and a piece cut off 'the instrument of his virility'. To cap it all, 'while Ala ad-Din had commerce with Hasan's wife, he did not avoid Hasan'. Gap-toothed, penis half cut off, buggered and cuckolded: this Hasan had reason enough to resent his master, and so did many others, including Ala ad-Din's own teenage son, Rukn ad-Din. 'In his insanity and melancholy madness,' wrote Juvaini, '[Ala ad-Din] would constantly torment and persecute [the boy] without cause.' He was made to stay with the womenfolk in a room next door to his father's, from which he escaped to wander the castle only in the imam's absences. Terrified of his father's drunken moods, he became convinced that the only hope of survival was to rebel, seize his inheritance and submit to the Mongols. The castle could have held out for years, delayed the Mongol advance, perhaps even retained its independence right through their occupation; but not with this dysfunctional pair at the top.

In November 1255 young Rukn ad-Din was in the midst of planning his move when the Assassin leader went to a nearby valley, apparently to check on a flock of sheep. On the last night of the month, an intruder attacked him and his two sleeping servants. He was found the next morning, 'his head having been severed with a single blow of an axe'. One servant was so badly wounded he died; the other recovered, but could throw no light on the identity of the killer. Some said Rukn himself had done it, but Rukn had been in bed with a fever. No: it had to be Hasan. Indeed, under persuasion, his wife confessed to a knowledge of the plot. Of course, Rukn may have been in on it; indeed, he probably was, because Hasan himself, while out surveying sheep, was decapitated by some unidentified axeman before he could be questioned. His family were all executed and burned, conveniently quickly. And Rukn ad-Din became the new and equally inadequate leader.

Rukn ad-Din was now free to parlay for survival. He decamped to another castle, Maimun-diz, and sent messengers to the local Mongol headquarters in Hamadan to say that he was ready to submit. Fine, came the reply, but Hulegu himself was on his way: submission should be made to him. Rukn began to stall. Five months passed. In May 1256 he sent his brother to Hulegu, now just five days' march away in Damarvand. Fine, said Hulegu, all Rukn had to do now was destroy his castles and come. Rukn wriggled again, begged for more time, made a few token demolitions but kept his main castles intact. As proof of good intent, he said, he would send his six-year-old son as a hostage. When the hostage turned out to be an illegitimate boy fathered on a Kurdish servant-girl, Hulegu sent the child back as of no importance.

Now it was November: Rukn had been prevaricating for almost a year, and the Mongols were upon him. The astronomer Tusi said the stars did not sanction resistance; better capitulate, which Rukn at last did. Hulegu did the proper thing: received him well, as befitted an imam, and handed out Rukn's gifts to the Mongol troops. Rukn was with Hulegu for long enough to fall for a Mongol girl, and was allowed to add her to his harem. He also became obsessed with fighting camels, to which Hulegu responded with a gift of 100 female camels. Apparently, now feeling secure as Hulegu's guest, Rukn did not show due appreciation for this favour. Females don't fight. 'How can I wait for them to breed?' he complained. Yet it suited Hulegu to be magnanimous, for if the imam were treated well he would save the Mongols the trouble of attacking castle after castle.

And it worked: most castles opened their gates. Alamut, Lamasar and Girdkuh did not. The last two held out for years – proof that these castles were indeed virtually impregnable, if determined to resist. At Alamut, the arrival of a Mongol force in November 1256 combined with Rukn's defection persuaded the commander to change his mind after a month. Out trooped the inhabitants; in went the Mongols and burned the place. All its contents would have been lost had not Juvaini, already serving the Mongols, suggested he check out the library, from which he extracted Qur'ans, astronomical instruments and a collection of historical works. The castle was, he noted, in very good shape, and would have been capable of holding out almost indefinitely.

Some 12,000 of the Nizari elite were killed. Rukn ad-Din himself had served his purpose, and eventually would also be despatched, for the Assassins had either resisted or been slow to capitulate. Nevertheless, Hulegu tolerated Rukn for a while longer, aware that the execution of a leader who had voluntarily surrendered would not be a good message to send to other potential vassals. Rukn, however, signed his own death warrant by requesting that he be allowed to present himself to Mönkhe in Karakorum. That suited Hulegu: it would get the young imam out of the way. So Rukn was guided all the way across Central Asia to Mönkhe's court, where, months later, he received the cold shoulder. Go home and destroy your castles, Mönkhe ordered. But on the way home, on the edge of the Khangai mountains, his Mongol escorts took Rukn and his party aside, put his companions to the sword, and – he was, after all, still a leader – kicked him to pulp, thus conferring upon him the honour, due to a leader, of a bloodless death.

That was pretty much the end for the Assassins, though a sub-branch in Syria endured until crushed by the Egyptians in 1273; the end of the Assassins themselves, but not of the Nizaris, whose later history is almost as strange as their origins.

Both Persian and Syrian groups split, following different claimants to the leadership.

The line of Syrian imams ended in about 1800. The Persian line endured. In the mid-nineteenth century the current Nizari imam was appointed governor of Qom, with the new title of Agha Khan, which became hereditary from then on. After being dismissed from a second governorship (of Kirman) and becoming embroiled in an uprising, the Agha Khan led his troops and family into Afghanistan, and allied himself with the British in India – who may well have been encouraging him in order to destabilize Persia as part of the Great Game of Anglo-Russian intrigue – just at the moment when the British were chased out of Kabul in the catastrophic defeat of 1842. He finally settled in Bombay in 1848, under British protection. There 'His Highness', as the British styled him, remained for the next 30 years, rebuilding his wealth and raising racehorses.

The present imam, HH Agha Khan IV, Harvard-educated, ministers to his scattered community of several million Nizaris through the Agha Khan Foundation in Switzerland and his headquarters near Paris, supervising the Agha Khan University in Pakistan, some 300 other schools and colleges, and a network of 200 health programmes and institutions, including six hospitals. The British link remains strong. His first wife was Lady James Crichton-Stuart, *née* Sarah Crocker-Poole, a top fashion model before the marriage; and the largest Nizari community, some 10,000 strong, is in London.

Of all the consequences of the Mongol assault on the world of Islam, this must be the most astonishing. In 1254

Mönkhe, scared by a rumour that a bunch of Assassins are after his blood, launches a campaign to destroy them. It succeeds. Assassins vanish. But in vanishing, they transmute, their imam in the end drawing good from evil, becoming a true father to a people reborn.

For the Mongols, that was half the problem solved. Now they could turn their attention to the rest of this part of the Islamic world: the Abbasid caliphate, and its centre, Baghdad, with which they had unfinished business, having tried and failed to take it in 1238.

In a sense, Hulegu had an easy target. The Abbasid caliphate was already a spent force, divided against itself in innumerable sects – Nusayris, Druzes, Qarmatians, Takhtajis, Zaydis, Sufis. Turks fought Persians, both fought Arabs. Syrians still resented the Abbasid conquest almost 500 years before, and yearned for a messiah to free them. To the east, the great Silk Road cities of Khwarezm – Bukhara, Samarkand, Urgench, Merv – were in ruins from the Mongol assault of 1219–22. At the centre, the royal line of Abbasids was debilitated by luxury. Rather like the Roman empire, as Philip Hitti says in his *History of the Arabs*, 'the sick man was already on his deathbed when the burglars burst open the doors'.

In September 1257 Hulegu, advancing 400 kilometres from the Elburz mountains, sent a message to Baghdad telling the caliph to surrender and demolish the city's outer walls as a sign of good faith. The caliph, al-Mustasim, must know the fate brought upon the world by Genghis Khan, wrote Hulegu.

What humiliation, by the grace of Eternal Heaven, has overtaken the dynasties of the shahs of Khwarezm, the Seljuks, the kings of Daylam [the region where the Assassins had been entrenched] ... Yet the gates of Baghdad were never closed to any of these races ... How then should entry be refused to us, who possess such strength and such power?

The caliph, a lacklustre character whose predecessors had been puppets dancing in the hands of their Seljuk masters, could only hope that this menace would pass, as the Seljuk menace had. He was, after all, the spiritual head of all Islam; God was surely on his side. 'O young man,' he foolishly blustered, 'do you not know that from the East to the Maghreb, all the worshippers of Allah, whether kings or beggars, are slaves to this court of mine?' Empty words, as it turned out. Of all the caliph's 'slaves' not a beggar, let alone a king, came to help him.

In November the Mongol army, leaving their families and flocks behind, started their two-month advance on Baghdad from several hundred kilometres away. They came in three columns. One, under Baiju, veteran of the 1238 assault on Baghdad, approached from the north, having crossed the Tigris near Mosul, 325 kilometres upriver. The second was commanded by one of the army's greatest generals, Kitbuqa, who was not a Mongol but a Naiman, one of the tribes blotted up by Genghis 50 years before. His group, the most southerly, advanced due west from today's Lorestan in Iran, while in the centre came Hulegu himself. Descending from the Iranian highlands along the Alwand river, Hulegu ordered his catapult teams to collect wagonloads of boulders as ammunition, since it was known that there were no stones around Baghdad.

There was scant opposition. A Muslim force on low-lying ground near Ba'qubah, some 60 kilometres north-east of Baghdad, met with disaster when the Mongols opened irrigation channels, flooded them out, then moved in on the floundering foot soldiers, killing 12,000 of them as they tried to escape the muddy waters. The three columns met at Ctesiphon, 30 kilometres south of Baghdad on the Tigris, aiming to take the newer eastern section of the city, with its Abbasid palace, law college and 150-year-old walls, and then the two bridges that straddled the river on pontoons.

By 22 January 1258, Baghdad was surrounded. With the Tigris blocked upstream by pontoons and downstream by a battalion of horsemen, flight was impossible; one official who tried to escape downriver in a small fleet was turned back by a barrage of rocks, flaming naphtha and arrows that sank three of his boats and killed many of his entourage. The assault began a week later. Rocks from the Mongol catapults knocked chunks off the walls, littering their bases with rubble. To gain better vantage points, the Mongols gathered the rubble and built towers onto which they hauled catapults, the better to aim at the buildings inside. Amid a steady rain of arrows that forced the inhabitants under cover, boulders smashed roofs and pots of flaming naphtha set houses on fire. By 3 February, Mongol forces had seized the eastern walls.

Inside Baghdad, panic reduced the caliph to mush. 'Truth and error remained hidden from him,' in Juvaini's scathing words. He tried sending envoys to sue for peace: first his vizier, along with the city's catholicos, the leader of its Christians, in the hope of appealing through Hulegu's Nestorian wife, the Kerait princess Doquz, cousin of his Nestorian mother Sorkaktani. Doquz was renowned both for her wisdom and for her stout defence of her faith, the outward sign of which was the tent-church she transported wherever she went. Hulegu, with an eye to his powerful, matchmaking mother, had a healthy respect for his wife and her creed. So when she interceded for the Christians of Baghdad, he listened. In messages shot into the city attached to arrows, Hulegu promised that the *qadis* – scholars and religious leaders – including Nestorians, would all be safe, if they ceased resisting. A second embassy sued for peace, and a third; Hulegu ignored them both. The caliph's vizier reported that there was no hope, telling his master that the efforts of his 'hastily gathered rabble are as ineffective as the twitchings of a slaughtered animal'. In the circumstances, he should surrender. 'It is the action of the wise to humble themselves and humiliate themselves.' Give up, he said, hand over the treasures, because that's what they're after; then arrange a marriage so that 'empire and religion shall fuse, so that sovereignty and splendour, caliphate and power become one'.

The caliph wavered, while the city's morale collapsed. Thousands streamed out, hoping for mercy; but since there had been no surrender, all were killed. With survivors cowering in nooks and crannies, the caliph saw he had no chance. On 10 February he led an entourage of 300 officials and relatives to Hulegu's camp to surrender. Hulegu greeted the caliph politely, and told him to order all the inhabitants to disarm and come out of the city.

This they did – only to find themselves penned and slaughtered like sheep for having continued their resistance. Sources speak of 800,000 being killed. All figures should be treated with scepticism, but the Mongols, who were used to mass executions, were quite capable of killing on such a scale. Even if the true figure was one-tenth that amount, it was a massacre of Third Reich proportions. No wonder Muslims refer back to it today as one of the greatest of crimes against their people and religion.

Three days later, the Mongols poured into the empty city and set almost all of it on fire. Mosques, shrines, tombs, houses – all went up in flames. The Nestorians, however, were spared, as Hulegu had promised. While Baghdad burned around them, they found sanctuary with their patriarch in a Christian church. Afterwards, the patriarch was awarded the palace of the vice-chancellor, and no doubt joined other Christians in celebrating Islam's astonishing collapse and their own renaissance.

To crown his victory, Hulegu chose to conduct an exercise in humiliation. Taking over the caliph's Octagon Palace, he threw a banquet for his officers and family members to which he invited his prisoner.

'You are the host, we are your guests,' he taunted. 'Bring whatever you have that is suitable for us.'

The caliph, quivering with fear, volunteered to unlock his treasure rooms, then found that none of his remaining servants could sort out the right keys. Eventually, after locks had been smashed, the attendants brought out 2,000 suits of clothes, 10,000 dinars in cash, jewel-encrusted bowls and gems galore, all of which Hulegu magnanimously divided among his commanders.

Then he turned on the caliph. OK, these were the visible treasures. Now: 'Tell my servants where your *buried* treasures are.'

There was indeed a buried treasure, as perhaps Hulegu already knew: a pool full of gold ingots, which were fished out and distributed.

Next the harem, 700 women, and the 1,000 servants. Oh, please, begged the caliph, not all the women. Hulegu was again magnanimous. The caliph could choose 100 who would be released; the rest were shared out among the Mongol commanders.

Next day, all the possessions from the rest of the palace – royal art treasures collected over 500 years – were stacked in piles outside the gates. Later, some of the booty was sent back to Mönkhe in Mongolia. The rest (according to Rashid ad-Din) joined booty from Alamut, from other Assassins' castles, from Georgia, Armenia and Iran, all of it being taken to a fortress on an island in Lake Orumiyeh (Urmia), a salt lake in Iran's far north-western corner.

And at last, the city foul with the stench of the dead, Hulegu ordered one more set of executions: those of the caliph himself and his remaining entourage. Al-Mustasim and five others, including the caliph's eldest son, met their ignominious deaths in a nearby village. Two days later, the second son was executed. Only the youngest son was spared. He was married off to a Mongol woman, by whom he had two sons. That was the end of the Abbasid line, and the first time in history that all Islam had been left without a religious head.

Now came the peace. Bodies were buried, markets restored, officials appointed. Three thousand Mongols began the task of reconstruction in Baghdad, while others set about securing the rest of Abbasid territory. Most towns, like Al Hillah, opened their gates. Some did not, with the usual consequences: in Wasit, 15 kilometres to the south-east of Baghdad, 40,000 died (according to one source, though again the numbers must be treated with caution; always vague, they were usually exaggerated by anything up to tenfold). Resistance made no difference. The region was Hulegu's from Afghanistan to the Persian Gulf. Georgia and the rump of the Seljuk sultanate – today's eastern Turkey – submitted. Beyond lay Syria and Egypt.

To finish this part of our story we must look forward a few more years before returning to Kublai. Syria, its coast a medley of Crusader states, with an Arab dynasty ruling Aleppo and Damascus inland, was next in line. As Hulegu advanced to the Mediterranean coast the Christians quickly allied themselves to the Mongol conqueror, seeing his anti-Muslim campaign as an extension of their own crusades; their Armenian co-religionists, too, came on board. Magnanimous as before to these Christian allies, Hulegu was as brutal as ever to Muslims. One petty emir ruling in Diyarbakir, in today's south-east Turkey, had made the mistake of crucifying a Christian priest who had been travelling with a Mongol passport. Understandably, he resisted Hulegu's forces, which made things worse for him. As a curtain-raiser to the campaign westward, the Mongols took his stronghold, captured him, and subjected him to a death by a thousand cuts, slicing his flesh away bit by bit, cramming the bits into his mouth, then cutting off his head, which became a sort of talisman as the campaign proper gathered pace. It moved across the Euphrates, reaching Aleppo on 24 January 1260. After a six-day massacre here, the lands were granted to the Crusader king Bohemund VI. Hamah and Hims capitulated. Damascus was abandoned by its sultan, who fled to Egypt, and Kitbuqa personally beheaded its governor. Christians rejoiced, bells rang, wine flowed and a mosque was restored to Christian worship. Six centuries of Muslim domination seemed over. Then the Mongols turned southward, to Nablus, whose garrison was exterminated for resisting, all the while making use of the good pastures on the Syrian borderlands.

Now, at last, for Egypt, which was led by Turkish former slaves, the Mamluks (*mamluk*, owned), who had murdered their way to power only nine years before. At this point, news arrived of an event in Mongolia that changed everything. In August 1259 Mönkhe had died (a development to which we shall return in chapter 5). On hearing this, Hulegu returned to Persia with most of his invasion force, leaving Kitbuqa in command of the remaining 20,000 men.

The current Egyptian sultan, Qutuz, now did something that seemed the height of folly, but turned out to be extremely smart. When Hulegu sent envoys demanding surrender, Qutuz cut off their heads. To the Mongols, the murder of envoys was an act of barbarism that precluded all further communication, including the possibility of capitulation. It was the grossest form of insult. Such an act, famously, had precipitated Genghis's attack on Khwarezm in 1219. Nothing could have been better designed to guarantee invasion. It was, perhaps, an act of defiance: better dead than slaves again! But it could also have been a deliberate provocation . . .

. . . because Qutuz could well have known that he had a window of opportunity to beat a Mongol force reduced by Hulegu's departure, and teetering on the very edge of sustainability. In Syria, in May, the main rivers – the Quwayq, the Orontes (Asi), the Barada, the A'waj – drop, the pastures wither. The remaining third of the Mongol army could only eat and drink at all because the other two-thirds had gone back eastward. They were shortly to learn a fundamental truth about campaigning in these parts, a truth baldly set out by John Masson Smith: 'Any forces that were small enough to be concentrated amid adequate pasture and water were not large enough to take on the mamluks.' In modern terms, the Mongols were too low on manpower, vehicles and fuel to fight a major battle. A wiser leader might have thought twice. But faced with such an insult, so blatant a challenge, the Mongols had no option but to fight.

In July 1260 a force of some 15,000–20,000 men, perhaps equal to, perhaps rather less than that of the Mongols (no-one knows the numbers for sure), left Egypt for Palestine, revictualled in Acre and on 3 September, during Ramadan, prepared to meet Kitbuqa's army near Nablus. This was a very different type of army from that of the Mongols. With Egypt's limited pasture, the average Mamluk would have had just one horse, well cared for, bigger and stronger than the pony-size mounts of the Mongols. The Mamluks depended not on speed but on weaponry: bows and arrows, of course, but also lances, javelins, swords, axes, maces and daggers. They were excellent bowmen, with weapons made by expert bowyers (Mongol bows were home-made) and arrows supplied by professional fletchers in amazing quantities. John Masson Smith has calculated that at the battle of Hattin, where Saladin's troops defeated the Crusaders in 1187, they used 1.3 million arrows. The soldiers trained in both speed of fire and accuracy, shooting from a stationary horse. Carrying so much weight, in the open country where the Mongols were at home the Mamluk horses would never have been able to catch their enemies and bring their arms into action; but in a shoot-out the Mongols would lose, as they had once already, at the battle of Parvan in Afghanistan in 1221. In addition, the Mamluk fighters were selected for their physical excellence, whereas the Mongols were ordinary citizen-soldiers, superb only as long as they could choose the terms of battle.

This time, they could not. The place was called Ain Jalut, the Spring of Goliath, because it is here, where the Jezreel valley ends up against the curve of the barren Gilboa hills, that David supposedly slung his fatal stone. No good account of the battle survives, but according to probably the most reliable one,[3] Qutuz arrived after a 50-kilometre march from Acre early on the morning of 3 September, choosing the site for its wooded ridges and good water supply. Behind him were the Gilboa hills, and the rising sun. According to one account, he scattered troops into the nearby slopes and under trees, and arrayed the rest of them at the bottom of the hills. The Mongols must have come around the hills from the Jordan, to meet the Mamluks as they advanced slowly, making a terrifying noise with their kettle-drums. Too late the Mongols, blinded by the sun, discovered that they had been outmanoeuvred. With reinforcements streaming in from Gilboa's side-valleys, the Mamluk cavalry, fresh and well-armoured, closed around the depleted and weakened Mongols. Two Mamluk leaders who had joined the Mongols redefected, reducing the Mongol forces yet further.

The Mongols died almost to a man. According to one account, Kitbuqa was magnificent to the end, spurring on his men until his horse was brought down, he himself

[3] An oral report by Sarim al-Din, assessed in Peter Thorau, 'The Battle of Ayn Jalut: A Re-examination'.

caught and taken before Qutuz. He refused to bow, proclaiming how proud he was to be the khan's servant – 'I am not like you, the murderer of my master!' were his last words before they cut off his head.

It was here, in today's West Bank, that the Mongols' war machine finally ran out of steam. They were not invincible after all. Mongol forces would mount several later attacks on Syria, but could never hold it because, once away from good pastures, they had no natural advantage. Genghis's ambition of a world under Mongol rule had reached its limits in the west. Future expansion would lie in the east, with Kublai.

The Mongols' defeat in 1260 has a peculiar resonance today. Muslims who see the Americans as the 'new Mongols' draw hope from Ain Jalut, for it proves to them that even an apparently overwhelming assault on Islam cannot succeed for ever. To quote one article on the second seizure of Baghdad: 'Fundamentalists believe they have every reason to anticipate victory in this battle, because the story of Baghdad did not end in 1258. The Egyptian mamluks were able to halt the tide of Mongol victories at the Battle of Ayn Jalut in Palestine two years later.'[4] History, of course, has no force apart from individuals willing and able to put its message into practice; and there is no reason to think that lack of fuel will limit the US-led coalition, as lack of pasture limited the Mongols. But Muslims see a message nevertheless, drawing further reassurance even from the subsequent

[4] Husain Haqqani, 'The American Mongols', *Foreign Policy*, May–June 2003.

century-long Mongol occupation of Persia and Iraq. For, long before their rule ended, the Mongols had converted to Islam – proof to some that, whatever the setbacks, Islam will always in the end be victorious.

3

THE TAKING OF YUNNAN

KUBLAI, MEANWHILE, WAS GAZING SOUTH, TOWARDS THE Song empire of southern China, a very much greater challenge than the world of Islam.

Over the 300 years since its foundation, Song China had become the world's leading power. Its stature had nothing to do with its geographical size. It had been cut almost in half when the Jürchen from Manchuria seized the north and its 40 million people in 1125, and was only one-fifth the area of China today – a good deal smaller than Kublai's homeland. But southern Song was everything that Mongolia wasn't: 70 million people, probably more, in scores of cities crowded in and around China's ancient heartland, the fertile plain of the river the Chinese call the Chang, and Europeans know as the Yangtze. From the edge of the Tibetan highlands, where it emerged from precipitous gorges, the river was, as it has remained, a blessing and a curse, its waters irrigating and sometimes drowning the rich paddy-fields along its course. It was also the country's major highway, navigable for 2,700 kilometres, within reach of which lay half a dozen of China's biggest cities. This was what the Chinese meant when they referred to China as the 'Middle Kingdom', the world between the sea and the mountains, and also between the northern deserts and the wet, hot south, where the forested hills flanking the Yangtze's basin fall away again to lush coastal plains. What a contrast with the Mongols: a people from treeless grasslands and barren gravel plains, with not a fence or a navigable river anywhere, who numbered scarcely 1 per cent of Song's population and had just one little town of their own.

Mere numbers give no clue to Song's real strengths: its cultural depth, economic drive and political unity. The Song had linked six independent kingdoms, creating a nation-state greater than all its neighbours – Tanguts and Tibetans in the west, Nanchao and two Vietnams (as now, but with different names) in the south. True, northern China was lost to its Jürchen conquerors in 1125, along with its capital Kaifeng; but the southern Song preserved their cultural identity, ruling from their new capital, Hangzhou (Linan as it was then). In any case, Jin was not a write-off, because the two Chinese populations shared language and culture, while the two governments, Chinese and Jürchen, rubbed along most of the time, their occasional disputes doing little to disrupt everyday life.

For artistry, wealth, inventiveness, depth of thought – for the quantity and quality of practically any cultural and social trait you care to measure – southern Song was unrivalled. By comparison, Islam was a novelty, an empire united by religion and trade, but divided against itself. Song China exploded with knowledge while Europe hardly stirred in its pre-Renaissance slumber. India? South-east Asia? Japan? Africa? Nothing comparable. The French scholar Jacques Gernet describes what happened under Song rule up until the Mongol invasions as a renaissance, in the European sense of the term – a return to a classical tradition, a diffusion of knowledge, an upsurge of science and technology, a new humanistic view of the world – some of which would flow westward and invigorate Europe. To use the word 'renaissance' invites a comparison between Song and fifteenth-century Italy – which is fair enough in some ways, except that the Song renaissance did not lead on to the outward-looking dynamism of post-medieval Europe: this was a society that favoured continuity and tradition over revolution.

Here is a brief sketch of the world the Mongols were about to challenge, a few flowers plucked at random from a garden that would take lifetimes to explore.

At bottom, the renaissance was fuelled by new methods of growing rice. Life seems to have become marginally easier for the vast mass of peasants, though they are virtually invisible in the records, which, like most official records in most cultures, were written by the literate elite for their masters. More and better food, population growth, trade, new industries (like cotton), people on the move in search of self-improvement, rising incomes from land, the spread of education, more civil servants – all these developments interacted to bring about the boom. Great estates provided income for absentee landlords, who took to living in town. The growth of wealth funded the arts, gardening, fashion, ceramics, architecture. Many peasant farmers, finding themselves landless as the estates of the wealthy expanded, chose to go on the road, taking employment in the army or as servants in the mansions of the rich, or in taverns and tea-houses, or as entertainers, or in one of the growing industries – coal-mining, metallurgy, paper-making, printing, salt-making, perhaps in one of the state-funded factories, some of which employed over 3,000 workers. Song porcelain became one of China's glories. Carters crowded the roads, boatmen the rivers and canals.

With the inland frontiers blocked by 'barbarian' kingdoms, Song China turned seaward. The Yangtze, its tributaries and their canals formed 50,000 kilometres of river highways, along which merchant ships sailed to a coastline dotted with ports that far outclassed their European counterparts and from which sailed ocean-going ships with refined sail-systems designed to take advantage of the regular monsoon winds. Quanzhou was the greatest of these ports, so well known to foreign merchants that it became known to them by its Arabic name, Zayton, possibly a corruption of an old Chinese name, with the advantage of meaning 'olive tree' in Arabic.[1] From here or from the mouth of the Yangtze, a Song captain, setting his course with a compass (an invention taken over from geomancers almost two centuries before it found its way to Europe) would take to the sea in his four- or six-masted junk, made safe with watertight compartments (a feature not seen in Europe until the nineteenth century), with 1,000 people aboard. Foreign trade spread Song coins from Japan to India. Chinese ceramics were exported to the Philippines, Borneo, even Africa.

The examination system for recruiting civil servants, already well established, was enlarged, giving new power

[1] Zaytun is supposedly the origin of the English word 'satin'. It's a neat idea, repeated in many books, but it's not true. 'Satin' predates Zaytun.

to the 20,000 'mandarins' and their 200,000–300,000 employees. Laws curbed the rich and helped the poor. State officials were paid well enough to limit corruption. The state, its income secured by taxes and by monopolies on salt and mining, looked after its people as never before, building orphanages, hospitals, canals, cemeteries and reserve granaries, even funding village schools. Taxes were reformed to win the co-operation of the peasant farmers. The revenues accruing to the state from taxation were immense, and carefully recorded. In the late twelfth century, annual revenues from maritime customs duty alone amounted to 65 million strings of 1,000 coins each – that's 65 *billion* coins. Now, coins are cumbersome things, and the monetary system was fraught with inconveniences. Every emperor issued his own currency, and 1,000 coins, strung through square holes, weighed about 6 kilos but were the equivalent of only about 1 ounce of silver (just over $7.00 today), with which one could buy about 60 kilos of rice.[2] Soon after the year 1000, Song had started printing banknotes. Later, commercial organizations began to use cheques, which could be cashed at exchange offices in all major cities.

And how was paper money made? The answer introduces a defining trait of Chinese society in general and Song in particular: the explosion of information. Money was printed as books were – with wood-blocks, images cut into wood in low relief. It was this technique that underpinned the explosion in records and reading matter that had started in the eighth century in China, Japan and Korea. The immense labour of carving each page in

---

[2] These coins are still so common that you can pick them up for a few dollars from dealers.

reverse inspired the next logical step: printing with movable type, an idea that did not occur – or, at least, was not put into practice – anywhere else until Johannes Gutenberg perfected the revolutionary technique in Germany in the mid-fifteenth century. The story is worth telling, because it would provide the Mongols with one of history's great missed opportunities.

The idea was attributed to a certain Pi Sheng, who in the eleventh century created characters by incising them in wet clay, then baking them. To print them, he chose his characters, fixed them in a frame, inked them, placed cloth or paper on them, and applied a little pressure, rather like taking a brass rubbing. It could not have worked very well, because characters cut into wet clay would hardly be great calligraphy. Still, it was ingenious – but also, in the context of Chinese culture, a dead end: first, because wood-block printing was cheap and efficient, a technology absolutely appropriate for China's script and illustrations; and second, because the use of movable characters was the exact opposite. A typesetter would have needed several thousand characters just to represent the full range of the Chinese script, let alone the extra copies he would need of the many common characters, amounting to tens of thousands of characters in all. The imperial printing works had 200,000 in the eighteenth century; indexed by rhyme, they were stored on several revolving round tables, each 2 metres across. Even then the technique, using ceramic or metal letters, was used only rarely, because it took so long to choose the characters and make up a page. It would not be adapted for mechanical use until the nineteenth century; and today's software has consigned the problem to history.

When Gutenberg devised a similar solution to the

problem of reproducing texts, he had several technical advantages – paper with a hard surface and a wine-press being two of them – and a supreme cultural advantage in the alphabet, which meant he only had to make a couple of hundred metal characters – the 26 letters in upper and lower case, in several different versions each, plus punctuation. Perhaps because their script was simpler, it was the Koreans who picked up the idea and ran with it, becoming the first people to use movable metal type in printing the 50-volume *Prescribed Ritual Texts of the Past and Present* in 1234. As it happens, this was shortly before Song fell to the Mongols, who at that moment had within their reach almost all the elements that might have allowed them to develop printing with movable type two centuries before Gutenberg – on which more in chapter 16.

The astonishing growth in books in Song China is proof of just how effective wood-block printing was. Pear wood, with its smooth and even texture, was the wood of choice for most ordinary work, while delicate illustrations were carved into the hard wood of honey locust trees, and for text alone block-cutters worked with soft boxwood. The output was phenomenal. The imperial library in Kaifeng had 80,000 volumes. Soon after the Song came to power, the whole Buddhist canon was published – 260,000 pages in two-page blocks. There were vast official text-collections and encyclopedias with up to 1,000 chapters. A fashion for collections inspired inventories of paintings, calligraphy, stones, coins, inks – anything and everything. Scientific treatises appeared on mushrooms, bamboos, peonies, fruit trees, birds, crabs, citrus fruits and all sorts of technical subjects, one of which (Shen Gua's *Meng-ch'i pi-t'an* or *Dream Pool*

Essays) includes the story of Pi Sheng and his movable type. Medicine, geography, maths, astronomy – there were treatises on them all. The print runs were astonishing, ranging into many millions of copies. Of one tenth-century Buddhist collection, 400,000 copies still survive.

Under the influence of the eleventh-century Si-ma Guang, historians developed both literary flair and a concern for good sources, with systematic notes of attribution. Scholars, seeking to escape the stultifying influence of Buddhist theology and stimulated by the fearsomely hard examinations that led to careers, status and income, sought to return to and move beyond Confucian traditions, asserting their faith in reason and evidence and the benefits of education: in short, in the possibility of progress in society and politics. These scholar-officials were deeply concerned with the nature of morality and its implications for life here and now – not, thank goodness, with the nature of God and his supposed ways, as so many Renaissance Europeans would be. Religious disputes bubbled up in plenty, but not religious wars, which are fought by governments, not churches. From these intellectual interests sprang many brilliant men and at least one genius: Shen Gua, a sort of eleventh-century precursor of da Vinci and Darwin who recognized the nature of fossils, theorized that mountains had once been sea-beds, improved astronomical instruments, pioneered advances in mathematics, described how compasses worked, wrote on pharmacology, and took a shrewd interest in politics, history and literature, to list but a few of his accomplishments.

The Song upper classes rejected violent sports – which recalled barbarian and lower-class pleasures – in favour of literature, painting and calligraphy. They loved antiquities: Hung Tsun's *Ku-ch'uan* (*Ancient Coins*), published in the 1190s, was the first book on numismatics. A catalogue of ancient stone and bronze inscriptions records 2,000 of them; it was made by a collector, Zhao Mingcheng, whose wife, Li Qingzhao, was one of the most brilliant poets of her age. In towns, shopkeepers and craftsmen loved storytelling, short musical mimes, puppet-shows and shadow-theatres: traditions that would later stimulate theatre and opera.

A great power culturally, then; but not so great militarily. It was not through lack of numbers – the Song had over a million soldiers in 1045. It was a matter of status and efficiency. The officers were scholar-officials, not professional soldiers, and the soldiers were mercenaries, social dregs raised by recruiters who were the scourge of the countryside. There were no barbarian mercenaries from the northern grasslands, and thus no cavalry to speak of. But inefficiency in the body of the army was countered by some extraordinary technology. As cities grew, so did siege warfare, with a variety of heavy-duty weapons, like the man-powered trebuchets and siege bows which the Mongols would soon adopt. This machinery was combined with the alchemical researches of a previous age. In the early tenth century, gunpowder – based on saltpetre – was used in incendiary devices called 'flying fires': primitive rockets. A century later, Song catapults lobbed bombs and smoke grenades.

It was this great culture that the Mongols were now about to assault, with an odd consequence. It was going to be like squirting water on an oil-fire. The fuel was scattered, along with Mongol forces, flowing westward, infusing Europe with Chinese ideas and discoveries. And the driving force behind this chain of events was Kublai.

Obviously a frontal assault on Song, over the busy, broad and well-defended Yangtze, would risk failure. The Mongols were not in the business of failure. Mönkhe needed something that would give him an edge. It so happened that to the south-west of Song, outside its borders, was a statelet that could, if taken, act as a base from which to open a second front.

Kublai was to be in charge, and about time too. In 1252 he was 37, and had never yet been given responsibility for anything but his own estates. His brother and father had led major campaigns while still in their teens and twenties. A first campaign, an untried leader: Mönkhe was careful to give Kublai the best of help, in the form of one of his most experienced generals, Uriyang-kadai, the 50-year-old son of the legendary Subedei, conqueror of half Asia and much of Russia under Genghis Khan.

Their target was a long way away, and very hard to get to. It was the core of what had between 647 and 937 been a great kingdom, Nanzhao, now reduced to a rump centred on its capital, Dali, after which it is known. Dali, which controlled the road, and thus the trade, between India (through what is now Burma) and Vietnam, was a knot of forested mountains and competing tribes, notoriously difficult to get into, let alone control. In 751, a Tang emperor tried to subdue it and lost 60,000 men.

Not surprisingly, information about Dali/Nanzhao remains scanty and contentious. Thai legends, for instance, refer to Nanzhao as the original homeland of the Thais, where they had ruled in glory until chased away by the Mongols; today, the consensus among scholars is that

Thais were insignificant warrior groups living in the far south. Dali's Bai people, a Tibetan–Burmese tribe, had emerged as the dominant group in 937, and since then had retained a sturdy independence for three centuries under its royal family, the Duans. For a region and a culture few westerners have ever heard of, this was no mean place. The Duans ruled an area some 800 kilometres across – half a million square kilometres, about the size of Afghanistan or Texas. Sichuan, to the north, is notoriously wet, so the Chinese dubbed Dali and its surrounding area Yun-nan, 'South of the Clouds'. Dali was a sort of Inner Asian cross between Afghanistan and Switzerland, its tribal rivalries held in check by rulers made rich by trade, and at peace with the Chinese, who had learned enough to leave the place alone to its tangle of tribes, its mountains, its glorious lake and its charming climate. Today, Dali still thrives on its ancient roots and individuality. The Bai inhabitants still wear traditional bright wrap-around shirts and top-heavy head-dresses. Stone houses decorated with wood carvings line cobbled streets. Buddhist pagodas recall old Nanzhao. Artists work the local marble. Tourists wander the old town, or the mountain trails and the lakeside. It reminds ageing hippies of Kathmandu as it used to be. For Mönkhe and Kublai, it was a stepping-stone to further conquest.

The details of this high-risk and challenging enterprise are obscure, but it is worth looking at it as closely as possible because it explains how Yunnan became part of the Mongol empire, and thus a province of modern China.

For strategists back in Karakorum, invasion must have looked a crazy idea. Dali, flanked on one side by the saw-toothed Azure Mountains and on the other by the Erhai lake, offered few approaches, and all were easily defended. But those three centuries of peace had made it complacent. It had no army to speak of. It was a plum, ripe for the picking – if only the Mongols could get there across Song. That would mean gathering their armies in territory newly conquered from the Tanguts, and then slicing southward for 1,000 kilometres along Song's weakly guarded western borders. It would have to be done well, which meant careful planning.

Mustering from the late summer of 1252 in the semi-desert of the Ordos, within the great northern loop of the Yellow River, Kublai's army took a year to gather itself together: a cumbersome process that must have involved assembling huge numbers of wagons and siege machines, all of which would have to cross rivers and valleys. Eventually, in the autumn of 1253, this great force headed south-west for 350 kilometres along the Yellow River to the Tao, then south across the foothills of the Tibetan plateau into what is today northern Sichuan. This was a pretty remote area, even for the Mongols, but it had been invaded (conquered would be too strong a word) by Ogedei's second son, Köten, in 1239. Kublai camped on the high, bleak grasslands of today's Aba Autonomous Region, with no trouble apparently from the locals, the notoriously wild and semi-nomadic Golok tribesmen, and was ready to attack Dali.

There would not be any need for destruction, if Dali capitulated. Later, the Chinese *Yuan History* told a story of how Kublai's Chinese advisers had managed to talk sense into his naturally violent Mongol soul. One evening, his main adviser Yao Shu told a story of how a Song general, Cao Bin, had captured Nanjing without killing 'so much as a single person; the markets did not alter their openings, and it was as if the proper overlord had returned'. Next morning, as Kublai was mounting up, he leaned over to Yao Shu and said: 'What you told me yesterday about Cao Bin not killing people, that is something I can do.'

Following normal practice, Kublai sent three envoys ahead offering Dali the chance to capitulate. Dali's leading minister, the power behind the Duan ruler, executed them. He must have been ill-informed, over-confident, or lacking all sense of history, or all three. Killing envoys was the worst of diplomatic crimes, a public slap in the face that guaranteed an all-out assault, and who knew what horrors thereafter.

Kublai divided his forces into three. One wing rode eastward, off the high grasslands, down into the Sichuan Basin, by today's Chengdu, replenishing supplies in the newly harvested fields of Dujiangyan, where dams and artificial islands dating back some 1,500 years controlled the Min river. Kublai himself headed south over the grasslands, meeting up with column no. 1 some 350 kilometres and perhaps three days later. All of this would have been well known to those in Dali. Meanwhile, Uriyang-kadai took a difficult – indeed, non-existent – path some 150 kilometres further west, deep into the mountains of western Sichuan, cutting across valleys and ridges to the main road between Dali and Tibet. This would give him a fast two-day run to Dali when the time came. Gao, Dali's leader, massed his forces on the Upper Yangtze, whose headwaters had formed a valley a day's march over a ridge to the east of the city. Dali's army would have looked formidable, but the Mongols had been in this situation many times. A river was no obstacle. They had crossed dozens on their way south. Some of the old hands would have been with Genghis in 1226, when he crossed the

Yellow River using sheepskins as floats for rafts. This had been standard procedure there for centuries; even today, you can try it for yourself in Lanzhou, or even further downriver in Shapotou, near the point where Genghis's armies crossed at the start of his last campaign. The crossing was made at night, of course, and in silence. Led by a general named Bayan, of whom more later when he steps into the limelight, the Mongols appeared at dawn on Gao's flank, attacked, inflicted terrible damage and forced a rapid retreat back to Dali.

With Uriyang-kadai galloping in along the lakeside from the north, Dali was now at Kublai's mercy. At this point, given the opposition, you might think that all-out slaughter would follow, in the spirit of Genghis. But Genghis was not all ruthlessness and barbarism. He slaughtered city populations for one main reason: to encourage other cities to surrender. It saves so much trouble when cities surrender. You get booty enough anyway, and it is easier to have subjects made grateful for their survival rather than made bitter and possibly rebellious by brutality. Here, there were no other cities to be conquered. Kublai ordered restraint, proclaiming that the common people should not be punished for the faults of their foolish leaders. Was this all down to his Chinese advisers? I think not. Kublai by now had enough experience of administration to have seen this for himself; but it is only natural that his advisers – and the writers of the *Yuan History* – should give the credit to China's civilizing influence.

It all fell into place quite easily. The leading minister and his underlings who had executed the envoys were themselves executed, but that was all. The king became a puppet in the hands of Kublai's officials. Rather like a prince in British India, he was pampered into sub-servience, being later awarded the grand-sounding but empty title of Maharajah. Uriyang-kadai, using Dali as his military base, went on to 'pacify' tribes further south and east, penetrating today's north Vietnam, taking Hanoi in 1257, then retreating rather hastily in the face of tropical heat, malaria and some spirited resistance. This is easily said, but it was an immense operation. Yunnan to Hanoi is 1,000 kilometres. In four years the Mongols had marched all the way round Song's western frontiers, meeting hardly any resistance; now they – more specifically, Kublai himself – had all the information needed to plan the next phase of the war against the south.

Yunnan was like a new weight placed on scales: it rebalanced China in interesting ways.

The place was left to its own devices with just a small garrison for almost 20 years, during which the only development of any note – more of a footnote really – was that local officers arranged a brief friendly contact with a tiny neighbouring chiefdom, Kaungai, which was on the upper Irrawaddy, and thus on the main route westward to the Burmese lowlands. This event, entirely insignificant at the time, would acquire significance much later, when Kublai turned an acquisitive eye on Burma.

In 1273 Yunnan's first high-level administrator arrived. Saiyid Ajall was a Turkmen who had survived Genghis's brutal assault on Bukhara in 1220 because his grandfather had surrendered at the head of 1,000 horsemen. Nine years old at the time, the boy was raised in Mongolia and China and went on to make a distinguished career in various government posts, culminating in Yunnan, which, with the help of his son Nasir al-Din, he brought fully into the empire.

The consequences endure in Yunnan's present-day multiculturalism. Here was an area inhabited by aboriginal populations who were no threat to anyone, and yet found themselves assaulted by Mongols leading a mainly Chinese army. The area was then handed over to a Muslim who made it part of a Mongol–Chinese empire, and was responsible for the introduction of Islam. As a result, it attracted Muslims. Today Yunnan has half a million Muslims as part of its rich amalgam of peoples.

4

IN XANADU

BACK ON HIS CHINESE LANDS, KUBLAI EXPERIMENTED WITH large-scale estate management, almost as if he were honing the skills he would need as a future emperor astride two worlds, Mongol and Chinese. His appanages were beginning to look less like estates and more like miniature kingdoms, especially his main one in the Wei valley. To oversee this substantial slab of territory – 50,000 square kilometres, with a mixture of Chinese and non-Chinese inhabitants – he appointed a 20-year-old Uighur, Lien Xixian, who in turn employed a venerable Confucian, Xu Heng. In the stylized words of the *Yuan History*, both men adopted the high-minded Confucian ideal 'to curb the violent and support the weak'. Together with one of Kublai's other advisers, the Zen Buddhist monk Liu Bingzhong, they re-established schools, banned Mongols from enslaving scholars and printed paper money. In a long memorandum Liu set out the steps

Kublai should take to keep society running smoothly and profitably, pointing out that good administration depended on good civil servants, which could only emerge from good schools. In effect, the polymath Liu advised Kublai to act like a Chinese emperor. He should codify the tax and legal systems, reintroduce the civil service examinations and finance the writing of the previous dynasty, the traditional task of a new Chinese ruler. Kublai, however, was not about to go that far. There would be no civil service examinations, because that would mean all his advisers would be Chinese; and there would be no dynastic history of the Jin, because that would be seen by Chinese as proclaiming a new dynasty, which would be seen by Mongols as an attempt to usurp his brother's authority. Perhaps that was what Liu wanted; but not Kublai.

Kublai was already straddling the two worlds, and in 1256 took the first big decision towards making this precarious balance permanent. He needed a better headquarters. He had no town of sufficient stature in his estates. He could not assert traditional Mongol values with a tent-city and mobile palace if he wished to retain the trust of his new Chinese subjects, on whom he now depended for his income. So, perhaps thanks in part to Liu, he decided to create a fixed base, a capital. Why not? Ogedei had one in Karakorum; his brother Hulegu had the choice of many Islamic cities; government in north China demanded no less. But it would have to be done with care. A true Chinese ruler, of course, would have taken over one of the old capitals, maybe Xian or Kaifeng, both within reach of his estates, or even Beijing, now regaining some of its self-respect after Genghis's assault in 1215. But Kublai was not Chinese, and could not afford to seem so in the eyes of his family and fellow Mongols. His Chinese advisers understood the problem, and set out to choose a suitable site.

Kublai knew the general area where his capital needed to be, because there was not a huge range of choices if he was to assert the two cultures equally. It would have to be within reach of Beijing, then known as Zhongdu, the Central Capital; it would also have to be on grasslands, in traditional Mongol territory.

The grasslands of Inner Mongolia, now colonized by Chinese spreading from the lowlands, are surprisingly close to Beijing on the map, a mere 250 kilometres, but a world away in practice, even with the fine new roads of today's booming economy. It's a seven-hour drive, which takes you on steep, slow climbs and a great dog's-leg to skirt mountains, stretching the journey by another 100 kilometres. You head north-west, away from the city's dense traffic and noodle-soup pollution, along the expressway that carries over a million tourists a year to the Great Wall. This wonder need not detain us, because it was built long after Kublai's time. Our attention should be on the undulating mountains over which the Wall floats. This was Beijing's last line of natural defences: two tree-covered ranges, the Jungdu and the Xi mountains, all sharp ridges and precipitous ravines, a landscape like crumpled tinfoil. The ancient route through was once a track along the Juyong Pass, just a few dozen metres across at its narrowest. It cannot accommodate all of an expressway: so while the northbound carriageway, with its tedious lines of bellowing trucks, is cut into the valley wall, the southbound one is out of sight, the other side of the mountains. It was easy to defend, and most armies could be stopped here; but not the Mongols in 1213. They went over the mountains and took it from behind. That's why the Ming, nervous of a Mongol revival, built the Wall across mountains, and why the Wall is actually many walls, its various bits and pieces guarding side-ridges where tough men and sturdy horses could sneak over.

You have now climbed several hundred feet, and are on the half-landing, as it were. It is an easy ride for the next 100 kilometres. Signs in English warn of the dangers of boredom: 'Don't try fatigue driving!', 'Do not drive tiredly!' The next stop, Zhangjiakou, used to be seven hours from Beijing; now it's two if the traffic is light. Zhangjiakou is a historic city, though you wouldn't guess this from the look of the seedy apartment blocks that now swamp the old town's huddle of single-storey houses and alleyways. It once marked the frontier between lowland China and the plateau lands of Mongolia, which is why Mongols (and foreign explorers) called it Kalgan, from the Mongolian for 'gateway'. Through here flowed the trade between Russia, Mongolia and China. A century ago it had 7,000 commercial enterprises, with ox-wagons by the hundred and camels by the hundred thousand passing through its narrow northern gate. In 1917, revolution in Russia killed the place, and its hinterland became famous for banditry. Now it has been resurrected by China's northward thrust into its frontier province, Inner Mongolia, while Mongol influence has vanished entirely, as far as I could see. The only sense of its historic role lies in the landscape, the long zigzag haul up on to the farmlands and villages of the Mongolian plateau.

Now you swing eastward, and your mobile beeps a message: Welcome to Inner Mongolia. The plaque on a huge statue of a hand holding a Mongolian horse-head fiddle urges us all to protect the grasslands – protection which they certainly need, because there is not much of them left. At Zhenglan Qi, a new northbound railway line is being built to bring in more farmers and civilize this frontier land with more ploughs and more towns.

Just beyond, though, there are still open spaces that would delight Kublai's soul. This too is a land rich in history, for it was Genghis's campsite on his way south to Beijing, and on his way back from its conquest. That's probably why Kublai directed his advisers' attention here. Led by Liu Bingzhong, the Golden Lotus Advisory Group, as Kublai's brains trust was called, followed the pre-scribed rituals of geomancy, and identified the site of the place English-speakers know as Xanadu, and which Kublai would soon call Shang-du, the Upper Capital (as opposed to Da-du, Beijing, the Great Capital, as it became under the Mongols).

There's a legend about the site. It was originally called Lung Gang, Dragon Ridge, so Liu and the Golden Lotus Advisory Group first had to cast a spell to evict the dragon and raise a tall iron pennant endowed with magic powers to prevent its return. There was also a lake in the middle of the open plain. This had to be drained and filled in.

There was nothing much around to build with – hardly a tree, no stone quarries. Xanadu's main palace, the temples, the government buildings, the sub-palaces and officials' houses all had to be started from scratch, with teams of pack animals and wagon trains carting timber and stone (and marble, as you will see) from hundreds of kilometres away.

* * *

Kublai was a little wary of calling his new place a capital, perhaps preferring to give the impression this was just a summer camp. For the three years it took to build, and for four years thereafter, it was known as Kai-ping, being renamed Shang-du only in 1263. But it was intended as a capital right from the start, though more for government administration and his own relaxation than a living city; more a Versailles than a Paris.

It had three sections, all squares, nested in the Chinese style of capital cities. The Outer City measured 2.2 kilometres to each side, almost 9 kilometres around in all: nowhere near the '16 miles' mentioned by the unreliable Marco Polo, but large enough to contain a huddle of mud-brick and wooden houses for the mass of ordinary people, crowded into a corner less than a square kilometre in size and carefully separated from its northern section. This was a rectangular parkland, the Emperor's Garden. Here, according to the notice at the site's entrance today, 'auspiciousness reigned'. Marco Polo left a description of it. Deer nibbled meadow-grass, wandering through glades of trees, drinking from streams and fountains. This was Kublai's Arcadia, an artificial version of the Mongolian grasslands, where he could pot a deer with his bow, send a tame snow leopard to seize another, and despatch falcons skimming in pursuit of songbirds. Here, too, he had a pavilion of bamboo, some 15 metres across, from which, sheltered against sun or rain beneath a roof of split canes laid like overlapping roof-tiles, he could watch displays of horsemanship. In these peaceful surroundings, Kublai would also raise his Great Palace Tent, the centre point of Mongol-style assemblies.

In the south-east corner of the Outer City was the Imperial City, 1.4 kilometres square, surrounded by a brick wall some 4 metres high, containing government department buildings, craft houses and several temples, Taoist and Buddhist, all laid out neatly along a grid of streets.

The heart of the place, the Palace City, lay within the Imperial City. Actually, the square that contained the palace was not *quite* a square, being 570 by 620 metres, just over two kilometres around. Six meeting-halls – the halls of Crystal, Auspiciousness, Wisdom, Clarity, Fragrance and Controlling Heaven – were gathered at the feet of the palace itself, the Hall of Great Stability, constructed like all the other buildings in the Chinese style, with curled-up roofs and glazed tiles. Rashid ad-Din says that the palace was built right over the lake that had been in the middle of the site, on a platform of rubble and melted tin, with the result that later the water escaped elsewhere in streams and springs.

After the Mongol dynasty fell in 1368, Xanadu was abandoned. For 600 years it decayed, its great palace, courtyards, buildings and walls eroding away until they were mere mounds, hardly visible in the rolling grasslands. A doctor at the British legation in Beijing, Stephen Bushell, stumbled on the ruins by chance in 1872, and reported seeing blocks of marble, the remains of large temples, 'while broken lions, dragons and the remains of other carved monuments lie about in every direction'. The Japanese did some work there when they occupied Inner Mongolia in the 1930s, after which not much remained. Both before and after the communist takeover of 1949 China showed no interest, for the Mongol dynasty – established by barbarians from beyond the Gobi – was a chapter of the country's history its new rulers would rather forget.

It was here, as every British and American schoolchild used to know, that Kublai decreed a stately pleasure dome, in the dream of Samuel Taylor Coleridge one summer day in 1797, before he was famously interrupted by an unwelcome visitor. Coleridge's vision, and his poem, are fantasy; so it is a surprise to discover that the place and the glory were real, and that by visiting the one you can still sense the other.

When I was first at Xanadu in 1996, there were no signs on the approach roads. My guide was unfazed. 'Under the nose is the mouth,' he remarked with the wisdom of ages, and proved it by asking the way from a couple of farmers. We were able to drive straight into the place, a glorious wilderness, eroded walls rising gently from waving grass and pretty meadow flowers. There was no fence, no entry charge; no custodians blocked the way along the track that cut through the outer wall. The sky was pure Mongolian blue, the breeze gentle, the only sound a cuckoo.

But we were not alone. Half a dozen men were measuring things and setting up bits of string in squares. They were archaeologists from Hohhot, beginning to pick up the threads of research at last. One of them, Wei Jian, an associate professor in the Archaeological Institute, briefed me through my guide. These were the walls, over there the palace. This whole basin used to be called the Golden Flower Plain, and you could see why from the profusion of buttercups mixed in with purples and whites of flowers I didn't recognize.

'You see what a beautiful site it is, protected by the hills.'

I looked at the low wall of hills to the north. They seemed to be very sharply pointed.

'This place was chosen for superstitious reasons. It is an auspicious site. To the north is Dragon Mountain, with Lightning River to the south.'

'The mountains, they look like . . . breasts.'

He laughed. 'They have shrines on the top, piles of stones. There is a story that those with shrines are arranged in the shape of the Seven Gods.' The term he used was the same as the Mongolian name for the constellation we call the Plough, Ursa Major. 'It is something we have to check. We have much to learn.'

I walked through the waving grass towards the palace, and came across a crude little out-of-place statue – Turkish, pre-Mongol – standing as if on guard, brought here perhaps by Kublai's people, or found here and simply left alone. The ground was strewn with rubble which threatened to twist an ankle if I wasn't careful. The base of the palace was still there, an earthen mound about 50 metres long standing some 6 metres above the grass. Despite Rashid's claim, there was no hint of underground dampness, except for what may once have been a well in what was once a courtyard. Or it may have been a flag-holder. The palace mound was flanked by two others – the remains of three great buildings creating a three-sided courtyard. Paths made through the grass by wandering tourists wound to the top of the mound at either end. The front, though, was an almost sheer earth face, punctuated by a line of holes, where long-vanished roof-beams must have held a canopy. I imagined visiting dignitaries dismounting in its shade, before climbing steps to the palace itself, to be received by the emperor himself on his dais.

There is nothing solid up there now, or down below either. It struck me as odd: a platform of earth has survived 700 years, despite the fierce summer downpours and rock-cracking frosts of winter, yet of the building itself not a trace remains. There is rubble, of course, strewn among the coarse grass. But what of the bricks and tiles? What of the remains of temples and monuments seen by Bushell in 1872? Had the Japanese taken the lot, leaving just the crude remains of stone? I picked up some, all shapeless bits and pieces, nothing about them to suggest what they had once been. A bit of glazing, from a pot, perhaps; the curve of a drab grey roof tile; stones that looked like just stones. But what rubble, what stones: the dust of Xanadu. How on earth would I do them justice?

I was back in 2004. Change was on the way, reflecting change everywhere in China. Now there's a spanking new highway leading east from Zhenglan Qi, and a sign in both Chinese and English to 'Yuan Shang-du', and a newly laid minor road, leading straight north across pasture to a tourist camp of round, white Mongolian tents. The road skirts the tourist camp with two right-angle bends, and leads you to a fence, a gate and a little museum, with two or three attendants and an entrance charge. After that, though, I was on my own, as before. Foreign tourists get no help, for the authorities have not yet appreciated the significance of the place, especially for English-speakers. The few signs were still in Chinese. I was still free to stroll the hummocks and the palace mound and the grass-covered rubble, still free to pick up rubble.

Not for much longer. The archaeologists had been at work. In the courtyard of the museum stands a glass cabinet containing an immense block of white marble, 2 metres high. It was found under the ruins of the palace in 2003, in the wake of two other similar finds which are now in the Hohhot museum. Probably the base of a pillar, it is gorgeously carved with a bas-relief of intertwining dragons and peonies, symbols of both war and peace. Finds like this are finds indeed. They hint at the magnificence of the place, and the skill of Kublai's Chinese artists, and the labour involved – the closest source of marble is 700 kilometres away. They are also new evidence in a rumbling academic dispute about whether the unreliable Marco Polo was ever actually in China at all. Yet he begins his description: 'There is at this place a very fine *marble* palace.' As a plaque near the palace mound states: 'These things testify to Marco Polo's presence.'

The greatest change is not at the site itself, but in the approach to it. The first glimpse of Xanadu is the tourist camp, some 40 small Mongolian tents (*gers*) and three huge concrete ones, with double domes. It is a hint of things to come. The camp is the creation of a local businessman, 'Benjamin' Ren (Chinese who deal with westerners often give themselves western names). Benjamin is remarkable in several ways: handsome, out-going, generous, ambitious, and driven by a desire to combine business with ecology. Conscious of the ruinous spread of industry and agribusiness into the grass-lands, he conceived a plan to plant forests and save pastures. Backed by a rich Indonesian, he bought up a county-sized tract of land, planted no fewer than 15 million trees on half of it, and would have put the rest to pasture had he not discovered it was disastrously overgrazed. Now he's letting it revert to meadowland.

One thing led to another. By chance, his land is right by Xanadu. Speaking good English, he at once saw the potential for tourism, especially with the new road.

The tourists would need somewhere to stay. His tourist camp opened in 2003, offering Mongolian *gers*, cunningly adapted with double beds, lighting, running water and toilets, and the double-domed restaurants that employ locals to cook Mongolian banquets and entertain with Mongolian music. In that first year of operation, he hosted 1,500 people, and in 2004 6,000, a number that should multiply sixfold by the time of the Beijing Olympics in 2008.

In the current climate of privatization, I can imagine Benjamin doing deals over the museum and access to the site and the flow of information. Soon, it will be easy, and comfortable, and crowded, and expensive. Unless you go soon, I'm afraid that Xanadu will not be an adventure any more, and you will certainly not be allowed to gather up bits and pieces of broken tile.

But where had they all gone, the remnants seen by Bushell? Benjamin had the answer. In the nearby town of Dolon Nur, many buildings have rather fine brickwork and tiles. This area, remember, was always short of building materials. It seems that Xanadu was mined, brick by brick, tile by tile, by local householders. All that's left is what they couldn't use.

I still have those bits I picked up, and I think I know what to do. I shall grind them to dust and use the dust to fill incisions in a table-top, forming two characters:

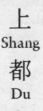

上
Shang

都
Du

* * *

The emerging capital, half-Mongol and half-Chinese in conception, was still too Chinese for traditional Mongols. Back in Karakorum, there were those who were jealous of Kublai's success and muttered that he was getting above himself, too ambitious by half, dreaming of his own empire by rivalling Mönkhe's capital. And far too rich. Could he perhaps be taking for himself some of the tax receipts that should by rights be coming to Karakorum? Mönkhe heard the talk, wondered if there was any truth in it, and was persuaded to act. In 1257 he sent two tax inspectors to audit Kublai's officials. They found fault, listed 142 breaches of regulations, accused Chinese officials, even had some executed and, with Mönkhe's authority, took over the collection of all taxes in Kublai's estates. What could Kublai do? He could let loose his guards, and arrest the malign accountants. But that, as his Confucian and Buddhist advisers pointed out, would be outright rebellion. Better to conciliate. He did, first with a two-man embassy that made no impression, and then in person, appealing to Mönkhe as brother to brother. That worked. The two embraced in tears, Kublai all contrition, innocence and loyalty, Mönkhe offering forgiveness and renewed trust. (He was as good as his word: three years later, he had his accountants executed for sedition.)

The fact was that the two brothers needed each other. Kublai's power depended on Mönkhe's support – and Mönkhe had a problem, created by Genghis himself 30 years previously. He had been so impressed by the aged Taoist monk Ch'ang-chun, the one whom Genghis had summoned from China all the way to Afghanistan to teach the ways of Tao, that he had granted Ch'ang-chun's sect freedom from taxation. The Taoists, once the juniors in the hierarchy of religions, had exploited their new-found wealth and status by seizing Buddhist temples. Wealth being a wonderful source of inspiration, Taoist sects had multiplied. There were now 81 of them, according to one account, with ascetics at one end of the scale and at the other fortune-tellers who were hardly more than hooligans, happy to rip paintings and statues from Buddhist shrines.

Buddhists objected, equally violently. They were much strengthened by an influx of priests from Tibet, a region that would soon form part of Kublai's empire (to which chapter 7 returns in more detail). In 1258 Buddhists were all too well aware of the importance of political contacts, and were desperate to have their revenge on the Taoists.

The row had to be stopped, because otherwise there would be no stability in north China, and no secure base from which to undertake the much more important matter of the invasion of Song. Kublai was the key to both problems. In Morris Rossabi's words: 'Though I do not rule out the possibility that the dramatic scene portrayed in the Chinese chronicles occurred, I believe it occurred only after both Mönkhe and Kublai had rationally evaluated the folly of a split between them.'

So the first thing on Kublai's agenda in early 1258 was to convene a conference of Taoist and Buddhist leaders, and knock their heads together. It was quite a conference. To Xanadu came 300 Buddhists and 200 Taoists, held apart by the presence of 200 court officials and Confucian scholars. Kublai was in the chair.

The Taoist case rested on two documents, both of which claimed that Lao-tzu, the sage who had founded Taoism, had undergone 81 incarnations – hence the number of Taoist sects – in one of which he was known as the Buddha. In addition, one document claimed Lao-tzu had died in India, the homeland of Buddhism, not in China. Therefore, they contended, Buddhism was actually Taoism. It was an insulting idea, made worse by the Tao agenda, summarized in their catch-phrase *hua-hu* (convert the barbarians). What they did not appreciate was that Kublai was already almost a Buddhist. His favourite wife, Chabi, was. He had been impressed by his clutch of Buddhist monks and their practical reasons for adopting Buddhist-style good government.

In fact, he did not need to bring his prejudice to bear. The Taoists were not used to debate, and proved a colourless lot. Kublai's Tibetan adviser, Phags-pa, cross-questioned the senior Taoist on the authenticity of their main 'convert the barbarians' text, with its claim that their founder, Lao-tzu, had died in India. How odd that Sima Qian (Ssu-ma Ch'ien in the old orthography), the great first- and second-century historian, did not mention this interesting claim or the document asserting it, the reason being – Phags-pa concluded – that Lao-tzu actually died in China and the document was a forgery. The Taoists, lacking both references and arguments, were left looking foolish. Kublai offered them one last chance: call upon ghosts and demons, prove your magical powers by performing supernatural feats. Naturally, they demonstrated no powers at all.

Kublai delivered his judgement. Buddhism was in, Taoism out. Seventeen Taoist heads were shaved, all copies of the fraudulent texts were to be destroyed, 237 temples were to be restored to the Buddhists. But he was wise enough not to be vindictive, for he knew he could not afford to alienate Tao's many adherents. There would be no executions, merely a return to the status quo earlier in the century, before Ch'ang-ch'un's sudden elevation three decades earlier.

The debate sealed Kublai's return to favour. He had imposed peace with firm executive action, displaying intelligence and moderation. Everyone approved, and he was all set for his next big task, the invasion of southern Song.

5

THE CLAIMANT

AS SUCCESSFUL DICTATORS DO, MÖNKHE DEPENDED ON RAPID and all-embracing foreign conquest as a way to pre-empt dissent. Not that anyone would have put it in those terms, because that motive was hidden by the overwhelming truth, as the Mongols saw it, that they had unfinished business with the world at large. By 1257 Persia and southern Russia were secure; so now for the rest of China – and then the rest of the world.

The Mongols were in strong positions, with armies based in Xanadu (under Kublai) and Yunnan, north China and what had been Xi Xia. But the task ahead was not simply formidable. It seemed frankly ludicrous, so vast was the difference between the two sides.

Song was a land of rivers and forests and mountains, with none of the open plains that gave the Mongol cavalry its advantage. The land between the Yellow River and the southern coast was then, as it is today, China's breadbasket, including a million square kilometres of fields and canals. Its capital, present-day Hangzhou (then called Linan) was the world's most populous city, with 1.5 million people – more than the whole population of Mongolia. A century of imperial spending had turned it into a boom-city. Dominating the southern end of the Grand Canal's exit into Hangzhou Bay, it was among the world's finest ports. Its setting – the Eye of Heaven Mountains, the West Lake – was as beautiful as its palaces. How could the Mongols dare to dream of victory over this one city, let alone the 41 other cities of 100,000 inhabitants or more, let alone the 50 million peasants who crowded the rich lands of the Yangtze basin?

The Mongols did not have resources of their own for such an enterprise. They would have to use north Chinese to fight south Chinese. With the Mongol cavalry virtually useless, everything would depend on Chinese infantry, Chinese siege engines, Chinese engineers. The climate was sub-tropical in summer, the landscape tortuous, the distances immense, diseases rife. Who would bet on success?

At least Mönkhe had a good HQ. Set up 30 years before by Genghis himself, it lay some 200 kilometres south of the Yellow River near the head of a tributary, the Qing Shui river in the billowing foothills of the Liupan mountains, where Genghis had spent the summer of 1227, before he had succumbed to the disease that killed him. It was a good site, because it was out in the open, yet within a day's gallop of the secret valley in the mountains – steep forests, fertile soils, a wealth of medicinal plants – where Genghis had probably been brought in a vain attempt to heal his fatal illness. Now a major archaeological site,

Kaicheng was the command centre where the last leader of Xi Xia had surrendered to the ailing – or perhaps already dead – Genghis, only to be murdered. It lay just 70 kilometres from the Song border.

Mönkhe knew well enough the immensity of the task ahead. His plan was to start big, by cutting his opponent in half. Three columns would converge on the Yangtze at Wuchang (now part of the mega-city of Wuhan), the key to the lower Yangtze and thus to the capital, Hangzhou. One of the columns would be Kublai's, advancing from Xanadu, a southward trek of some 1,400 kilometres. Actually, Kublai's involvement was in doubt for a time because he was suffering from gout, the disease that would afflict him all his life. When Mönkhe suggested he be replaced by one of Genghis's nephews, he was indignant. He had just finished sorting out the dispute between Buddhists and Taoists, and was eager for action. 'My gout is better,' he protested. 'How is it fitting that my elder brother should go on a campaign and I should remain idle at home?' Mönkhe let him get on with it. In Wuchang, Kublai would meet up with the two other columns: one under Uriyang-kadai, arriving from Yunnan (almost 1,500 kilometres away), and a third from Kaicheng. Mönkhe himself would be on a separate campaign into the centre of this region, striking south-west for 650 kilometres, taking Chengdu in the heart of Sichuan, and finally turning south-east for 250 kilometres to Chongqing, the river port that was the link between the Yangtze's downriver trade and the overland route to Tibet.

Mönkhe arranged for the correct rituals to ensure that Heaven would be with him, honouring his grandfather's spirit at his grave on Burkhan Khaldun and scattering milk from his herd of white mares around his palace. Then he headed south, across the Gobi, through what had once been Xi Xia and was now imperial land, to Kaicheng. The summer of 1257 he spent in the Liupan mountains, gathering his forces. The following spring, his army took Chengdu and moved on through Sichuan's mists – so thick, it was said, that dogs bark when they see the sun.

But progress was slow, because conquest had to be accompanied by administration; so it was early 1259 before he reached Chongqing. Then, further delay: to take Chongqing, he first had to overcome a formidable fortress 60 kilometres to the north. Set on a sheer 400-metre-high ridge called Fishing Mountain over what is now the town of Hechuan, it dominated three rivers which flowed together before joining the Yangtze. This operation brought Mönkhe to a dead halt. Weeks turned to months, spring to summer. The heat mounted. Disease struck. Several thousand of his men died. Yet, despite urging from his generals, Mönkhe refused to give up.

In August, escaping the heat in the nearby hills and drinking far too much wine with the excuse that it would stave off sickness, he went down with something very serious, probably cholera. If that was it, he had little chance. His bowels turned to water, cramp racked him, and in ten days he was dead.

At this point all military action should have ceased as Mongol leaders refocused their attention on the succession. First came the rituals of burial, which took at least a month, perhaps two: the preparation of the body for travel; the 1,800-kilometre, month-long return to Karakorum, where official mourning took place over four consecutive days in the palaces of high-ranking women;

then the final 500-kilometre procession eastward over the grasslands, past the hills that flank present-day Ulaanbaatar, into the Mongols' original heartland, up the Kherlen river, over the ridge that guards its headwater valleys and thus at last to the sacred mountain of Burkhan Khaldun, the burial place of Genghis and his son Tolui. This immense act of reverence should have involved every prince, every noble, every princess, each with his or her entourage of horses and wagons, ending with the pitching of many tents in preparation for the interment. The final burial would have been in the Great Forbidden Place, with its permanent corps of mounted guards patrolling the approaches. A final, smaller group of mourners would have wound along the 20-kilometre valley of the Bogd river, then up the forested slopes to the open plateau that lies beneath Burkhan Khaldun's great arched summit. The site itself was designed to be kept secret: horses trampled the graves, then saplings and coarse grass slowly covered the spots where the earth had been disturbed, while summer rains and winter frosts churned the graves back into the permafrost. So where exactly Genghis, Tolui, Mönkhe and later emperors lie is still a mystery.

Next on the agenda would be the great assembly of the princes and the clan leaders, the *kuriltai*, that would elect the next khan. But by now winter was coming on; so the election would not take place until the following spring, allowing the claimants time to ensure they had the backing they needed.

And what, meanwhile, of Kublai? He had been about to cross the river now known as the Huai, 250 kilometres into Song territory, when news came of Mönkhe's death.

He had been on the road for several weeks, covered 1,000 kilometres, opted for speed over security by avoiding the great fortress-town of Xiangyang, and had another 400 kilometres – perhaps ten days' march – to go to reach his rendezvous. There was a Song troop ahead. Scouts were bound to hear of his brother's death, and spread the good news, and inject new heart into the Song opposition. So he had a choice: to sit about doing nothing, and allow the Song time to mount a counter-offensive; to retreat, and abandon conquered territory; or to advance. He knew from experience what was right. When his grandfather had died, he had been twelve: old enough to be part of the plan to keep the death a secret from his main enemy, the Tanguts, in case the news should put new heart into them. He talked the matter over with his number two, Batur. Batur, the same age as Kublai, came from an eminent military family, being the grandson of Genghis's great general Muqali (Mukhali in an alternative spelling). He understood, and between them the decision was made.

They would pretend the news was merely gossip designed to spread fear and despondency. 'Let us pay no attention to this rumour,' Kublai said, according to Rashid ad-Din. 'We have come hither with an army like ants or locusts. How can we turn back, our task undone?'

His advance continued, to the universe of water that was the Yangtze. From the point where it leaves the Three Gorges, 400 kilometres upstream, the Yangtze becomes Amazonian, meandering lazily across rice-rich plains, dropping just 2.5 centimetres every kilometre. It's more inland sea than river, as variable as wet ink on blotting paper. In Kublai's day it hardly had banks at all, so regularly did it spill over them. At this point, it was a maze of meanders and lakes, making a barrier over 10 kilometres wide. It must have taken quite a fleet to cross; but cross he did, because he laid siege to Wuchang, to be joined some three weeks later by Uriyang-kadai's 20,000-strong force from Yunnan. They'd had a hard time, taking fortresses on the mountain passes, losing 5,000 men to disease. Their arrival nearly knocked the heart out of Wuchang. The town must have been on the brink of surrender when, in early October, Song contingents, released from fighting Mönkhe by his death, arrived to confront Kublai. Somehow, they managed to bypass the Mongols – by river, probably – and enter the city, proof that the besiegers' grip was not as tight as it should have been.

Stalemate.

Kublai faced a tricky decision: to continue the siege of Wuchang, or return to Mongolia to engage with the business of the succession. Increasingly, imperial strategy was being trumped by affairs back home. In December, Kublai decided he could hesitate no longer. But which to choose: finish the job, or pull back?

The Song commander, Jia Sidao, a wily diplomat who undoubtedly knew of the pressures on his adversary, tried to nudge him into withdrawal. Jia, one of the most famous and controversial men of his age, has an important role to play in Kublai's story. His grandfather and father had been men of medium-grade military rank; nothing exceptional, but good enough to put silver spoons in Jia's young mouth. In his home town, the Song capital of Hangzhou, he had been one of the *jeunesse dorée*, with a penchant for pretty girls, drinking and gambling. He was also lucky. His sister had been chosen as an imperial concubine; she became the emperor's favourite, bearing him a daughter, his only surviving child, and rising to the high rank of Precious Consort in the harem. In 1236 the emperor had fallen ill and some senior official was going to suggest pensioning him off. Jia heard of the plot and told his sister, who told the emperor, who acted to save his throne. Good jobs followed, and by the time he was 40 Jia was powerful and rich. He dabbled in art and antiques. He had a glorious estate in the hills overlooking the West Lake, where he threw parties for guests by the thousand. With time and wealth to spare, he was able to indulge a very strange hobby: he loved to set crickets fighting each other. Indeed, he became such an expert in crickets and their aggressive ways that he wrote a handbook on the raising and training of champion crickets. He had literary pretensions. Another work, a commonplace book of his thoughts and experiences, was called *Random Excerpts from the Hall Where One Enjoys Life*, which he signed pseudonymously 'The Old Man Who Is Half Idle'. His rivals (of course) called him arrogant and frivolous, and muttered about the way he siphoned off state cash to cram his own Xanadu, the Garden of Clustered Fragrances, with art treasures. In 1259, when he was 46, he was appointed Chancellor of the Empire, with responsibility for upgrading Song's shaky finances and armed forces. He thus found himself in charge of the defence of Wuchang, and in a position to influence Kublai in his next decision.

Jia chose a high-risk strategy. He made a secret approach to Kublai to propose terms, an act of duplicity for which he would pay dearly later. What if the Song paid an annual tribute, in exchange for the Mongols agreeing that the Yangtze should be the new frontier between the states?

Kublai would have none of it. 'Your intentions may be

good because you are in favour of peace for the sake of living beings,' he replied through his envoy. 'But now, after we have crossed the Yangtze, what use are these words?'

The Mongols didn't need an agreement to receive what they could simply take; and a treaty designating a new frontier would be a diplomatic inconvenience when the time came to complete the conquest. Better simply to pull back and then return in their own time, especially – and this was the deciding factor – because something rather ominous was afoot back home.

As Kublai learned in a message from his worried wife, his younger brother, Ariq Böke – Ariq the Strong – master of the empire's nomadic heartland, was raising troops, for some unknown reason. It must be to do with the succession, because of the surviving three brothers, Hulegu, ruler of Persia, was not in the running; only Ariq and Kublai were left. Could Kublai possibly return? If Kublai needed a further reason, he had it two days later, when messengers came from Ariq himself, bringing nothing but innocuous greetings and enquiries about Kublai's health. Kublai was suspicious. He asked what their master was doing with the troops he had raised. Disconcerted by the fact that he had heard of Ariq's actions, they wriggled. Troops? What troops? 'We slaves know nothing. Assuredly it is a lie.' Kublai smelt treachery. In a secret meeting with his top generals, he told them he was heading north to find out what was going on.

The fact was that Ariq was a traditionalist. He didn't like to see his brother abandoning the old ways – a Christian wife here, Chinese estates there – and he was seeking support at home to make sure that he would be elected khan at the assembly next spring. But obviously he didn't want Kublai to know his plans. A couple of weeks later, Kublai, having decamped 600 kilometres northward back to the Yellow River, sent Ariq a message asking about the troops – What were they for? Why couldn't they be handed over to him, Kublai, for use against the Chinese? One of Ariq's aides pointed out that Kublai seemed to have guessed what was up. Better to send messengers telling him recruitment had been stopped and reassure him with gifts of falcons and hunting animals.

So it happened. Outwardly, Kublai expressed relief – 'Everyone's mind is set at rest' – but he wasn't fooled. Politics now trumped empire-building. He ordered his generals to abandon the siege of Wuchang instantly, leave a token force as a bridgehead, and head back to Mongolia.

It was, at last, the end of this invasion. Jia soon re-captured what had been taken. Song would remain unconquered for another 20 years. Kublai found all his attention focused on a dispute that would rapidly escalate into civil war.

As 1259 turned to 1260, ploy was followed by counter-ploy, with messages being carried back and forth across the steppes and the Gobi at full gallop, the two would-be emperors dicing for advantage as if they and their supporters were pieces on a vast chessboard. Ariq tried to call an assembly to elect himself khan. It didn't work. It was so obviously intended to bend the rules that several princes did not respond. He tried another stratagem. Come at once, he begged, to mourn our brother. Kublai, now in Beijing, saw that if he did he would be walking into a trap, and stalled. His men were only just back from the campaign, he said. They needed a break. No sooner had Ariq's messengers left than Kublai sent for the force Mönkhe had been leading when he died. Where were they, anyway? Keeping out of the way, apparently, in the land of the Tanguts – what had once been Xi Xia before Genghis took it over.

By now it was spring. Ariq, newly arrived in his summer quarters in the Altai mountains in Mongolia's west, saw he could not afford to wait any longer, could not risk a journey to Karakorum, perhaps because it was within too easy reach of Kublai's armies. He gathered what princes he could, had himself declared khan and sent off messengers proclaiming, as Rashid puts it, that Hulegu, Berke (the new ruler of the Golden Horde in southern Russia), the current ruler of Chaghadai's realm in Central Asia and other princes had all agreed to raise Ariq to the khanate and 'You must pay no attention to the words of Kublai.'

Kublai was incensed. This was outright rebellion, not so much against him personally as against the practice by which the new khan was elected by a conclave of a majority of the princes. It was also a lie. The two khans of Persia and the Golden Horde were not in Mongolia, and anyway were now bitter rivals over both territory and religion. Hulegu had indeed set off for Mongolia after Mönkhe's death, but the disaster of Goliath's Spring had turned him around. Berke had converted to Islam the better to rule his Muslim subjects; Hulegu had been killing Muslims by the thousand. Both princes, one pro- the other anti-Muslim, claimed what is now Azerbaijan. As Hulegu returned to save what he could, Berke took advantage of his cousin's weakness to declare war. What chance such bitter rivals would agree on a new khan?

Ariq had shot himself in the foot. Kublai was not the only one angered by his presumption. Princes and generals who had not responded to Ariq's call rallied to Kublai. To save the empire, there was only one thing to be done: he had to declare himself khan, with as much validity as possible. This could not be done with *total* validity, because that would take a full assembly in Karakorum, which he was not yet ready to hold. So in early May 1260, those who backed Kublai were called to Xanadu for the ceremony.[1]

The two sides were evenly balanced. Kublai could count on Hulegu; but Hulegu was busy trying to fight off Berke. Then again, Kublai had the resources of north China behind him, which he did his best to secure with a proclamation pointing out his virtues: he would rule with goodness and love, lower taxes, feed the hungry, revere the ancestors, and in brief be everything a thoroughly Chinese emperor ought to be. A flurry of orders set up Chinese-style institutions. Under guidance from his Chinese adviser Wang O, he gave his reign a title: Zhong Tong, 'Moderate Rule'. Some scholars think that this was done to assert Kublai's pro-Chinese credentials by making a link between his rule and the *I Ching* (*Yi Jing* in pinyin), the *Book of Changes*, the 2,000-year-old oracle.

This historical snippet, I think, throws a sharp little spotlight on the choices facing Kublai. His roots were in the grasslands, yet he had Chinese estates; he had been

[1] This is Rashid's order of events. Other sources have Kublai's coronation coming first, followed sharply by Ariq's. It doesn't matter very much. Being first would not have affected matters either way.

part of the conquest of the north and some of the south, and was set on conquering the rest. Now here he was in a Chinese-style city built on the grasslands, about to declare himself emperor – of what, exactly? A Mongolian empire? A Chinese empire? He needed help to sort out how best to handle this. But he did not, as far as we know, summon Mongolian shamans to examine the scorched and cracked shoulder-bones of sheep. Instead, he called upon a Chinese adept who knew how to cast the *I Ching*.

The *I Ching* holds a unique place in Chinese culture. Both Confucianism and Taoism find themselves reflected in it. At heart, as Kublai would have known from his advisers, *I* (*Yi*), Change, means the stream of life, symbolized as the Way of Water or Tao, in which, if we can only read the symbols aright, we can see what is arriving from the future and what is of the past and finished. This hugely complex system of divination, which integrates myths, symbols, rituals, landscapes, character, language and many other human qualities, has roots that reach back 5,000 years into pre-Shang, pre-Bronze Age, pre-writing times, its complexity and (some would say) wisdom growing with each age thereafter. It was one of the Six Classics, the foundation for all study. Everyone, from emperor to street-cleaner, consulted it at times of change and decision, especially at crucial moments when the Mandate of Heaven falls upon a new dynasty, for it offers insight into the unseen world, where events in the physical world are foreshadowed. Depending on your levels of scepticism and creativity, it is either a very impressive piece of mumbo-jumbo or full of astounding truths. Like a vast and complex ink-blot, you can read in it your heaviest problems and find the most startling insights. Nowadays many say, as Jung said, that it is a 'method of exploring the unconscious', of cutting through the clamour of rival thoughts to arrive at a decision. The problem is how to understand what it says, which is where the experts come in.

What Kublai was told was exactly what any Chinese emperor would wish to hear. Imagine the scene. Kublai, in his new palace, is agonizing over what to do. He knows that he must claim the throne, sometime, somewhere. Moreover, he must assert his claim by giving his reign a name, thus imposing a new calendar, as all new Chinese emperors had done. But should he do it here? Now? And what name should he choose?

The sage prepares his consultation, with the 50 yarrow stalks that will be used to produce one of the 64 six-line diagrams (hexagrams), which will in turn yield a Judgement, an Image and a Commentary. This will be complicated by the fact that the sage speaks Chinese and Kublai doesn't. Everything goes through an interpreter. Each of the six lines that will produce the hexagram must be made by combining random decisions, ritual acts and complex numerical transformations. This is, remember, all about understanding change. One stalk is set aside (I can't discover why; perhaps to produce an odd number). The 49 remaining yarrow-stalks are divided into two random heaps. Obeying ancient rules, Kublai slowly transfers stalks from pile to pile and from pile to hand, until he is holding either nine or five stalks between the fingers of his left hand. The stalks are set aside, and given new numerical values. This he does three times. Then the three selections are integrated to produce a final figure, which in turn produces either a broken or an unbroken line, which, depending on the figure, will or will not undergo further transformation. In this case, it is a 'young yang' line, a positive line, unbroken, a line that will not undergo further change. Six times he repeats this procedure, producing six lines. And lo! All six lines are the same. The hexagram is the very first in the time-honoured catalogue, 'The Creative', Qian:

―――――――――
―――――――――
―――――――――
―――――――――
―――――――――
―――――――――

This is highly auspicious. The creative urge emanates from heaven. It consists of two trigrams, both called Qian. The doubling represents action. So the whole sign represents primal power, the power of Heaven, the creative action of both the Deity and his earthly image, the leader. Kublai knows about Heaven, because it was from the Mongol Heaven or sky-god, Tenger, that his grandfather Genghis had received his mandate to rule. If Kublai makes the right decision and becomes ruler, he will inherit that mandate, first as Mongol khan, but then as world conqueror, which will include being Chinese emperor, who, of course, rules only by Heaven's Mandate. Is this his destiny? If so, how best is he to achieve it? He waits, agog.

The sage proclaims the Judgement: 'The Creative works sublime success, furthering through perseverance.'

I can imagine Kublai's inner reaction. '*What??*'

The sage draws breath to explain. When an individual

draws this oracle, it means that success will come to him from the primal depths of the universe and that everything depends upon his seeking his happiness and that of others in one way only, that is by perseverance in what is right. One of the attributes of this oracle is a word which is sometimes translated as 'sublime', but which also means 'origin, prime, first, great'. That word is *yuan*.

The sage hasn't finished. The khan's destiny is to display the four attributes of sublimity, potential, power and perseverance. The movement of Heaven is full of power. Thus the superior man makes himself strong and untiring. Because he sees with great clarity causes and effects, he completes the six steps at the right time and mounts towards heaven on them at the right time, as though on six dragons. He towers high above the multitude of beings, and all lands are united in peace.

And more of the same. It is obscure, and mystical, and sounds wonderfully wise in almost any version (this one is from the Cary Baynes translation of Richard Wilhelm's German translation from the Chinese). What Kublai surely got out of it was reassurance that he was on the right track. He also took from the reading a name for the period of his reign: Zhong Tong, an obscure term meaning something like Central or Moderate Rule. Eventually, once he had been crowned, he would have to assert himself even more firmly with a name for what would surely become a new dynasty. To take such a step now would have seemed too arrogant; but the reading gave him an idea for a dynastic name that would stay with him until the time was right to assume it, a name that expressed everything he wished his dynasty to become: the sublime, the first, the great, the Yuan.

On 5 May 1260, Kublai took the plunge. The princes

assembled in Xanadu begged Kublai three times to accept the throne. As tradition dictated, he declined twice; the third time, he graciously accepted. The princes swore their oaths of allegiance, and proclaimed him the new emperor.

Now the empire had two Great Khans, rather as the Christian church had two popes, pope and anti-pope, during the Great Schism of 1378–1417. Here were a khan and an anti-khan. Which would turn out to be which?

Military operations in Song went on hold. Kublai did try for a diplomatic solution by sending envoys to Hangzhou, but Jia's reaction was to arrest them. Through the summer of 1260 the two opposed brothers did more jockeying, each tit-for-tat move raising the stakes. One of Ariq's men, Durchi, who was at Kublai's coronation, fled with the news, only to be chased and captured. Ariq returned to Karakorum to assert his rule from there. Kublai tried to put his own man, Abishqa, the grandson of one of his cousins, in charge of Chaghadai's Central Asian realm, only to hear that the mission – Abishqa, two other princes, 100 men – had all been caught by Ariq, who then had his own candidate crowned khan of Chaghadai's territory. Then came the first armed clash, at an unidentified place, which apparently Ariq lost. In revenge, Ariq had Abishqa, his two royal companions and their 100-man escort all executed.

Kublai closed down the Gobi trade routes, starving Karakorum of the supplies that until then had been imported from China. He could do this because his cousin, Khadan, controlled Xi Xia and the Uighur regions further west. The two of them could blockade the whole 2,300-kilometre arc from Beshbaligh, on the border of Chaghadai's realm, to Xanadu, forcing Ariq as winter came on to turn to the rough farmers and craftsmen of the Siberian valleys to his north. Kublai took no chances. He recruited more troops, bought 10,000 extra horses, ordered 6,000 tonnes of rice – a year's supply – then led his well-supplied army northwards into the heart of Mongolia. Not far from Karakorum he learned of the executions, in revenge for which he executed Durchi.

Ariq, forced to retreat to the valley of the Yenisey, the source of his supplies in Siberia, was becoming desperate. He offered apologies and obedience: 'We, your younger brother, committed a crime and transgressed out of ignorance. You are my elder brother, and . . . I shall go whithersoever you command.'

But he didn't. Skirmishing continued, until the next showdown the following autumn in the grasslands of eastern Mongolia. Two battles were fought, with great loss of life on both sides and no decisive outcome. But Ariq was badly damaged. 'Distraught and bewildered, with a lean and hungry army,' in Rashid's words, he pulled back into the forests and mountains of Siberia. Allies abandoned him. Alghu, his puppet ruler of Chaghadai's realm, refused to help and executed Ariq's officials; the khanate collapsed into raid and counter-raid, and its capital, Almaligh, became a place of 'dearth and famine'. That was where Ariq now fled, hounding his former ally into the depths of Central Asia, while Kublai occupied Karakorum for the winter. In the spring, Ariq found his support draining away, symbolized for his aides when a whirlwind – May in the Central Asian steppes is famous for its winds – tore his audience tent from its 1,000 pegs, smashed its support post and injured many of those inside. To his ministers, it was an omen of coming defeat.

At which moment – early 1262 – he was saved by

rebellion against Kublai back home. The trouble came from Shandong, the heart of north China, a rich coastal area near the mouth of the Yellow River. The local warlord, Li Tan, was the son-in-law of one of Kublai's top officials and had helped Mönkhe fight the Song. Kublai thought he was a staunch ally and backed his raids with injections of cash. It seemed a good bet, because Li's son was at court, in effect a hostage. But Li, in control of the local salt and copper industries, was more interested in feathering his own nest than in keeping in with Kublai. He decided that he, as a Chinese, had a better future with the Song than with the Mongols. So he arranged for his son to slip away from Kublai's court, then turned his army loose on local Mongols, seized warehouses, and was clearly intent on establishing his own breakaway kingdom. It took several months to crush him – literally, for his punishment was to be sewn into a sack and trampled to death by horses, the traditional fate reserved by Mongolians for those of princely rank. Kublai followed up by having Li's father-in-law executed as well, and then turned back to the business of dealing with Ariq.

The revolt in Shandong had been a nasty episode, but Kublai came out of it well. Though he would always in future be wary of trusting Chinese, he still consulted his Chinese advisers carefully, and instructed his troops to look after civilians. But he now saw that he needed a better organization to run his war machine. The Bureau of Military Affairs, set up in 1263, drew a clear distinction for the first time between civil and military administration. War would be a sort of Mongol *cosa nostra*, with Chinese excluded, a Mongol-run combination of war ministry and secret service. In establishing this body Kublai was taking an important step away from his grandfather's steppe-based empire, bound together by personal loyalty to Genghis. The Bureau would become a whole parallel bureaucracy, with an elite body of officials owing loyalty not to the person of Kublai, but to his creation, the state.

The winter of 1263–4 was a harsh one for Ariq's army, trapped in Central Asia. Food, weapons and friends were all in short supply. Men and horses starved. Allies – even some members of Ariq's own family – defected. On the wings, Alghu regathered his forces to fight back.

In 1264 Ariq faced the inevitable and came begging for peace, brother submitting to brother. As Rashid describes it, the meeting was full of emotion. Ariq approaches Kublai's huge palace-tent in the traditional manner, raising the flap that covers the door and letting it hang over his shoulder, awaiting the call to enter. Summoned inside, he stands among the secretaries, like a naughty schoolboy. The two brothers stare at each other. If this were a novel, I would tell you that memory carries them back to their childhood, to the years spent under Sorkaktani's stern gaze, to recollections of her virtues: restraint, tolerance, forgiveness. Even Rashid makes it, as they say in film scripts, a moment. Kublai softens. Tears come to the eyes of both men. Kublai beckons.

'Dear brother,' he says, 'in this strife and contention, were we in the right or you?'

Ariq is not quite ready to admit the fault is all his: 'We were then and you are today,' he says. It is almost good enough for Kublai.

Not, however, for the brother of Abishqa, the prince executed by one of Ariq's generals, Asutai. He protests. 'I killed him by the command of the then ruler, Ariq the Strong,' says Asutai, heatedly. 'Today Kublai Khan is ruler of the face of the earth. If he so commands, I will kill you too.'

Another leader utters soothing words. Today is not a time to rake over the past. Today is a time for merrymaking. Kublai approves. Ariq is assigned a place among the princes.

But he is not free. The following day, there is an examination to establish how things had come to this pass. There follows much finger-pointing as commanders dispute who had influenced Ariq the most. These are difficult matters, because Kublai wishes to establish guilt, yet find cause not to execute his own brother.

In the end, ten of Ariq's associates were put to death, while Ariq and Asutai were spared, though remaining under arrest. What to do about Ariq? Kublai summoned his three junior khans – Hulegu, Berke and now Alghu – to discuss the matter, but all three demurred. Hulegu and Berke were still at war, and Alghu only newly restored to power. None of them dared leave home.

Who, then, would rid the khan of his troublesome brother? Not, it seemed, his family; nor Eternal Heaven, either. Ariq was not yet 50 and in fine fettle, a constant reminder that Kublai's claim to the throne was not unchallenged. Then, suddenly, out of the blue, in unexplained circumstances, as Rashid baldly states, Ariq 'was taken ill and died'. Was he murdered? Some suspected so at the time and others have claimed so since. It was certainly a wonderfully convenient solution to an intractable problem.

And then Heaven really did step in. Within a few months of Ariq's death, Hulegu in Persia, Berke of the Golden Horde and Alghu the restored khan of Chaghadai's realm were all dead too. What a waste the past five years had been – all as a result of Ariq's opposition to his brother. The great task of invading China had been put on hold, the stability of Mongol rule across all Eurasia threatened, the Mongol heartland divided against its Chinese territories, the rulers of the three western khanates set at each other's throats. Now, at a stroke, all seemed to be resolved. Never mind that his coronation had not been strictly legal: Kublai was now in direct command of Mongolia, north China, much of Central Asia and some of Song, and overlord of his subsidiary khans in Persia and southern Russia. A portrait of him around this time shows him aged 50, in his prime, in a simple wrap-around gown without adornments. There is something of the sage about him, but his expression is that of a man of uncompromising commitment to the task in hand.

It was time to look south again.

II

SUMMER

KUBLAI'S HEARTLAND

A stone tortoise (*below*), once a pillar-base, is the sole relic of Karakorum, the capital built on the Mongolian grasslands to administer the empire founded by Genghis Khan. The stupas in the background, built in the seventeenth century from Karakorum's bricks, form the monastery of Erdene Zuu, now one of Mongolia's top tourist attractions. In the mid-thirteenth century, this was the empire's heart for Genghis's children, including his youngest son, Tolui, Kublai's father. In this Persian portrait (*above*), Tolui is shown with his wife, Sorkaktani – Kublai's hugely influential mother.

Striking at the Heart of Islam

In 1253 Kublai's brother, the khan Mönkhe, sent his other brother Hulegu to resume the conquest of Islam and extend the Mongol empire westward. Here (*right*) Mönkhe holds a celebration on the eve of the campaign. Hulegu first eradicated the notorious sect of Assassins, whose head, Hassan, supposedly initiated his followers by drugging them (*above*) before despatching them on murderous missions from his main HQ, the formidable castle of Alamut in Iran's Elburz mountains (*below*). In 1258, after destroying the Assassin castles, Hulegu launched a devastating assault on Baghdad (*below right*) which is still remembered by Muslims today as one of Islam's greatest disasters.

IN XANADU, HINTS OF VANISHED SPLENDOUR
Today, Kublai's summer HQ, Xanadu – Shang-du, 'Upper Capital' – is a long-abandoned site of ridges, grassy plains and distant hills. The palace where Marco Polo met Kublai is an eroded mound (*above*), with little to suggest past glory, except a marble pillar (*left*) displayed in the nearby museum. An original gateway is blocked by a wall of rubble (*below*).

A nearby hill (*above right*) is capped by an *ovoo*, a stone shrine. Xanadu will not remain so wild for long. Nearby is a new, comfortable, Mongolian-style tourist camp (*right*), set up by the energetic and imaginative 'Benjamin' Ren (*below*).

THE COMING OF BUDDHISM

Kublai's commitment both to rule China and to extend his empire led him to build on Mongol contacts with Tibet and with its universalist religion, Buddhism. The link was established in 1244 when the head of Tibet's Saskya sect was summoned from Tibet (*top left*) by Kublai's cousin, Köten (*left*).

The two met near Liangzhou (today's Wuwei), at a place now marked by 100 pagodas, built after an earthquake destroyed the originals in 1927 (*below*).

Here a museum commemorates the occasion and emphasizes the importance of the Mongol– Chinese–Tibetan link, with fine though inauthentic artworks, like murals and bronze busts of the main participants. With the Saskya lama came his two young nephews, one of whom, Phags-pa (*top right*), would become Kublai's Buddhist guru and chief religious adviser.

In Kublai's New Capital, a Great Buddhist Temple

In 1271, under Phags-pa's guidance, Kublai built the White Pagoda (*below*), which was the largest structure in his new capital, Dadu. The pagoda survives today as one of Beijing's most impressive monuments, and the only Yuan one. Its architect was a Nepalese named Arniko (*inset*), one of many foreign artists and intellectuals employed by Kublai, and now a symbol of Chinese– Nepalese cooperation. The White Pagoda is still a living centre of worship, as the presence of two Tibetan monks showed when I was there in 2005 (*right*).

6

A NEW CAPITAL

SOME CAPITALS SEEM TO BE BORN GREAT: ROME, PARIS, London. Some have greatness thrust upon them: Brasilia, Canberra, Washington – and Beijing. For 3,000 years Chinese culture was focused by the two great rivers of central China, the Yellow River and the Yangtze. Beijing was no-one's first choice – too far north, no good rivers – until the Mongols' predecessors, the Jin, invaded from Manchuria in the 1120s. With the southern Song ruling from Hangzhou, Beijing became one of three capitals of north China – Zhongdu, 'Central Capital', as it was known.[1] So it was northerners from outside the Chinese heartland who made it a seat of government, and thus drew Genghis's attention to it.

---

[1] Only for a time. Beijing has had many names, and other cities have also been a Beijing (Northern Capital). I have kept these references to a minimum, preferring to call the place Beijing throughout.

The city that the Mongols seized and devastated in 1215 was small by modern standards, a square of 3.5 kilometres per side. Today a nondescript area just southwest of Tiananmen Square, with hardly a trace to hint at its former existence, it had by 1260 still not recovered from the destruction meted out by Genghis's army. No doubt the sights and sounds of medieval Beijing would have returned to its alleyways: the twang of tuning forks by which travelling barbers signalled their arrival, the clang of copper bowls from soft-drink sellers, bells sounding the day and night watches, cries of street-vendors everywhere. But the walls and the burned-out palaces were still in ruins. An estate agent showing Kublai's people around would have muttered about its potential. A potential purchaser would have seen nothing but a hopeless mess.

In the 1260s, holding north China as a potter holds unformed clay, Kublai might have made any number of choices. He might have ignored Beijing and ruled from Xanadu. But if he did that he would declare himself for ever an outsider. Seeing the benefits of governing from a Chinese base, he might have chosen to revive an ancient seat of government, like Kaifeng or Xian. But Beijing had two major advantages: of the many possibilities for a Chinese capital in the north, it was the closest both to Xanadu and to Mongolia. In 1263, only seven years after starting to build Xanadu, Kublai decided to make Beijing his main capital. This would complete a sort of stepping-stone progression from the Mongolian grasslands into China, from Karakorum to Xanadu to Beijing. He would abandon Karakorum altogether, henceforth commuting between his two bases, spending summers in Xanadu and winters in Beijing, which was his way of straddling his two worlds. That's why Beijing is China's capital today.

But how best to handle this dilapidated piece of real estate? Incoming dynasties have often made their mark by total demolition and reconstruction (as the Ming would do to Mongol Beijing). Perhaps there was a year of indecision, for in 1261 the walls of the old city were mended, as if he was on the verge of building on the past. But new life in these ancient alleyways, as Kublai's advisers pointed out, would be seething with resentment. To work on the ruins within would have been to accept the agenda of a defeated dynasty and, perhaps, nurture rebellion. Kublai decided on an entirely new capital.

Just north and east of the Jin capital was a perfect site, where runoff from the Western Hills fed Beihai (the North Sea). Here, for 30 years before the Mongols arrived, there had been a playground for the wealthy. The 35-hectare lake at the heart of the parkland had come into existence as the result of a legend. Once upon a time, in the East Sea, there were three fairy mountains where the immortals lived on the miraculous Potion of Immortality. Many searched for the mountains and the potion, but none were successful. In the second century BC Emperor Wu Di of the Han had a lake dug by his palace in his capital, with three islets representing the fairy mountains. Later emperors did the same in their respective capitals. So did the Song in Beijing in the late tenth century, excavating a lake fed by a river from the Western Hills and giving it the by-now-traditional three islands. It was this carefully landscaped beauty spot that the Jin emperor chose for a summer palace in the twelfth century, the Palace of a Myriad Tranquillities; he also built a second retreat on top of today's Jade Island, the city's highest point (now crowned by the seventeenth-century White Dagoba, Beijing's equivalent of the Eiffel Tower). The imperial buildings had been ransacked when Genghis had assaulted Beijing in 1213–15, but the lake was still at the heart of the abandoned and overgrown park. It was natural that Kublai should choose it as the centrepiece of his new city.

With Xanadu representing Kublai's Mongol aspects, the new capital would be thoroughly Chinese. That would have been hard to credit in the autumn of 1263, when the emperor arrived from Xanadu to reclaim an area that would have been half-wilderness after 50 years of neglect. Imagine the lake choked with silt and plants, summer-houses decaying round its edges, and here and there some smallholdings where farmers had dared colonize what had once been royal parkland. With the old capital in ruins, Kublai had nowhere to stay but his tents. Saplings and bushes were cleared and an imperial camp sprang up: a royal area of several grand *gers*, lesser establishments for princes and officials, and hundreds more for contingents of guards, grooms, wagoners, armourers, metalworkers, carpenters and other workers by the thousand, including, of course, architects.

Overall authority for the design was borne by Liu Bingzhong, the mastermind of Xanadu. But among his team of architects was one of particular significance who is not mentioned in the official Chinese sources, for he was an Arab named something like Ikhtiyar al-Din (a rough re-transliteration from the messy Chinese version of his name, Yeh-hei-tieh-erh-ting). We know of him at all only thanks to a Chinese scholar, Chen Yuan, who in the 1930s came across a copy of an inscription dedicated to Ikhtiyar's son, Mohammad-shah. Ikhtiyar had, presumably, proved his worth in Persia after the Mongol conquest a generation before, for he was summoned by Kublai – or, more likely, Liu Bingzhong – to head a department in the Ministry of Works which had something to do with tents (no-one knows what; their manufacture for the imperial household, perhaps). Whatever his duties, he had over the years become an expert in town planning. Now, in his old age, he was selected to oversee Kublai's grand new scheme.

The inscription is worth quoting at length, because it gives a feel for the size of the project and makes explicit Kublai's political aims, as well as honouring its senior architect. In autumn 1266, it says, the court ordered the construction of the new capital's walls and palaces, and it continues:

> As the Great Enterprise [whatever that was – perhaps the building of Xanadu] has come to its conclusion, the national influence is in the process of expansion. If the palaces and metropolitan adornments are not beautiful and imposing, they will not be able to command the respect of the empire. Following his appointment, Ikhtiyar laboured at his task ceaselessly, until he had drawn up a grand scheme. The grand astrologer selected a propitious date, and the director of supplies assembled the necessary materials. Detailed plans were prepared for passes and gates, audience halls, roads and residential quarters, informal reception rooms and detached courts, administration offices, shrines, guard houses, storerooms for clothes, food and utensils, quarters for officers on duty in the imperial household, and so on up to pools, ponds, gardens, parks and places for dalliance, high storeyed structures and beamed pavilions and unadorned verandahs with flying eaves ... In the 12th month [28 December 1266–26 January 1267] a decree was issued ordering [three officials] and Ikhtiyar al-Din to take on

together the duties of the Board of Works and carry out the programme of constructing the palaces and city walls. Measures were taken to provide the necessary equipment, to put in place the pillars and beams, to transport thither stone and brick, timber and earth. Multitudes of artisans participated. Foundations and terraces were laid, solidly and firmly. All met with imperial approval. The services of Ikhtiyar al-Din were highly appreciated, but he was beginning to feel the weight of his advancing years.

Yet in the official Yuan history Ikhtiyar's name is omitted, only his three Chinese junior colleagues being mentioned. 'Either it was left out on purpose,' says Chen, 'or the omission was due to the low regard in which architecture was formerly held.' Well, it sounds to me more like deliberate racism. Kublai, like his grandfather, was happy to employ talent wherever he found it. But Beijing would soon be the vastly imposing imperial capital, with Kublai himself a Chinese monarch. Look at it from the Chinese point of view: Kublai had imposed a class system with Mongols at the top, followed by Muslims, northern Chinese and southern Chinese. Here was an Arab employed by Mongols showing Chinese how to build a Chinese city. It does not take much to imagine a clique of Chinese official historians wishing to take revenge for their humiliation. Ikhtiyar was simply written out of history – until Chen Yuan deciphered the inscription honouring Mohammad-shah and his father. 'Visitors to Peking in these days are amazed at the grandeur of the palaces and the city walls,' wrote Chen, 'but who would suppose that the man who worked this out was from the country of Arabia?'

* * *

Today Beihai Park, once a playground for emperors and princes outside the city walls, is a playground for everyone, right at the heart of the city. For that, Beijingers, picnicking on its banks and paddling its rowing boats, owe Kublai some gratitude. It was he who turned it into an Arcadia that is now a tourist cliché; he who first built a bridge across to Jade Island (replaced late in his reign by the marble Eternal Peace Bridge visitors see today, with its graceful curve); he who landscaped its slopes with rare trees and winding staircases and poetically named temples and pavilions – Golden Dew, Jade Rainbow, Inviting Happiness, Everlasting Harmony; he who made the lake and its island a sight at which foreigners gasped. Marco Polo remarked on the stock of fish, and the metal grating that stopped them escaping into the river at either end. Almost 50 years later, Friar Odoric from Pordenone in north-east Italy admired its multitudes of swans, geese and ducks.

Naturally, Kublai replaced the old palace on the top of Jade Island with a new one, having increased the height of the hill with soil excavated from the lake-bed. This, presumably, was where he held court for a decade (1264–74) while the city proper was under construction.[2] The hilltop palace is now long gone, but recalled by a surprising object standing in its place. In one of the palace's seven halls was a second, miniature palace, and in this was a bed, inlaid with gold and jade, on which Kublai liked to recline as he held court. Beside the bed was an immense jade urn, weighing 3.5 tonnes, intricately carved with dragons cavorting in waves. From this Kublai would

[2] See G. N. Kates, 'A New Date for the Origins of the Forbidden City'.

dispense wine, 3,000 litres of it. Tossed away by the whirl of events, this extraordinary vessel was rediscovered in the eighteenth century and placed again at the top of the hill, sheltered by its own little pavilion and standing on a new jade base. Rather oddly to western eyes, the stand sports a swastika – not in its malign Nazi version, but with its arms set anti-clockwise in the symbol's original beneficent Zoroastrian form (卍 is the symbol used to represent a temple on Chinese maps). Everyone recognizes the urn's good-luck value. Tourists buy little red charms to hang from the surrounding fence: Good Luck All Life! A Prayer for the Whole Family's Happiness!

Ikhtiyar planned a city that would have the traditional form of previous capitals, including Xanadu. It would be three-in-one: a palace, inner city and outer city in nested rectangles. This design recalled the ground-plans and glory of several previous Chinese capitals, most notably Changan (today's Xian), the Tang capital in the seventh to tenth centuries, possibly the world's greatest city at the time. Kublai would not have known anything of the Terracotta Army that draws tens of thousands of tourists to Xian every year, but he would have known of the power of its dead commander, the First Emperor, unifier of China in the third century BC, builder of roads, canals and the Great Wall. This was the mantle of power and glory to which Kublai now laid claim.

In August 1267, several thousand workers under Ikhtiyar's direction started to build ramparts over the hills and along the three winding rivers. They used earth, not stone, digging out a moat to give them the raw material. 'It is the custom of that country,' writes Rashid ad-Din, 'to put down two planks, pour damp earth in between, and beat it with a large stick until it is firm. Then they remove the planks and there is a wall.' This was unskilled work, and it went fast. The 382 smallholders who had moved into the area during the years of dereliction were thrown out, with the equivalent of compulsory purchase orders – they all received compensation in 1271. After a year, rammed-earth walls 10 metres thick at the bottom rose for 10 metres, tapering to a 3-metre walkway at the top, so that in cross-section they looked like a decapitated triangle. They made a rectangle of just over 5.5 × 6.5 kilometres, 28 kilometres all the way round, punctuated by eleven gates. Inside, a second wall rose to conceal the Imperial City, and inside that a third wall, within which in due course would lie the palace and its attendant buildings. Actually, Ikhtiyar went one better than Xian, making a fourth set of walls to create a palace-within-a-palace.

From March 1271, 28,000 workers began to build the Imperial City's infrastructure, setting out a network of roads at right-angles, Manhattan-style, each block the property of a top family, complete with its grand house. At the heart, off-centre, just to the right of Beihai lake, was the palace. The nest of walls was designed only in part to provide security. Its unstated purpose, like that of the Kremlin and the Alhambra in Granada (both of which, incidentally, had been built not long before), was political and psychological: to impress all who entered with the awful majesty of the occupant. Imagine your approach, through a gate in the outer bastions, along crowded streets, through another gate – passage through which demands an escort and written permission – into the enclave of the rich and powerful, with their great mansions and gardens and armies of servants, and finally to the empire's innermost sanctuary, the jewel-box that contained the all-powerful embodiment of power, Heaven's own choice to rule the greatest political entity since the Fall of Rome, against which the Arab and Russian empires would have paled. Kublai had his opponents and insecurities; but approaching him would erase thoughts of such things. Long before you were ushered into the divine presence, you would be overwhelmed by a whole thesaurus of royal attributes: might, majesty, power, mystery, and wealth untold.

These were the feelings described by Marco Polo when, in 1275, he came to the place known informally by its Mongol-Turkic name, Khan-balikh, the Khan's City, or Cambaluc as Polo spelled it. To the Chinese, it was Da-du, the Great Capital. He made a particular point of describing the palace and its gardens, all surrounded by 10-metre walls that linked eight fortresses, each a storehouse for its own article of war – bows, saddles, bridles, weapons. Beneath the trees – rarities carried in from distant parts by elephant – grazed deer and gazelle, overlooked by walkways, which were gently slanted so that the rain drained fast before it could soak aristocratic feet. The palace, with a roof of red, yellow, green and blue tiles, was a single-storey building with a vast central hall where 6,000 dinner-guests dined beneath animal frescoes set off by gold and silver decorations. Off limits to all except the elite of the elite lay unknown numbers of private rooms.

Eventually, when all China fell to the Mongols, this would become the capital of the whole united nation, and so it has remained. The heart of today's Beijing, the Forbidden City, was built right over Kublai's creation, its entrance facing south, like the door of any Mongolian tent. The 800 palaces and halls, the 9,000 rooms, the entrance from Tiananmen Square – all these are where they are because Kublai chose to place his palace there.

As the chequerboard of streets and new buildings began to turn a building site into a capital, Kublai had a decision to make. To help his rule become total, to fulfil the ambitions inherited from his grandfather, he needed to make a public statement that Heaven had granted him its mandate, that a new dynasty had been founded. It needed a name. Clearly, a Mongol name would not go down well with his Chinese subjects, especially the southern subjects who would soon be his, if his plans worked out. It was his adviser Liu Bingzhong who came up with the perfect Chinese name, the one that had first suggested itself when Kublai was considering the decision about when to declare himself emperor. It springs straight from the great book of divination, the *I Ching*. The word had been embedded in the Qian oracle cast in Xanadu. Now it found greater justification in a set of words, a magical incantation, associated with the Way of Water or Tao, a formula that evokes life's flow. The words are *yuan heng li zhen*. Each recalls for initiates the sequence of ages through which the *I Ching* evolved; each holds universes of meaning. Right now, it is the first we are interested in: *yuan*.

The dictionary definition of yuan is first, chief, principal, fundamental. But there is much more to it. This, in summary, is what Stephen Karcher has to say about *yuan* in his *Total I Ching: Myths for Change*: Yuan is the ultimate source, the *primum mobile*, the movement behind the absolute origin of the universe. It is the power of spring, and of the east. As well as implying primacy, it also suggests the concepts of 'eldest' and 'the source of thought and growth'. It signifies the good man and a connection with fundamental truths. It is linked to ideas of fundamental rituals, greatness and founding acts.

So Yuan it was, the new name being proclaimed in December 1271. It was chosen with deliberate originality: no previous emperor had chosen a name for his dynasty that was not a place name. Yet its pedigree was impeccable. No name could have better appealed to Chinese sensibilities (which is why, incidentally, it is also the name of today's Chinese unit of currency). Moreover, its vaguely religious overtones hinted at the sublime, linking it to Tenger, the Mongol Heaven. All Kublai's subjects, Chinese and Mongol, would be impressed by their new emperor's choice.

Beijing today is a lagoon swamped by modernity. But below the murky surface of traffic, pollution and new building is a faint image of the old city, a ghostly rectangle defined by one of the innermost road-systems. One hot summer's day, I took the plunge in an attempt to make the ghost real. I decided to follow in the tracks of Emil Bretschneider, botanist, physician at the Russian legation and assiduous historian of the city. In his day, around 1875, Mongol ramparts reared up from countryside crisscrossed by paths and cart-tracks. Forty years later, when the historian Lin Yutang wandered over it, he found it 'completely rural in aspect, with farmsteads and duckponds'. It sounded charming.

All charm has long since vanished. Four kilometres north-west of Beihai Park, a tree-covered ridge divides a dual carriageway. It looks like nothing, but it is the remains of Kublai's earthen ramparts. You reach it by dodging cars. Paths of grey brick flanked by ranks of tired grass-clumps led me to the top, for a fine view of high-rises, carriageways and traffic through the soupy air. A notice urged: 'Take care of the grass, because the grass is alive.' There was not much else alive here, and not much of the past either. A modern temple was unused, except for a man with a close-shaven head playing a single-stringed fiddle on his knee. Traffic whizzed where once guards marched and courtiers strolled. A block north there's a canal, once the moat marking the northern limit of Kublai's new estate. I followed it, past what would soon be the main Olympic site, and came upon Yuan Dadu Park, after Kublai's dynasty and the name of Mongol Beijing. Garish little pleasure boats awaited day-trippers. A young man dozed on a bench. Paving stones fringed the ex-ramparts, now nothing but slender trees and pathways. A pillar displayed a bas-relief of Genghis attended by a cloud-borne orchestra and his heirs. This was not real history, but heritage: it was made in 1987, along with the park. But here at least something had sur-vived from the thirteenth century – two stone tortoises bearing rectangular pillars, those symbols of power favoured by the Chinese and adopted by the Mongols. Behind them, Kublai's palatial grounds overflowed with apartment blocks. If you want to get a feel for Kublai's Beijing, best avoid the streets and search for something to set your imagination free.

By 1274 the palace by Beihai was near enough com-pletion for Kublai to hold his first audience in the main hall (though work continued on both walls and palaces for the rest of his reign). He now had a theatre in which to stage the drama of power.

One secret of power is to make a display of it. The modern world has become a bit half-hearted about power-displays. Democracies are embarrassed by it; royalty, if preserved, is pickled in heritage, very pretty but devoid of power-content. But autocrats, the alpha males and sometimes alpha females of history, have always known that power and display work well together. From ancient Persia to Nazi Germany, political dominance has been made palpable by the use of symbols, rituals and ceremonies to act out the ideals with which rulers identify themselves, and through which they assert themselves. Different societies have their own ways of doing this. Roman emperors became gods at their funerals; Nepalese kings proved themselves embodiments of the universal god Vishnu by acts of generosity; in Bali the king showed his power by acting in pageants; Hitler had himself turned into an epic hero by the theatricality of the Nuremberg rallies. As one historian, David Cannadine, points out, kings have ruled as much by divine *rites* as by divine *right*. But underneath the different rites lie fundamental similarities (much debated by anthropologists and historians).

Such rituals and ceremonies assert several things:

- the stability of the state;
- the power of the state over the individual;
- the importance of the power-structure: the hierarchy of ruler, family, court, people;
- the legitimacy of the ruler;
- the ruler's superhuman qualities, connecting him (or occasionally her) with the divine.

One piece of theatre which crops up in several societies is the ceremonial hunt. It was, for instance, one of the most significant events in Charlemagne's Frankish empire after he was crowned emperor in the year 800. It was the natural conclusion to an assembly in which major political crises were resolved, for 'the hunt was an exercise in, and a demonstration of, the virtues of collaboration'.[3] In dramatic form, and in the feast that followed, it symbolized the advantages of collective action, of military and political co-operation.

Kublai, smart enough to see the benefits of ritual but with no experience in their form within Chinese culture, had teams of advisers to guide him. There were precedents galore, notably an immense three-volume corpus of imperial rituals recorded half a millennium earlier during the Tang dynasty (618–906), when China was unified, rich and stable.[4] Tang scholars believed these rituals originated in remote antiquity, some 2,000 years BC, and were then modified by the introduction of Confucian practices in the second and first centuries BC. The 150 rituals, the symbolic essence of government, combined cosmology, ethics, and Confucianism, with admixtures of Buddhism and Taoism. Here were rules for sacrifices to gods of heaven and earth, of the five directions, of the harvest, sun, moon, stars, sacred peaks, seas and great rivers; to ancestors; to Confucius. There were rites for

[3] Janet Nelson, 'The Lord's Anointed and the People's Choice: Carolingian Royal Ritual', in David Cannadine and Simon Price, eds, *Rituals of Royalty*.
[4] David McMullen, 'Bureaucrats and Cosmology: The Ritual Code of T'ang China', in David Cannadine and Simon Price, eds, *Rituals of Royalty*.

recurrent and non-recurrent rituals, for use on sacred Mount Tai, where human and spirit worlds met; rites for the sovereign and for those taking the place of the sovereign, for receiving and entertaining envoys, for the proclamation of victories, for the marriage of dignitaries, for royal congratulations, for investitures, for coming-of-age ceremonies (for all levels down to the sons of sixth-grade officials), for the despatch of memoranda by provincial officials, for procedures to be conducted after bad harvests, illness and mourning . . . and variations of all of these, and more, depending on whether they were conducted by the emperor or a proxy, and for every rank of official from the emperor down to the lowliest, those of the ninth grade. Propitious rituals demanded abstinence at two levels, relaxed or intensive, spread over seven, five or three days, depending on whether the ritual was major, medium or minor. Rules specified the tents, the musical instruments, the positions of participants, the words of prayers. Here were instructions on how villagers should offer cooked meat, jade and silk to the gods of soil and grain. The rituals had their own huge and complex bureaucracy, with four divisions – looking after, respectively, sacrifices, imperial banquets, the imperial family and ceremonies for foreigners – and a Board of Rites within the Department of Affairs of State. These demanded hundreds of specialists in ritual; but all the 17,000 scholar-officials of all the other departments were expected to have intimate knowledge of particular rituals in their own areas of expertise.

All of this immense, vastly expensive and horribly cumbersome apparatus was considered absolutely vital to the workings of the state, because it provided a context for human actions and linked these to the cosmos. It maintained the social hierarchy, restrained man's unruly appetites. It picked up where the criminal code left off, for it did not coerce people or punish them. It affirmed the benevolence of the cosmic order, and the emperor's role in mediating between earth and heaven. It was, as it were, a vast social gyroscope that kept society stable (which is one reason why dynasties so often kept going even when moribund, until an end that seemed to come suddenly). Later dynasties followed the Tang lead, producing their own ritual codes. If Kublai wanted to be taken seriously as a Chinese ruler, this was what he had to take on board.

So, in late middle age, Kublai displayed and regimented for all he was worth, which was more than any monarch on earth at the time. If you rule one-third of inhabited Asia and have family ruling the rest; if at the same time your original claim to power is a little shaky; and if you are ageing, overweight, easily out of breath, and wincing on gouty feet – then you would naturally wish to put on as much of a show as you possibly could. In the years after 1274, Kublai commanded more wealth than any monarch in history, and, by heaven, he knew how to use wealth to display and reinforce his power. But he would not pretend to be Chinese, slavishly following Tang precedents in his ceremonies and rituals; his aim was still, as it had long been, to balance Mongol and Chinese, and his techniques were the well-tried means of inspiring awe – ritual and display that raised him from man to monarch, from monarch to demi-god.

His power base at court, through which his influence spread through China and beyond, was his 12,000-strong court of family, officials and officers; and every individual in this throng had at least three different sets of clothing, each a less lavish match for Kublai's own costumes, one for each of the three main state occasions, the khan's birthday at the end of September, New Year's Day and the annual spring hunt.[5]

Take New Year's Day. This was a festival designed to emphasize both the emperor's Chinese and his Mongol credentials. One of the greatest of Chinese festivals, it was doubly significant under Kublai because his dynastic title, Yuan, means among other things 'first', particularly the first month of the lunar calendar. (Today, the two calendars, lunar and Gregorian, run in parallel.) It was also one of the most important of Mongolian festivals. Still, as always in the countryside, on the first day of the first month – 'White Month' day – one gets up early, puts on one's best clothes, goes out of one's tent, bows to the east and then the other cardinal points, sprinkles milk or vodka to the Blue Sky, flicking some into the air, and returns to honour Buddhist images or – more likely these days – photographs of departed family members. The father of the household tosses some fermented mare's milk to the Blue Sky, children offer silk scarves to parents, hands placed just so in the correct fashion. There are bows and benedictions. Tea is drunk, visits made, old ways recalled, the social network reinforced.

Kublai's court ceremony mixed these simple old private rituals with Chinese court festivities to create a celebration of gargantuan proportions, an overwhelming assertion of personal and state power. Marco Polo describes it. Thousands – 40,000, he says, though we must always remember his habit of tossing out suspiciously

[5] The number of these occasions rose in the sources with the passage of time, often to 4, sometimes to 12 or 13 (*trois* and *treize/tres* being easily interchanged in versions of Polo).

large round numbers – dressed in white, all in due order behind the royal family, overflow from the Great Hall into surrounding areas. A high official of some kind – top shaman, Buddhist priest or senior chamberlain, Polo is not sure – calls out 'Bow and adore!' and the whole assembly touches forehead to floor, four times, in a mass kowtow. A song follows, then a prayer from the minister: 'Great Heaven that extends over all! Earth which is under Heaven's guidance! We invoke you and beseech you to heap blessings on the Emperor and the Empress! Grant that they may live ten thousand, a hundred thousand years!' Then each minister goes to the altar and swings a censer over a tablet inscribed with Kublai's name. Officials emerge from every corner with presents of gold, silver and jewellery, many of them in 81 examples, 81 being the doubly auspicious number of nine times nine; treasures are displayed in coffers mounted on contingents of richly adorned elephants and camels.

Then comes the feast. Kublai sits at the high table, which is literally high, placed on a platform, with the princes and their wives immediately below. To one side is a huge buffet table, decorated with animal carvings. The centrepiece is a golden wine-bowl the size of a barrel with four dispensers, from which servants draw wine into golden jugs. Down the hall range ranks of small tables, several hundred of them, flanked by carpets on which sit the guards and their officers. To one side of the dais is an orchestra, its leader keeping a close eye on the emperor.

Polo mentions an odd element in this scene, a significant detail that recalls Kublai's nomad roots. Anyone travelling in Mongolia today would understand. When entering a *ger*, you must take care to step right over the threshold, the bottom bit of the door-frame, without touching it. No-one knows the origins of this superstition, but there's no denying its force. If you kick the threshold by mistake, it is a bad omen; done on purpose, it would be a deliberate insult. Now, it's unlikely that Kublai's Great Hall had actual thresholds to step over. Nevertheless, at each door stand two immense guards, armed with staves, who watch for infringements. Back in Mongolia, a serf might be killed for stepping on a prince's threshold. Nothing so brutal would occur at Kublai's state banquet. But it's still no joke. The guards have orders to humiliate those who infringe the rule, stripping them of their finery or giving them some nominal blows with a stave. To be spared you have to be an ignorant foreigner, in which case a senior official will pounce upon you to explain courtly ways. Once all are seated, the banquet begins, with those at tables being served by butlers. Again, the khan uses ritual to assert his status, for his butlers 'have the mouth and nose muffled with fine napkins of silk and gold, so that no breath or odour from their persons should taint the dish or the goblet presented to the Lord'.

The Lord graciously receives a cup from a butler. The orchestra proclaims the significance of the moment. The cupbearers and the foodbearers kneel. The Lord drinks. When he deigns to accept food, the same thing happens. These observances punctuate the feast, until the end, when the dishes are removed and it's time for entertainment, a cabaret provided by actors, jugglers, acrobats and conjurors.

Kublai's new Beijing was the centre of hunting on an industrial scale. Under the control of 14,000 huntsmen, the countryside out to 500 kilometres – 40 days' journey, as Polo says – from the city in every direction was dedicated to the business of supplying the court. All large game was the emperor's: boar, deer, bear, elk, wild asses (which can still be found in Mongolia's far west), wild cats of various species. For his own hunt, Kublai had a zoo of cats, cheetahs and tigers specially trained to hunt and kill larger prey. Cheetahs had long been kept as hunting animals by kings across Asia, but the tigers – Siberian tigers from the northern borders of Kublai's empire – seem to have been a novelty. Polo, who didn't know about tigers, called them lions 'whose skins are coloured in the most beautiful way, being striped all along the sides with black, red and white'. There were eagles, too, trained and deployed by Kazakhs to hunt not just hare and foxes, but deer, wild goats, boar – even wolves, which an eagle attacks with claws and beak, while battering its prey into stupefaction with its wings (hunting with eagles is still alive today in Kazakhstan and western Mongolia). All of these came into their own in spring.

Marco Polo tells us all about it.

It is 1 March. Winter is over, spring approaching. The court prepares for its annual spring hunt, a hunt of such staggering size and opulence that it is easy to forget its underlying purpose. Hidden beneath Chinese wealth lie Mongol roots, the old idea of disparate clans united under one leader. In this ritual, Kublai, grandson of the man who claimed to remain a simple nomad at heart, is playing the nomad himself. The palaces and much of Beijing empty into wagons by the hundred, onto horses by the thousand. For Kublai himself, four elephants are harnessed together, carrying an enormous howdah, a room made of wood, lined on the inside with gold leaf and dressed outside with lion skins. A dozen senior aides ride beside him in attendance. There are 2,000 dog handlers and 10,000 falconers, so Marco says, each with his bird, but we shouldn't take this as exact, because there are also 10,000 tents; it's just an impressively large number. In order not to clog the gateways and the roads, they leave in bunches of a hundred.

Marco says they head south. But if so, the vast array soon swings eastward over the plains and rivers that run between Beijing and the sea. The emperor makes stately progress on his elephants, say 30 kilometres a day, arriving every evening at a campsite that is a tent-city. Along the way, birds of many species scatter and soar from their new nests.

And sometimes as they may be going along, and the Emperor from his chamber is holding discourse with his Barons, one of the latter shall exclaim: 'Sire! Look out for Cranes!' Then the Emperor instantly has the top of his chamber thrown open, and having marked the cranes he casts one of his gerfalcons, whichever he please; and often the quarry is struck within his view . . . I do not believe there ever existed in the world or ever will exist, a man with such sport and enjoyment as he has.

Some hunts involve the dogs, huge mastiff-like creatures trained for hunting by their handlers, known as 'wolf-men' (Polo gets the Mongol term right, but thinks it means 'keepers of mastiffs'). 'And as the Lord rides a-fowling over the plains, you will see these big hounds coming tearing up, one pack after a bear, another pack after a stag, or some other beast.'

They are heading towards the spot where the Great

Wall now swoops down from highlands to the Pacific. There is no Wall yet, of course, and no danger from the nomads, because the land is all Kublai's. Ahead, through the narrow strip between hills and sea, lie the Manchurian grasslands. After a week, Kublai's elephants bear him into the camp that will be the court's HQ for the next three months. It is a traditional spot, chosen for broad expanses and wealth of game. Falconers and hawkers, with their hooded birds on their wrists and whistles at the ready, scatter over the billowy ground for several kilometres in all directions. The emperor's three tents are ready – a huge one which can hold a whole court of 1,000 people; sleeping quarters; and a smaller audience chamber. Polo does not tell us what shape the tents are, but each has three poles, which probably support the centre of traditional round tents to remind Kublai of his grassland origins.

What impressed Polo was the decoration of these mobile palace-chambers. They are weatherproofed with tiger skins – Siberian tigers at this stage not being endangered – and lined with ermine and sable, the most valuable of Siberian furs. Consider. A tent that could hold 1,000 people has a circumference of about 125 metres. To cover its walls would take 16,000 pelts, each today costing $50–100 each. That's the equivalent of $1 million, just to line the main tent – without the tiger-skin waterproofing. Spread out all around are the tents of the royal family – Kublai's senior wife Chabi, the three subsidiary wives, and the princes, and the girls from the Ongirad (the Mongol clan that traditionally supplied Genghis's family with mates) brought in for the harem – and the tents of the senior ministers, the attendants, the falconers, grooms, cooks, dog handlers, household staff, secretaries, all with their families, and all of course protected by contingents of soldiers. This was a tent-city, with a population of many thousands, sustained by blood-sport. Every day hawks and falcons bring down cranes, swans, ducks, geese, hare and deer, which the soft-mouthed dogs mark and fetch. Hare, stag, buck, roe – these are designated as royal game, which ordinary people are banned from hunting at this time to ensure a good supply for the imperial forays onto the plains of north-east China.

Meanwhile, the business of the court continues, with conferences and audiences and messengers coming and going and the receipt of ambassadors from abroad. And at the centre of this vast array is the emperor: overweight, gout-ridden, but still eager to reconnect with his roots by riding out over the plain. A portrait of him by the court artist Liu Guan-dao shows him perched heavily in the saddle, wrapped in an ermine coat, with Chabi at his side. He has two attendants. It is a scene of deliberate pseudo-casualness, like a Cartier-Bresson snapshot, for all four have had their attention caught by something off-camera – someone calling, perhaps: 'Your Majesty! Cranes! Over here!' But there is no bird on the royal wrist, and a whippet awaits an order.

So it continues for two and a half months, until, in mid-May, the immense operation reverses itself, bringing emperor and entourage back to the capital, where, as the summer begins to build, preparations start for the haul northward to Xanadu.

7

EMBRACING BUDDHA,
AND TIBET

UNHAPPILY FOR THOSE WHO WISH IT WERE NOT SO, TIBET IS now part of China: threatened, dominated, invaded, colonized, occupied and developed out of any possibility of regaining its independence – or *gaining* it: for China says that Tibet was part of China from way back. But it depends how far back you wish to go. We can see the roots of China's involvement in Tibet by looking back 750 years, which is where Kublai fits in. But there are deeper roots, which take us back another 500 years. It is worth digging them up, because they explain Kublai's role in Tibet's history and thus help us to understand the presence of Chinese troops and colonists in Tibet today.

First, some background to show how thoroughly independent Tibet used to be.

In the seventh century Tibet was an empire, spanning the high heartland and deserts of the north-west, reaching from the borders of Uzbekistan to central China, from halfway across Xinjiang down to the Bay of Bengal. That's 2,250 kilometres from east to west, 1,750 from north to south: an area larger than the Chinese heartland. Indeed, in 763 a Tibetan army briefly captured the Chinese capital Chang-an (today's Xian). Trouble arose around the same time, when Buddhism became the state religion. It made little headway against the Tibetans' original shamanistic faith, Bon. Tensions increased when a ninth-century king became a fanatical advocate of Buddhism. Buddhist monks, deriving wealth and power from their newly founded monasteries, challenged traditional rulers. Bon nobles revolted. In 838 they killed the king by twisting his head off his body and installed his younger brother, who was himself assassinated five years later. Buddhists were persecuted, monasteries destroyed, and the empire collapsed into a patchwork of squabbling minor kings and feudal lords. Politically, Tibet fell into a historical black hole. Without central rule, with the monasteries in ruins, there were few records.

From this wreckage Buddhism re-emerged, in several sects; predominant was the stream called Mahayana, with its complex, mystical belief in the multiple manifestations of Buddha and transcendent beings or *bodhisattvas*. All the sects embraced Tantric Buddhism, with its spells, mystic syllables and diagrams, as the highest and best type of practice, and all took on peculiarly Tibetan forms by adapting Bon chants, rituals and deities.

The seed of revival grew in the east from the action of three Buddhist scholars, later known as the Three Men of Khams, who escaped the persecutions and fled with their books to Amdo, the present-day Chinese province of Qinghai, on the headwaters of the Yellow River. There they lived in a cave, devoting themselves to re-establishing monastic life. From about 950 onwards, a monk from Amdo named Klumes (or kLu-mes in one of several possible transliterations) drove forward the Buddhist renaissance, carrying Buddhism west to the Tibetan heartland. In what is known as the 'second introduction of Buddhism', old monasteries were repaired, new ones founded.

A similar revival occurred in the far west, where a member of the royal family had fled when the empire collapsed. He and his descendants created three tiny kingdoms on the upper Sutlej river, near the borders of present-day India. One in particular, Gu-ge, became a centre for the Buddhist revival in the western Himalayas, then populated by Tibetans. The Gu-ge king became the 'royal monk', Ye-shes-'od (or Yeshe-Ö). He arranged for twenty-one young Tibetans to study in India. Nineteen died there. One of the survivors returned after seventeen years, and went on to become Tibet's most famous medieval scholar, Rinchen Zangpo (958–1055), the 'Great Translator', who founded a monastic complex at Thöling, which remained in use until it was partly ruined in the Cultural Revolution in 1967.

The tenth and eleventh centuries saw intensive programmes of building and restoring monasteries, and translating Sanskrit texts, including one that set out Tibet's 60-year calendar, with its cycle of twelve animals and five elements. The greatest expert on this system was an Indian teacher and master, Atisha. Ye-shes-'od issued an invitation to Atisha, who arrived in Gu-ge at the age of 60 in 1042 – a vital date, because it acts as the base-line for Tibet's lunar calendar. Atisha stayed in Thöling monastery for three years, then travelled in Tibet until his death in 1054. In that time he laid the foundations for

Buddhism's fully fledged revival, confirmed in 1076 by a great council in Gu-ge, linking eastern and western Buddhists. The translation of Buddhist literature into Tibetan accelerated. This was to prove vital work for a religion that was to decline in India under the pressure of Islam. Atisha's influence, the translations, the revival of monastic discipline: all this ensured that Tibet was to become the chief inheritor of Indian Buddhism. (Not that this gave Tibet political unity under a single ruler. The struggle between Bon and Buddhism continued until the seventeenth century, when members of the Gelugpa sect killed the last political claimant to the throne, opening the way for the joint spiritual and temporal kings, the Dalai Lamas.)

All of this shows that historically, up until the early thirteenth century, China had no claims on Tibet. Indeed, the opposite applied: Tibet ruled half of present-day China, but looked westward to India for its most significant influence, Buddhism. So on what basis does China claim authority? What is the justification for what happened in the 1950s, the liberation by Mao's army, when 30,000 battle-hardened Communist troops crushed 4,000 Tibetans, the military occupation, the crushing of the 1959 uprising, the flight of the Dalai Lama, the death of hundreds of thousands of Tibetans – over a million, some say – the bombing of the Jokhan, Tibet's most revered religious institution, the subsequent sacking of over 6,000 monasteries, the ruin of a nation?

The justification was, of course, that Tibet became Chinese when it fell to the Mongols.

How did that takeover start? Not in the way that most

books claim. Standard accounts say that Genghis's coronation was enough to inspire Tibet to tender voluntary submission. Not so, as Luciano Petech states in the most authoritative recent analysis,[1] calling the suggestion 'a tissue of absurdities'. Nor is there any evidence for a claim that Sorkaktani made an approach in 1215 – the year in which she was supposed to have given birth to Kublai in Zhangye.

The first verifiable link was made in 1239, by Ogedei's second son Köten (Kublai's cousin), who, after campaigning in Sichuan, was given an appanage on the Tibetan borderlands, centred on present-day Wuwei. He invaded briefly the next year, damaging a monastery. The death of Ogedei delayed any further advance, but in 1244 a rather pressing invitation arrived from Köten for the 62-year-old lama of the Saskya monastery, the other side of Lhasa, not far from the Nepalese border. His words suggest that he had identified Buddhism as the key to political dominance. 'I need to have a master to tell me which path I should take. I have decided to have you. Please come in total disregard of road hardships. If you find excuses in your old age . . . don't you fear that I will answer the matter by sending troops?' With little choice in the matter, the lama started a long journey from the Tibetan highlands, accompanied by two nephews, aged nine and seven, one of whom will be of peculiar significance in Kublai's story. Bear in mind that these events occurred over immense distances: it was 1,700 kilometres from Saskya to Wuwei, across some of the toughest landscapes on

[1] 'Tibetan Relations with Sung China and with the Mongols', in Morris Rossabi, ed., *China Among Equals: The Middle Kingdom and its Neighbours*.

earth. The lama arrived at Köten's base in 1246, only to find the Mongol absent attending the great assembly that elected Güyük as the new emperor. On Köten's return, the two agreed that the lama would act as the Mongol agent in Tibet. The lama wrote to various Tibetan leaders suggesting they co-operate: 'There is only one way out, which is to submit to the Mongols.' To seal the pact, the lama's seven-year-old nephew was married to Köten's daughter. As Petech says, by this agreement 'Köten laid the foundations of Mongol influence in Tibet', the influence that one day China would inherit.

Now three deaths occurred in quick succession: of the new emperor Güyük, Köten and the senior lama. The new emperor, eager to assert his rights in the area, sent troops into Tibet, with attendant destruction. He and several princes assumed the patronage of a number of Tibetan sects. One of the princes was Kublai, who thus found himself competing for influence in Tibet with (among others) his brothers Mönkhe, Hulegu and Ariq.

Kublai now made a small gesture of immense significance. He was still only a prince, still under the thumb of his brother Mönkhe, but with ambitions to extend his influence in north China. Kublai had already realized that he needed to balance his Chinese Confucian and Taoist advisers with a strong Buddhist one, and by happy chance one of the late Saskya lama's two nephews was at a loose end in Köten's HQ. His name was something that looks totally unpronounceable to westerners (Blo-gros rGyal-mtshan), but he would shortly acquire a title, Phags-pa (Noble Guru), which is how he is known to history. Kublai invited the 16-year-old Phags-pa to court. It must have suited them both – the boy grateful to have a sponsor in a chaotic world, already halfway Mongol, and eager for whatever was on offer in Kublai's expanding empire; Kublai well aware that this young priest, the heir to the senior lama of Tibet's most powerful sect yet too young to be viewed with suspicion by Mönkhe, could be the key to the whole country.

In 1251–2 Kublai was back and forth in China's western regions – the Ordos, or Zhangye, or Wuwei – preparing for the invasion of Yunnan. And he had a problem. He needed a rather better justification for conquest than he had inherited from his grandfather and father. Genghis and his immediate heirs had had a powerful but rather limited idea of what the empire was all about. They believed – no: they *knew*, with the utter, impregnable certainty of true believers – that Heaven had given the world into their hands. True, Genghis himself had moved beyond mere brutality to administer his new estates. But still the justification for conquest was, as it were, God's command. Of course, rulers have always claimed divine backing. Certainly every Chinese dynasty had done so, arguing that the very fact of a successful change of dynasty meant that the new emperor had been granted the Mandate of Heaven, and that he and his heirs alone were qualified to apply correctly the rules of good government, the age-old system of Confucian ethics and bureaucracy. But, as Herbert Franke points out in his magisterial analysis of this subject, the Mongols were different. Whatever may or may not have filtered into Genghis's mind from his Chinese neighbours, he was totally uninterested in any Chinese-style Mandate-of-Heaven nonsense, with its goody-goody Confucian veneer. As far as he and his heirs were concerned, the bottom line was that Heaven had given them the world. The Mongols' task was to dominate, and all everyone else had to do was submit. It's there in *The Secret History*: 'Together Heaven and Earth have agreed, Temujin [Genghis's original name] shall be the lord of the land . . . The whole earth is prepared for you . . .' It's there in many statements from the first Europeans to make contact with the Mongols. John of Plano Carpini reported in 1247 that the Mongols intended to conquer the whole world, that only then would there be peace, that Genghis was seen as 'the sweet and venerable Son of Heaven' – *filius Dei dulcis et venerabilis* – and as the only lord on Earth, as God is in Heaven. William of Rubrouck made the same point: *Super terram non sit nisi unus dominus Chingischan* – 'Over the Earth there is to be only one lord, Genghis Khan.' Note the sense of present and future. Genghis remained in some sense alive, in spirit; still does, actually, as anyone can see if they visit his so-called mausoleum in Inner Mongolia, or witness the adoration released by the 800th anniversary of his coronation in 2006.

Even in his life this had proved a rather over-simple prescription. Conquest is not the same as government. Genghis himself had moved beyond conquest, introducing a script, written laws, bureaucracy and some of the rules of administration; and his heirs, overriding the objections of reactionaries, had for the most part drifted in the same direction. As it happened, the fundamental Mongol belief in Tenger proved quite adaptable. Islam and Christianity both acknowledge Heaven. Hence Genghis's religious tolerance, and hence the relative ease with which Mongol rulers in Persia and Central Asia adopted Islam. As Herbert Franke suggests, it is not hard to imagine that, if the Mongols had remained in Hungary after 1242, they would in due course have become Christian.

It was the same with Kublai. The needs of government

in his Chinese territories had already demanded that he acquire the trappings of Confucianism. But that was not enough. His gaze was looking beyond traditional Chinese lands, to Yunnan, to Tibet. He had to legitimize his rule in the eyes of Mongols, Chinese and *any other culture that would, as Heaven decreed, form part of the Mongol world-empire*. He found what he was looking for in Buddhism. You may think of Buddhism as a peaceful religion, and therefore unsuitable for an empire dedicated to world conquest, but it is not necessarily so. In Lamaist Buddhism, one of the four god-kings who preside over the four corners of the earth is Vaiśravana, a warrior armed with a lance or cudgel with which to defeat non-believers. He was, if you like, a Buddhist god of war. There is nothing in Lamaist Buddhism incompatible with Mongol imperialism.

It was the teenage Phags-pa who showed Kublai that Buddhism could serve his needs well. For Buddhism offered something that did not exist in the Chinese view of history, or in Islam, or in Christianity: not only did it claim to be a religion of universal truth, it also contained a model of the 'universal emperor', the *cakravartin-raja*, who ruled people of many languages and 'turned the wheel of the Law'. Some previous rulers had experimented with this idea, equating themselves with Buddha, having themselves addressed as a *bodhisattva*, an enlightened being – Emperor Bodhisattva or Saviour of the World Bodhisattva. Buddhism was, in brief, the best way for Kublai to attach himself to a religion that not only was much more than Chinese but also offered an ideology that justified world conquest and world rule. Kublai would become both Caesar and Pope, head of both church and state, the fount of both worldly welfare and spiritual salvation.

The process started in about 1253 – the date is slightly vague, because Kublai was involved with the conquest of Yunnan at the time – when he received a consecration from the 18-year-old Phags-pa, being initiated into the rites of the highest deity of Lamaism, Hevajra, whose cult centred on the Saskya monastery, in which Phags-pa had been raised.

With Yunnan conquered, Kublai returned to Xanadu, bringing with him Phags-pa, a key both to his evolving ideology and to Tibet. Phags-pa concluded his studies, became a full monk, and in 1258, now aged 23, became Kublai's Buddhist guru; for Kublai, shortly to declare himself emperor, needed formally to establish his credentials as a universal ruler.

Phags-pa's status was confirmed when, that same year, he took part in the third and decisive debate set up by Kublai between Buddhists and Taoists. This left him in a strong position when Kublai had himself declared khan in 1260. In the civil war with Ariq that followed, rival sects in Tibet were suspected of siding with Ariq and silenced (temporarily, as it turned out). In 1261, Kublai conferred on Phags-pa the title of National Preceptor and made him the supreme head of the Buddhist clergy in his Chinese domains. Three years later, Kublai gave his protégé the so-called Pearl Document, by which the Buddhist monks were exempted from taxation and granted various other privileges. Soon after, he sent Phags-pa home as abbot of the main Saskya monastery, along with his younger brother. While Kublai sent a scattering of troops to 'pacify' remote corners of Tibet that had hitherto remained beyond Mongol reach, Phags-pa and his brother were supposed to establish Kublai's moral sway over the whole country.

This was not so easy. Locals objected, apparently seeing in Phags-pa not so much a brilliant young mind as a turncoat who had adopted Mongol clothes and manners. The whole project foundered when his brother died in 1267, aged 29; so an army marched in from Qinghai, cowed the opposition and established a Pacification Bureau that would run the country directly. Politically, Phags-pa was sidelined, spending the next few years engaged on a task which we shall get to in a moment. A Mongol named Dashman was given the job of establishing a postal system, with 27 relay stations, and of proclaiming Kublai's sovereignty. By 1269 Tibet was an integral part of Kublai's empire, where it remained for the next 80 years, until the Mongol empire fell apart.

Meanwhile, Kublai had had a startling cultural insight. He had identified a problem that sprang from the nature of Mongol achievements, and from his own ambition; and he wanted Phags-pa to provide the solution.

Kublai had grown up in two worlds, Mongol and Chinese. He spoke Mongol, but struggled with Chinese. Now Xanadu was rising around him, he was surrounded by Chinese advisers, and the vast majority of his subjects were Chinese. Soon, if all went well, there would be millions more.

His problem was this: how to form an administration that actually spanned the two worlds? Sure, Mongol edicts could be written in Mongol, Chinese in Chinese, but the two systems were incompatible.

Mongolian had a fine vertical script, introduced on Genghis's orders by his new vassals the Uighurs, of what is now western China. It was an alphabetical script, which means it could represent most of the sounds of almost any language fairly well (as Latin script does in, for instance, the Latinized version of Chinese, pinyin). However, since the vertical script was devised for Uighur, not Mongolian, it has a number of faults, among them an inability to capture some Chinese sounds. In addition, it has three versions of most letters – initial, medial and final – which gives it about 80 characters (our alphabet having 52, if you count upper and lower case as separate). Still, it works well enough to have survived. It is in everyday use in Inner Mongolia, and quite common in Mongolia itself, if only in academic circles and as a designer-chic escape from the standard and rather less exotic Cyrillic.

Chinese script is infinitely more complex, with thousands of characters, each one representing a syllable, governed by the rule that each must begin with a consonant and end with a vowel or 'n'. In its favour, it works, for Chinese; it is as expressive as any other script; it is beautiful, an art form in its own right; and it has tremendous cultural momentum, in that it has been in existence for 4,000 years – a few characters can be traced right back to their origins in Shang times around 2500 BC – and the Chinese are not about to change it (Mao once played with the idea of trying, but backed off). For Kublai to try to impose Mongolian script on China would have been impossible; it was equally impossible to use Chinese script to write Mongolian. So a system arose whereby documents were first written in Mongol, then translated. But Kublai was wary of allowing Chinese scribes too much authority, so they were not allowed to learn Mongol, and had to rely on non-Chinese interpreters. It was a tedious and cumbersome business.

It gets worse. Genghis had conquered Xi Xia, which

was inhabited by Tangut-speakers. Tangut had its own script, which had been invented at the behest of the state's founder, Li Yuan-hao, in the eleventh century. As a model, he chose the script of the region's dominant culture, China. But he also wanted it to be unique to Tangut, a Tibetan language that had no relation to Chinese at all. So he instructed his scholar, Yeli Renrong, to devise something totally new. Tangut's characters, some 6,000 of which are recorded, look like Chinese, but are no more Chinese than the language itself. Since Genghis virtually destroyed the Tangut culture, the language eventually vanished from history. As a result it has only been deciphered quite recently, and Tangut is still in the process of emerging from the darkness into which Genghis cast it. Kublai had many thousands of Tangut subjects. They, too, needed to read his edicts.

Then there was the script of the Khitan, the Manchurian people who had been the Mongols' predecessor dynasty in north China. And Sanskrit, the language towards which his new subjects the Tibetans looked as the fount and origin of their religion. And Tibetan itself, of course, already some 600 years old. Not forgetting Korea, which the Mongols had already attacked once in 1216, and to which Kublai would soon return. And what of those languages of people under the control of Kublai's brother Hulegu, principally Persian?

That's just the languages in which Kublai was directly involved around 1261. If things went as he hoped, if all south China fell to the Mongols, they would be in contact with Burmese, Vietnamese, Japanese and who knew what other cultures. A bureaucratic nightmare loomed. If it went on like this, all administration would be suffocated by translation work.

Once he saw the problem, Kublai also saw an instant solution. Chinese had unified China, welding together diverse dialects with a common script; Kublai wanted a script that would unify the world. Xanadu was ready, Ariq's rebellion had been crushed; Kublai was already thinking about a new capital in what is now Beijing and planning the long-delayed invasion of southern China. He needed to consolidate, to ensure the most efficient management possible as a basis for expansion. On hand was just the man: young Phags-pa, just back from his abortive trip to Tibet. In 1267, Kublai told him to invent the new script, a script in which any language under Heaven could be written.

Phags-pa, fluent in Tibetan, Mongolian and Chinese, and probably with a good knowledge of Uighur and Sanskrit as well, analysed their phonetic demands and modified his own Tibetan script into a sort of International Phonetic Alphabet of some 60 signs, most representing individual vowels and consonants, but including some common syllables. Tibetan reads from left to right, but Phags-pa designed his script to be read vertically, in deference to the Uighur system introduced by the great Genghis. The letters are mostly made of straight lines and right-angles, hence its name in Mongolian: square script. For representing Mongolian and other languages, it is certainly a big advance on Chinese: 'Genghis' in Chinese transliterates as *cheng ji si*; in Phags-pa it is *jing gis*.

After two years of work, it was done. Phags-pa presented his master with his new script in 1269. Kublai was delighted, and conferred on Phags-pa the title of Imperial Preceptor, with income to match. He ordered that all official documentation be recorded in the new script – the

'State Script' as he called it – and set up schools to teach it. It was used on seals and the metal or wood passes – *paiza*, as they are known – which gave authority to high officials to demand goods and service from civilians. 'By the power of Eternal Heaven, by the protection of the Great Blessedness [of Genghis],' ran the text on one of them, 'whoever has no reverence [for this] shall be guilty and die.'

That was the high point of Phags-pa's international influence. He returned to Tibet shortly afterwards as head of the Saskya monastery and sect, which exercised an uneasy sway over the others. Suddenly, in 1280, he died. He was only 45, and there were strong suspicions he had been poisoned. The Tibetan civil administrator was suspected. There was no proof, but justice being rough and Kublai being emperor, he had the man executed anyway.

You can see Kublai's problem, and his solution, set in stone today. If you visit China's prime tourist attraction, the Great Wall at Badaling, just outside Beijing, you will see behind the Wall an ancient arch, Cloud Terrace (Yun Tai), built in 1342 as a gateway to the pass. Its flagstone floor is scarred with parallel tracks by an infinity of wagon-wheels, making it look like an abandoned railway tunnel. If you stand inside and look up, you see that you are surrounded by five flat surfaces carved with intertwining bas-reliefs of warrior kings, buddhas, elephants, dragons, snakes and plants, all framing a Buddhist text in six languages: Sanskrit, Tibetan, Mongol, Tangut, Chinese – and Kublai's answer to this Babel, Phags-pa's 'State Script'.

In fact, the monument confers a significance on the new

script that it lacked in practice. It looked good on seals, stone slabs, coins, even porcelain. You still see it today on Mongolian banknotes and the occasional statue, but this is only for display. For routine records it never really took hold. Four more times in the 15 years after his initial proclamation Kublai repeated his order, backed by the creation of a special academy to study and teach the script. His officials handled his demands as bureaucrats always handle orders that make life harder: they said yes, and did nothing. The special schools lacked teachers, because no-one wanted to learn the script, and anyway the officials refused to send their children there.

The trouble with Phags-pa's script had nothing to do with its quality. The problem lay in human nature. Learning a script, however easy, is a demanding business. Writing has grown from nothing only four times in history: in Mesopotamia, Egypt, China and Central America. Each script took many centuries to refine. Once they reach maturity, they spread to other cultures, because they are vital to complex societies. They are incredibly tenacious. Changing a script is the cultural equivalent of growing a new limb. There have been examples of script change by authoritarianism: Kemal Atatürk forced Turkey to shift from Arabic to Latin script in the 1920s; Mongolia's Soviet-style rulers replaced Genghis's vertical script with Cyrillic in 1941. But in both cases the government wielded overwhelming power over tiny bureaucracies and unsophisticated societies. Kublai could employ his officials to control taxes, armies and records, but he couldn't control their minds. Trying to overcome the cultural inertia of his Chinese bureaucracy was like trying to row an iceberg. It just wasn't going to happen.

* * *

In a sense it didn't matter. Kublai's involvement in Tibet had already done more for his empire than a new script would ever achieve. By bringing Phags-pa on board, he added a vast new territory to his domains and established a link between China and Tibet that was a foundation for their relations from then on. Under the Manchus it was the Dalai Lama who ruled, maintaining a nominal independence with Manchu support, and occasional intervention, until the dynasty's overthrow in 1911 briefly restored the independence that Tibet had lost almost seven centuries before. After the 1949 revolution, Mao and his propagandists could thus argue, and did, that Tibet was an 'inalienable part of China', that Tibet's independence in the previous 40 years was an illusion based on China's weakness, and that the Communists were merely restoring the status quo. It is not an argument that seizes the moral high ground; go this route, and Britain could reclaim its empire. In fact, the foundation for the Chinese claim to Tibet is even shakier than Britain's claim to the USA or India. At least India and America were seized by the British. The Chinese claim is based on the fact that Tibet was first occupied by the troops of Genghis's son Ogedei and then his grandson Kublai, both Mongols. As far as Mongols were concerned, it was Mongolia that conquered China, Mongolia that occupied Tibet, Mongolia that established a Mongol empire. That's what they still assert. Fortunately for China, Kublai decided to establish a Chinese dynasty, making his grandfather its posthumous founder, thus turning history upside down, and allowing official pronouncements like this one in a recent book: 'The Chinese emperor enjoyed paramount authority in the areas under his sovereignty, and these areas included Tibet.'[2]

In Chinese eyes, Genghis and Kublai were actually Chinese.

And so, therefore, is Tibet.

End of story.

[2] Wang Jiawei and Nyima Gyaincain, *The Historical Status of China's Tibet.*

8

THE KEY TO CONQUEST

SOME THINGS ARE NON-NEGOTIABLE. FOR KUBLAI, CONQUEST of Song was one of them. He had tried invasion, and failed. Like his grandfather, Kublai was not to be put off by failure. He would give anything a go if it might work. So when his armies were dealing with Ariq in the north, he turned to soft talk and generosity in the south, hoping to win by charm what he could not yet win by force. But when in 1260 he sent an embassy to Hangzhou to suggest a deal, the envoy never even made it through Song lines. He was detained, and would remain under house arrest for an astonishing 16 years, until released to Kublai's invading armies.

Now why would Song do such a thing? Scholars have tended to put the arrest down to pure dimness, because it gave Kublai a *casus belli*. But more likely the affair grants us an insight into the shadowy world of espionage and

counter-espionage.[1] The envoy, Hao Jing, was the protégé
of a northern Chinese general who had gone over to the
Mongols after the conquest of Jin in 1234. As a Chinese,
and a turncoat, he would make an effective secret agent.
The Song general in charge of the frontier region set his
spies to work, and somehow learned the contents of a
memo from Hao Jing to Kublai, in which he suggested
what Kublai's policy should be. 'There are two ways to
conquer countries,' he began: 'by the use of force and by
the use of strategy.' Force hadn't worked, therefore
strategy was advisable, and this would take a great deal of
patience. 'We should thus buy time and gain the confidence of the Song and request that they cede to us some
territory and present us annual tributes of cash. When the
time is ripe for the conquest we should then first—' and
he sketched out an attack plan that was, in essence, the
plan eventually adopted by Kublai. So the terms he had
come to propose would have been merely a delaying
tactic, because Kublai had no intention of keeping the
peace long-term. Of course he didn't. His aim was
conquest, as Genghis and Heaven had ordained. Hao Jing
was on a phoney mission. That's why he was arrested.
And once arrested, he could not be released because he
would tell Kublai that the Song now knew Kublai's long-
term strategy.

Kublai gritted his teeth – he had little choice, given that
almost all his troops were dealing with Ariq – and continued to appease. He released unasked 172 merchants
who had been arrested for clandestine trading across the
Mongol–Song border. He granted land, clothes and oxen

[1] This paragraph is based on Jennifer W. Jay, *A Change in Dynasties:
Loyalism in 13th-Century China.*

to Song defectors, of which there were many. But this was not real peace, as both sides now knew. As soon as he could, Kublai would turn on the south again.

The previous campaign had shown that the Mongols were not yet up to the task. Song was all rivers and cities, exactly what Mongolia and most of north China were not. Cities were the prizes, because that was where the rich lived and the powerful administered – there were no castles such as the European nobility had, no manorial estates to be plundered. As a result, cities were tough nuts, well supplied with explosives, many of them positioned on rivers, the better to trade and feed themselves. Mongol horsemen might move fast over open land, but as the assaults on Fishing Mountain and Wuchang had shown, horsemen could not guarantee victories against cities set in rivers and mountains. The Mongols needed to beat the Song on their own terms, with (a) better means to take cities and (b) ships. Though they had known of the first – the principles of siege warfare – since Genghis's time, they would now need a vast increase in the scale of their siege machinery. But ships? The only ships they knew were ferries for crossing rivers. To build warships that would carry armies and weapons up and down China's river roads, they would have to start from scratch.

The key, of course, was the mighty Yangtze, beyond whose lower reaches lay the capital, Hangzhou. Now, the Yangtze flows from west to east, while Kublai's armies would be invading from the north. But right in the middle of the Mongol–Song borderland a major tributary, the Han, swung southward, making a river-road straight down to Wuchang, the lower Yangtze – and Hangzhou.

There was just one problem. The Han had its own key,

in the form of the town of Xiangyang,[2] which lies on the Han at the junction of two other rivers. Today, Xiangyang and its sister-city across the river, Fancheng, form the super-city of Xiangfan, a knot of roads and railway lines; it thrives on industry and tourists heading for the Wudang mountains to the west, famous for their 72 pinnacles, their Taoist temples and their boxers, who date their *tai ji*-like skills back to Song times. In Kublai's day, Xiangyang was a moated fortress-city and a major trade hub of 200,000 people, linked to Fancheng by a pontoon bridge consisting of boats moored between posts driven into the river-bed. In summer, when bloated by rain, the Han, wide and languid, rolls on southward between the Jing and Dahong hills then meanders out on to lake-spattered lowlands around Wuhan. Xiangyang would have to be eliminated by any army heading south by river.

This was common knowledge on both sides, because the city had been a prime target before – in a Jin assault in 1206–7 and in Ogedei's 1235–41 campaign. It had not fallen either time, but surrendered in 1236 to the Mongols, who held it only briefly before returning north. So Xiangyang was used to taking punishment; and besides, thanks in part to the discovery of Hao's memo, it had been busy rebuilding its defences. It had 6 kilometres of solid stone walls, some 6–7 metres high, set in a rough square just over a kilometre across. Three of the six gates gave directly on to the river, which was a high road for supplies and communication half a kilometre wide when it was in flood, and far too deep to wade; in winter,

---

[2] Xiangyang has been through all sorts of different versions and spellings – Saianfu in Marco Polo, Sayan-fu in Rashid, Hsiang-yang in more recent, but pre-pinyin times.

when the water was low, it became a maze of channels and sandbars; and the moat, fed from the river, was 90 metres across. All of this meant that attackers could not get close enough either to assault the walls with ladders and towers or to undermine them.

This chapter is largely about the answer to this problem – the first of several problems whose solution led on to Kublai's greatest achievement, the recreation of a unified China. In reverse, the argument runs like this: the key to all China was the south, the kingdom of Song; the key to the south was the Yangtze, with its vast population, numerous cities and agricultural wealth; the key to the Yangtze, if approaching from the north, was the Han river; the key to the Han was Xiangyang; and the key that would open Xiangyang to the Mongols was – well, I don't want to give away the story just yet. Let's just say it could not possibly be the old-style Mongol cavalry.

The evidence, I have to admit, is patchy: sources relate the overall progress of the campaign, the difficulties and significance of the siege, a mention of the engineers who solved the problem, the hugely influential consequences. But my reasoning has a step-by-step logic that leads inexorably to a conclusion I would very much like to be true: that, in effect, modern China owes its existence to the device that broke the siege of Xiangyang, a device such as China, and perhaps the world, had never seen before.

Very little of this was in Kublai's mind as he rebuilt his forces after dealing with Ariq. It was four years before his generals told him they were ready, which made it nine years since Kublai had been forced to give up on his first assault on Song. You would think nine years would have been long enough to prepare, but he had no way of knowing that Xiangyang would be such a challenge, and certainly no way of knowing in advance how to deal with it.

It began with Mongols approaching the city in early 1268, under the command of the young (32) and famous Aju – famous because military glory was in the family; he was the son of Uriyang-kadai, who had won Yunnan for Kublai fifteen years before, and the grandson of the now-legendary Subedei, who had masterminded Genghis's and Mönkhe's western campaigns. Almost as soon as he started his advance, Aju found he needed help. 'The forces I am leading consist entirely of Mongol military units [i.e. cavalry],' he wrote to the emperor. 'Encountering barriers of mountains and rivers, stockades and forts, without Chinese army forces I can do nothing.' Kublai complied: infantry arrived, boats were captured and built, and Aju had the amphibious force he thought he needed.

Aju and his army would not have found much in the way of loot to sustain them, because in preparation for a siege city rulers customarily ordered a scorched earth policy, clearing the surrounding countryside of anything that might help the enemy: high buildings, trees, stones, metals, tiles, vegetables, straw, animals, grain. Much of this went into storage inside the walls. A military handbook, *Wu-pei ji-yao* (*The Essentials of Military Preparedness*),[3] lists what had to be stored: lamps, oil, axes, charcoal, sulphur, lime, rafters, nails, needles, mats, hemp, shovels, pestles, stones for pounding textiles, vessels to deal with 'night-soil', brushes, ink, ink-slabs, writing tables – and

[3] About 1830, but the practices it quotes are ancient ones.

on and on. Civilians would be trained as militiamen, women organized in cooking gangs, children trained in delivering food and materials. Particular care would have been taken to pre-empt trouble from the disaffected poor – espionage, sabotage – by avoiding harsh treatment: 'The poor are our children who may carry weapons and stand up against the enemy with all their strength,' says the *Essentials*, then quotes the words of a sage, Xu Dong: ' "If a town is besieged, one must first look to the interior peace and only then consider the external enemy." ' The townspeople must draw together. Innkeepers must vouch for their lodgers, abbots for their monks. Itinerant musicians, magicians and fortune-tellers are expelled as potential spies. Families are grouped in tens, with every-one vouching for everyone else. Only long-established employees are kept on, new ones fired. Curfews are kept. Every quarter has its fire-brigade, with its huge water-jars, ladders, and hooks and pulleys to deal with demolition. Specialists prepare their double and triple crossbows, which could shoot 2-metre arrows some 200 metres, while engineers check their trebuchets.

This is the moment to introduce the trebuchet, a subject that will shortly seize our attention in a big way.

The backbone of Chinese siege technology was the 'traction trebuchet', which has been resurrected in re-constructions. A typical trebuchet consists of a frame about 4 metres high on which pivots an 11–12-metre pole. The pole is on an axle, off-centre, with one section longer than the other. On the long end is a sling, on the short end are ropes, usually attached to a T-bar. The sling is crucial: it lengthens the pole and magnifies its power without increasing the weight. One end is nailed to the head of the pole, the other is attached to a simple hook. In release, it acts like a whip, being dragged up and over like a weighted hook on the end of a fishing line. Centrifugal force carries it in a semi-circle. As it reaches its topmost point, its momentum frees the unattached end, which flies clear, releasing the missile. Each trebuchet has a team of 5–15, depending on its size. A rock weighing no more than a couple of kilos or some sort of incendiary device is loaded in the sling, the team hauls on the other end – hence the term 'traction' – the lever rises, the sling whips round, slips its hook, and releases the rock. The whole operation takes no more than 15 seconds (modern reconstructions show that a good team can fire 5–6 rounds per minute). It is all rather primitive, but effective at close range: over a city wall, and anything up to 100 metres. In the thirteenth century, this was utterly standard siege technology. Traction trebuchets could be made on the spot, or carried in bits on horses, or mounted on wagons. Any army worthy of the name would muster scores, sometimes hundreds of them.

On campaigns, trebuchets formed a whole branch of siege warfare, as the artillery does in modern armies. For one thing, working a trebuchet was demanding, rather like rowing a racing eight. Teams needed to rest. As well as needing its own transport – a few horses, an ox and wagon – each trebuchet had to have several teams, working in relays. These specialized soldiers needed their own food, armour and horses. So each trebuchet, simple as it was, had quite an entourage – large versions demanded 200 men – with tremendous implications for commissariats planning advances, camps, sieges and retreats. They were often made on the spot, and they often needed repair, so imagine also contingents of carpenters. Ropes were of both hemp and leather, alternating, because their qualities varied with the weather (in wet weather, leather shrinks, hemp swells).

Trebuchets were, of course, standard weapons in defence as well as attack. In the siege of 1206–7 Xiangyang had 114 of them. Trebuchet teams would work in relative safety from inside the walls, with an artillery spotter up above to direct them. Before a siege, defenders gathered huge quantities of stone from surrounding areas, for their own use and to deprive the opposition of ammunition.

Whether in attack or defence, trebuchets lobbed more than simple rocks, for all Chinese armies employed experts in explosive devices and chemical warfare. The techniques, based on some 700 years of experimentation by alchemists, had been developed from the first use of gunpowder in war in the early tenth century – a flame-thrower. Rapidly, a whole range of gunpowder-based weapons had appeared: exploding arrows, mines, and bombs thrown by trebuchets. One of these consisted of gunpowder packed into bamboo and surrounded by broken porcelain: the first known use of shrapnel. By the early thirteenth century, about the time of the first Mongol invasions, this had evolved into the much more deadly 'thundercrash bomb', which detonated inside a metal or ceramic casing 5 centimetres thick. The Mongols experienced these when they took the Jin capital Kaifeng in 1232–4:

Among the weapons of the defenders there was the heaven-shaking thundercrash bomb. It consisted of gunpowder put into an iron container; then when the fuse was lit and the projectile shot off there was a great explosion the noise whereof was like thunder, audible for more than

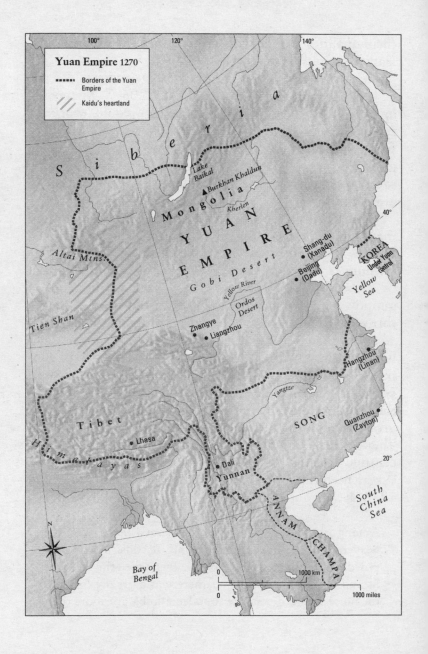

Yuan Empire 1270

- ▪▪▪▪ Borders of the Yuan Empire
- ⫽⫽⫽ Kaidu's heartland

100°   120°   140°

S i b e r i a

Lake Baikal

Burkhan Khaldun ▲

Mongolia

Kherlen

YUAN

EMPIRE

40°

Altai Mtns

Shang-du (Xanadu)

KOREA
Under Yuan control

Gobi Desert

Beijing (Dadu)

Tien Shan

Yellow River

Yellow Sea

Ordos Desert

Zhangye
• Liangzhou

Hangzhou (Linan)

Tibet

Yangtze

SONG

Quanzhou (Zayton)

• Lhasa

H i m a l a y a s

20°

• Dali
Yunnan

South China Sea

N

ANNAM

CHAMPA

Bay of Bengal

0   1000 km

0   1000 miles

a hundred *li* [*c*.50 kilometres], and the vegetation was scorched and blasted by the heat over more than half a *mou* [400 square metres].

In self-defence, the Mongols dug themselves trenches, covered by cowhides; but the Jin lowered the bombs on chains: 'When these reached the trenches . . . the bombs were set off, with the result that the cowhide and the attacking soldiers were all blown to bits, not even a trace being left behind.'

These bombs were made in large quantities, 'one or two thousand a month', according to a Song official in 1257. He was complaining that current production was down. 'They used to despatch ten or twenty thousand at a time to Xiangyang and Ying-chou,' he said, but now there were not enough. 'The government supposedly want to make preparations for the defence of its fortified cities . . . yet this is all they give us! What chilling indifference!'

The exploding poison devices, the first steps in chemical and germ warfare, are worth a diversion. There were many types. The most repulsive must have been the original dirty weapon, the excrement bomb.[4] I'm inclined to call it the 'shit-and-beetle bomb', after its most bizarre ingredients.

Here is the recipe:

• *7 kilos powdered human excrement.* First gather about 70 kilos of human shit. Dry it, and sift it into a fine powder. This will be the bulk of your poisonous

---

[4] From Robert Temple, *The Genius of China* (London: Prion, 1999), a distillation of Joseph Needham's massive *Science and Civilisation in China*.

cloud, searing lungs and infecting open wounds. To this add:

- *400g root of aconite*, the herb with hood-shaped flowers whose roots produce some of the deadliest of poisons. Absorbed through the skin, it numbs. Once breathed in or swallowed, it brings on nausea, breathing difficulties, convulsions and heart failure.

- *200g croton oil*. The croton tree grows in India and Indonesia. The oil of its seeds blisters the skin and, if swallowed, inflames the stomach and produces instant diarrhoea.

- *400g white arsenic (As_2O_3) and its compound, arsenic sulphide*. These, in the explosion, would form something like an insecticide spray, which when inhaled in sufficient doses would produce long-term diarrhoea, stomach pain, blood and kidney damage, and death.

- *100g beetles, of the genus Mylabris*. This is the oddest element in this extremely odd mixture. When I first saw it, my imagination went into overdrive. Were the beetles alive? Would they survive an explosion and its poisons? What on earth would be the use of a cloud of poisoned beetles in warfare? A beetles man at the Natural History Museum, Lee Rogers, put me right. *Mylabris* beetles have long been used in traditional Chinese medicine, because in small amounts the chemical they produce, cantharidic acid, stimulates certain organs, including the sexual organs. Indeed, it is the active ingredient in the aphrodisiac known as 'Spanish fly'. A quick bit of Googling reveals that there is a good deal of interest in the chemical at the moment in China because it may be anti-cancerous. But in larger doses, if it gets on the skin, the chemical is a toxin that produces blisters. Hence the common name for these creatures, 'blister beetles'. Once you have gathered your 100g (a few dozen only) of *Mylabris phalerata* or *M. cichorii*, you mash them up, dry them, powder them and add the powder to your poison-bag.

These ingredients were packed into gunpowder, from which ran a fuse. The whole lot was then wrapped in thick paper, tied up with string and covered in a layer of resin, like candle-wax, leaving the fuse sticking out. Weighing some 10–15 kilos, the shit-and-beetle bomb would be placed in its trebuchet sling, lit and fired. This was a specialized weapon, needing a large trebuchet and a team of perhaps a dozen men, who had to cast their lethal package a good 100 metres, or risk being affected by their own poisons.

On both sides all the effort might well end in a balance of forces. For one thing, trebuchets had one huge disadvantage, especially for the defenders. If they used rocks, the cheapest ammunition, they simply supplied ammunition to the other side. The same rocks arced back and forth over the walls, shattering heads, breaking arms, smashing roofs, on occasion in such numbers that the missiles crashed together in mid-air. Whether in defence or attack, think of the rock you would need to attack a city: two shots a minute per device, 100 devices – that's 12,000 rocks per hour, hour after hour, day after day. Where would it all come from? How many men and horses would it take to find it, cut it, transport it? There was thus an incentive to develop more effective projectiles – that is, explosive ones which could scatter poisons, chemicals and shrapnel. But even these were anti-personnel devices, useful only in close-up artillery exchanges, seldom reaching over 100 metres.

* * *

It was with these weapons, then, that the siege of Xiangyang began early in 1268, and Aju's advance stopped. The siege was to become a five-year epic, a sort of Chinese Trojan war, with its assaults and attempted break-outs and acts of heroism. The siege even had its equivalent of Troy's dramatic end, though in an act, not of cunning, but of overwhelming force. Unfortunately, since we are in history not prehistory, no bards sang of Xiangyang's heroes, no local Homer spun epic verse; and so, for the first three years of the siege, since we have no tales of heroism to tell, a paragraph of description will have to do.

A proper blockade required boats, 500 of them, built under the supervision of Kublai's admiral Liu Cheng, a senior Song officer who had defected. They took several months to build. Through the summer, the Mongols built fortifications downriver on either side of the Han to bombard Song boats ferrying in supplies. As winter came on again, Aju extended the siege across the river to include Fancheng. An attempt by the Chinese to break out ended in disaster for them: hundreds were captured and beheaded. After that, the Chinese sat tight, with enough supplies reaching them to survive. In spring 1269, Kublai sent in another 20,000 troops to strengthen the besiegers. In August, after 18 months of action and inaction, 3,000 Song boats came up the Han to attack the new Mongol fortifications, and were repulsed with the loss of 2,000 men and 50 boats. Now the Mongols somehow connected up the two sets of downriver fortifications, probably with a chain on pontoons. It could not have worked very well, because the commanders requested another 70,000 troops and 5,000 boats. Even making allowance for the normal inflation of military statistics, this was a massive increase. No doubt, like generals on the Western Front or in Vietnam, they claimed that they could see light at the end of the tunnel, that with one more push it would all be over. The Chinese defenders, reassured by secret-service officers smuggling in orders, cash and letters sealed inside balls of wax, were equally adamant: there would be no surrender! Several more times the besieged tried to break out. Once, in March 1270, a battalion-strength force – a 'Ten Thousand' – of infantry and horsemen, with 100 boats, mounted an amphibious operation to break through the downriver fortifications; after suffering heavy losses, they retreated back behind the city walls. The catalogue of useless thrusts continued, the Chinese losing 1,000 men in October 1270, 2,000 in August 1271, most of a 3,000-strong force the following month.

What could break the stalemate? As a Mongol general, a Uighur named Ali-haiya, told Kublai, what the Mongols needed was the right sort of artillery. Now, the Mongols already had artillery of many kinds – mangonels, trebuchets, arrow-firing ballistas – having acquired the technology and specialist troops after the siege of Beijing in the year of Kublai's birth. The problems were Xiangyang's moat and stone walls. The Mongol-Chinese artillery simply didn't have the range or the power to tackle these defences, and no-one in Mongolia or China had the expertise to build bigger, more powerful siege engines.

Kublai, hearing of the problem, also saw the solution. He needed the empire's best siege-engine designers, who happened to be in Persia, 6,000 kilometres away, two-thirds of the way across the empire. This he knew, because he had to hand reports of the siege of Baghdad by his brother Hulegu in 1258. Had not Hulegu had catapults that breached walls? Rashid's words must surely have been echoed by reports in Kublai's archives: 'They set up catapults opposite the Ajami Tower, and breached it.' Ordinary old traction trebuchets could not breach walls. These were machines of a different order.

But even this new secret weapon would not guarantee success. As yet, Xiangyang remained untaken; victory over Song hung in the balance. Yet failure was unthinkable. How could Kublai best fulfil the will of Heaven? Phags-pa advised him what to do. He should seek help from the world of the spirits. Spirit-helpers needed to be approached in the right way, with the correct rites performed in a place impressive enough both to act as a sanctuary for the deity concerned and to assert the emperor's authority as spiritual leader.

Kublai commissioned a temple such as no-one had seen before: Baita Si, the White Pagoda, which still reaches up over central Beijing just to the west of the Forbidden City (it has no connection with the other White Pagoda in Beihai Park). In 2005 I paid the place a visit, vaguely hoping it would bring Kublai to life in some way. It did, mainly because there was one question I had not even thought of yet: to whom or what was Kublai going to pray? I came face to face with the answer, and, without giving away too much, I can tell you it was – well, not scary exactly, but certainly a surprise.

The site on which the White Pagoda would stand was a place of power. People avoided it, because there were reports of fireballs bursting from its low-lying soil (perhaps flares caused by marsh gas). Kublai ordered a dig to see what lay under the ground – and by happy chance someone found ruins, and coins, and a stone tablet engraved with dragons. That was the good omen he needed. Clearly, a dragon-palace had once stood here, making it the ideal location for a royal temple.

Now to define the temple's borders. This he did by means of an ancient Mongol practice for marking a new base. He – or perhaps one of his officers – fired arrows to the four points of the compass, each 200-metre shot specifying the distance to a wall. The original temple was therefore a complex of buildings in a compound about 400 × 400 metres. Later dynasties and the passage of time condemned the outer buildings and walls, reducing the compound to a fraction of its original size, but the pagoda itself, a great inverted ice-cream cone towering over its surrounding huddle of exhibition rooms and offices, remains pretty much as it was in Kublai's day.

Tourists go there to see Buddhas en masse, all official symbols of China's readiness to make everyone part of one great family. The Hall of Ten Thousand Buddhas claims to be one of the greatest collections in the world, with miniature Buddhas from every Buddhist country glittering like jewels. The Hall of Seven Buddhas now has three, four having vanished during the Cultural Revolution. In the Hall of the Great Enlightened One, Emperor Qian Lung's eighteenth-century calligraphy reminds visitors that 'the mind of the Buddha is as bright as a shining pearl'.

The heart of the place is the pagoda itself. To build this, and the complex that would surround it, Kublai naturally chose a Buddhist: a 27-year-old Nepalese architect and painter named Arniko, who had established his reputation as a teenager in Tibet and then come to China as one of Phags-pa's protégés, making his mark with Kublai in

1265, aged only 21, by rebuilding a bronze statue showing the acupuncture points. He went on to create many
other temples and statues around China, continuing
almost until his death in 1306 at the age of 62. Everyone
is rather proud of Arniko – not surprisingly, given that in
the thirteenth century the pagoda, at 374 metres high, was
Beijing's tallest building. A statue of him – slim, youthful,
fine-featured – stands at its foot, placed there by the
Arniko Society of Nepal, unveiled in 2003 in the presence
of Nepalese government bigwigs.

I wanted to see inside. With my guide, Silver as she
called herself, I climbed steps beside Arniko, and found
the way blocked by a wall of corrugated iron. The pagoda
was closed for renovation. But there was a door open in
the wall. We sneaked inside. To my surprise, I saw two
red-robed monks, one solid as a wrestler, the other a lightweight, setting out prayer-flags. Apparently, rituals were
still observed here. The monks seemed shy, and I didn't
like to intrude with questions. So I wandered round the
other side of the pagoda, and was staring up at the huge
fat curve of white plaster soaring into the bright autumn
sunlight, wondering at the lack of windows and doors, when
I heard low chanting. The two monks were performing
some sort of a rite; by the time I had hurried back to
the front of the building they were closing the door of
what looked like a cupboard, and began burning incense
and rice. This time there was eye contact, a smile, a nod.
Encouraged, I asked Silver to introduce me. The monks were
Tibetan. The big one was Tu Dan, the lean one Ganga. How
strange, I said, that such a place should still be in use. It
always was, came the reply, always protected, always a place
to strengthen the relationship between Chinese, Mongols
and Tibetans . . .

. . . At which moment we were joined by a man with the soft, round features of the Beijing professional, who instantly revealed a fine command of English. Benjamin Li was an English graduate and a businessman. He was here because he was an admirer of the temple, and because he was a friend of the two monks. It struck me that he was also some sort of a benefactor, because he pointed out that they lived entirely from donations. A small contribution and an offer to buy lunch produced smiles, and opened the way to more conversation.

Benjamin loved the temple. 'This is a very, very good place, to me, the most important place in Beijing, maybe all China.' He nodded at my look of surprise. 'A *really* good place. Even the Dalai Lama has worshipped here.'

I wanted to know more about its original purpose.

'It was to defeat the Song and unify the country. It was not the only one, you know. There is another, also built by Arniko, in Zhuozhou, Hebei' – 75 kilometres south-west of Beijing – 'called the Protecting-the-Country Temple.'

Still there was something I couldn't quite get. What made this temple and its twin in Hebei so special, then and now? What or whom had Kublai actually worshipped?

'This was created for Kublai, his private family place of worship.' Benjamin paused. I don't think there had been any conscious attempt to keep anything from me, but suddenly the truth about the place came with a rush. 'This temple, you know, was for the worship of a guardian called Mahakala.'

'Mahakala? Who on earth is Mahakala?'

'Mahakala is like . . . a god of war.'

So this was the deity Kublai had hoped to summon to aid him in the struggle with Song. I had never heard of him, but millions across Asia from India to Japan revere him as 'the great black one'. Hindus know him as a form of Shiva, the destroyer. In Tibet, he consumes those who fail to show Buddhism proper respect. I didn't know yet what he looked like, but he was clearly not a god you would wish to meet on a dark night.

As luck would have it, a few days later I was in Ulaanbaatar with the Mongolian scholar and leading Mongolist Shagdaryn Bira, who had researched this very subject. Mahakala was a guardian connected in some way with Hevajra – the deity who was an object of special veneration by Phags-pa's Saskya monastery; the one into whose cult Kublai had been initiated by Phags-pa in 1253. Now, eighteen years later, imperial power had qualified Kublai for the protection of his own personal god. Or, as Bira put it in a paper he was preparing for publication: 'The Khan, having gotten into direct spiritual contact with his tutelary deity Mahakala, the most powerful defender of religion, could pretend to have acquired all his mysterious power in the cause of ruling his empire. Thus the Mongolian khan could enjoy not only the favour of Tenger, but also the favour of the powerful Tantric god.'

And it wasn't just Kublai, as Benjamin explained: 'For Kublai Khan and Phags-pa, and for all the masters since, right down to the tenth Panchen Lama today, the guardian was always Mahakala.'

'And still is?'

'Still is. He is right here. Look behind you.'

And Tu Dan opened the door I had seen him closing earlier, to reveal a little altar surmounted by a peculiarly vivid portrait of Mahakala: a black face, three staring eyes, a ferocious snarl, fangs, a head-dress of skulls set in yellow hair. So that was what the monks had been doing while I was wandering round the pagoda: ministering to Mahakala.

On a shelf along the front of the shrine was a little silver dish of pale liquid. 'Alcohol,' said Benjamin. 'For other bodhisattvas, you may offer flowers, fruits, but nothing alcoholic. But for guardians, especially powerful ones like Mahakala, you give alcohol. With the right prayers it is like, like' – he tapped a word into an electronic Chinese–English dictionary, the type of thing that students and guides tend to carry with them – 'nectar. And food, like the incense and the rice, which gives off the smell that feeds the spirits. We are satisfied by food, but spirits – how can they be satisfied? By smell! Then Mahakala will become your guardian. He brings good luck.'

'He doesn't look like good luck. He looks like a nightmare.'

Benjamin translated, and all three laughed.

'If he is on your side, that's good. He scares away all other spirits.'

I paused, hoping for more insights. 'Can we see inside the pagoda?'

'Not possible. It will not be ready for months. But you can go around again. This time, go the right way, clockwise.'

'What's inside?'

'Mahakala! The real Mahakala!'

One day, I promised myself as we circled the bulbous mass, I would be back, to see him face to face. He may be just a statue, but I shall take no chances. There will be prayers from the likes of Tu Dan and Ganga, and alcohol. I shall make sure he's on my side – as he must have been on Kublai's in 1271, if events are anything to go by.

* * *

By way of understanding the problem posed by the walls of Xiangyang, let me introduce you to the strange world of counterweight trebuchets. These machines were the heavy artillery of their day, against which the man-powered traction trebuchets paled into comparative insignificance. In the counterweight trebuchet, manpower was replaced by a box filled with ballast (rocks, earth or lead), the advantage being that the weight could be enormous, the throwing arm lengthened, the missile heavier, the sling extended (without increasing the weight), the range increased, and – if the counterweight and missile remained unchanged between shots – accuracy improved.

Size demanded expertise, which took time to acquire. So the counterweight trebuchet came on the scene quite late, emerging in the Islamic world in the twelfth century and spreading to Europe soon after crusading armies came across it in about 1200. Actually, no-one is quite sure which way it spread. The Chinese called the new engines 'Muslim catapults'; the Muslim writer Rashid ad-Din referred to them as 'Frankish'. Wherever the idea originated, information soon flowed both ways, the machines developing in both Europe and the Islamic world into specialized devices that not only destroyed walls but seized imaginations, influenced strategy and made stars of their engineers (who therefore had a good reason never to record their secrets).

By the end of the fifteenth century, they were gone, blown away by gunpowder. They were only wood, after all, and they took up a lot of space. Once redundant, they became junk, good for beams or planks or firewood. No counterweight trebuchet survived into the twentieth century. One was found during the 1890s in a church in what was then eastern Prussia (now part of Poland), but by the time a museum heard of it, the locals had burned it. No accurate plans have ever been discovered either (probably thanks to the secretiveness of their elitist designers), and all the illustrations are heavily stylized, with vital details of the triggers and pivots omitted by non-technical artists.

Down the years, only very few military-historical specialists have devoted much thought to these machines. To understand them, you have to resurrect them. Today, there is an international sub-culture of 'treb' enthusiasts who do just this. Combining theoretical science, history and practicality, they are all keenly, many obsessively, and some eccentrically dedicated to the business of hurling huge loads as far as possible without the use of explosives. Much of this work is serious reconstructive archaeology, but it also generates extremely odd behaviour, because the forces involved are immense and the results hard to predict, making each machine an individual, often with its own name: Cheesechucker, Son of Cheesechucker, The Flinger Thinger. In 1991 Hew Kennedy, English landowner, inventor and military historian, became intrigued by a machine portrayed by Leonardo da Vinci which appeared to be able to throw dead horses. He designed and built a 30-tonne trebuchet with which he threw half a dozen cars, 60 pianos and many dead pigs, earning himself a good deal of notoriety. Pianos, for some reason, are popular ammunition for hurlers, perhaps because their strings wail wonderfully in mid-throw and they land with a glorious crash of exploding keys. TV channels, which love the combination of power, drama and craziness, have shown keen interest. The US TV programme *Northern Exposure* filmed a catapult built by John Wayne Cyra flinging 200-kilo upright pianos, nine of them, one after the other. The programme went on air in October 1992, the pianos soaring in 100-metre arcs to the tune of 'The Blue Danube'. Ron Toms, a Texan (there are quite a few Texans in this business; they like the power and size), came to trebuchets as a teenager, building a trebuchet and using himself as ammunition, shooting himself 30 feet into the air and landing in a river. He and his friends spent a happy afternoon lobbing themselves into the water, until he increased the counterweight to toss himself further and, as he says, 'The machine self-destructed in mid-throw.' Toms went on to build the big daddy of them all for the TV show *In the Name of Science*. He called his iron monster T. Wrecks: its namesake ate diplodoci; this one spat cars. Websites speak of plans for Thor, with a 100-foot arm and a 25-tonne counterweight, which will supposedly toss Buicks as the war-god tossed thunderbolts. At the time of writing, Thor was still a dream.

Now I, too, am a trebuchet addict because of a visit to Caerphilly Castle, south Wales. The castle contains four reconstructed working catapults, one being a counterweight trebuchet. On the grimly overcast Easter Sunday of 2005 I watched a team of hefty blokes in medieval costume get the machine ready to lob missiles into the moat before a crowd of tourists. They were under the expert eye of Paul Denney, engineer, who with his wife Julie work at the serious, archaeological end of treb research. This is not a huge machine, weighing in at 10 tonnes, with a counterweight of 2 tonnes. Even so, priming it is quite an operation. It took two men winding the capstan and six others hauling on a rope to cock the machine. With all that weight, all that power being slowly stored, there was a sense of a great beast being harnessed. A hook held the trigger-ring. Someone laid out the sling with its missile. Usually, it's a 2-kilo ball of concrete. In this pre-exhibition test, Paul was using a 5-kilo rock.

'You want to pull the trigger, John?'

'Fire it? Sure.'

'Not "fire". We don't say that. There's no fire involved. That's to do with gunpowder artillery. We say "loose" or "shoot".'

So I did.

There is beauty in what happens when this pent-up energy is released, because it involves only natural elements – wood, iron, rock, rope, gravity – carefully managed. A jerk on the trigger frees the arm. The counterweight drops, the arm rises, the sling follows with its missile. The only sounds are soft, like a giant exhalation: a whisper from the greased axle, the swish of the sling. I had expected a whiplash action, but it's all in slow motion, rather graceful. Away the missile flies. Then the beast resettles with little sounds of satisfaction – sighs from the counterweight swinging back and forth, the clunk of heavy stones rearranging themselves inside, the slap of the empty sling against the waving lever-arm. High up, the rock soars lazily away, spinning in a huge, high arc for seven seconds (I timed it) to splash into the moat 80 metres away.

There was a long moment of awed silence. I was seduced. I wanted more. Not that I yearned to launch pianos and Buicks. That takes metal, which is cheating. What I wanted was to answer a historical question: how big and how powerful did medieval wooden counterweight trebuchets get? This would take me back to the matter in hand, Kublai's conquest of Song.

King Edward I, Edward Longshanks, almost answered my question, because he was responsible for what was perhaps the biggest European trebuchet. In 1304 he attacked Stirling castle, a key element in Scottish resistance. His army made no impression on its massive walls and well-stocked inhabitants. Edward's response was to order his engineer, named Reginald, to build the biggest counterweight trebuchet he could. Five carpenters and five assistants laboured for three months, and produced the machine called Lup de Guerre, Warwolf. Details are lacking, but it must have had the potential to batter down Stirling's walls. At the very sight of it, so one story goes, the castle surrendered – though Edward refused their surrender until he had tried his giant machine and proved that it worked.

A wooden treb that must approach this size has been built, by a French designer, Renauld Beufette. Its design is authentic, based on the only known plan of a trebuchet, a sketch by a French artist, Villard de Honnecourt, about whom virtually nothing is known except his portfolio of drawings. Beufette's trebuchet is a monster, with a 10-tonne counterweight that can toss 100 kilos 220 metres.

So we know what Kublai was after. We know it was possible. We know the expertise did not exist in China; it had to come from Persia. Nothing could have better shown the advantages of having an empire all run by one family, bound together by a network of transcontinental communications. Off went his letter by pony express. Five weeks later and 6,000 kilometres away, his message was in Tabriz, northern Persia, at the HQ of Kublai's nephew, Abaqa, the Il-khan (subordinate khan) since the death of his father Hulegu in 1265. Abaqa had on hand several designers who had built the counterweight trebuchets used in the sieges of Baghdad, Aleppo, Damascus and Syria's crusader castles. He could spare two of them, Ismail and his assistant Ala ad-Din.[5] In late 1271 the two arrived with their families at Xanadu, and were given an official residence for the winter. The following spring, after building a catapult to demonstrate the principles to the emperor, the two men – plus, apparently, Ismail's son, whom he was training to follow in his footsteps – found themselves in the battle zone, staring at Xiangyang's solid walls, the moat, the broad river and Fancheng, Xiangyang's sibling-city across the river.

Let us put ourselves in the shoes of Ismail. Our task is to sling 100-kilo balls of rock at Xiangyang's walls, given that the moat places us at least 100 metres away. So we are already dealing with a machine too large to be manoeuvrable. That means we must place ourselves and our crew yet further away, out of the range of arrows and poisonous, explosive bombs slung from the walls. So we are at a range of about 200 metres. Beufette's giant would fit the bill nicely. Ismail's machine must have weighed 40 tonnes and towered almost 20 metres high.[6]

There are all sorts of other variables to be assessed, like the exact weight of the counterweight if it happens to get wet; and what happens to the properties of the newly cut lever-arm as it slowly dries out; and at what moment the

[5] Rashid gives completely different names: Taleb and three sons, which sounds like another family altogether. I have not seen a resolution to this, and follow the Chinese sources in the *Yuan History*.

[6] You can get an idea of what was required by checking the website of an Australian group, the Grey Company. Here you will find a link to 'The Algorithmic Beauty of the Trebuchet', which, with the computerized application of some tricky maths, allows you to become a virtual trebuchet engineer.

sling should disengage (earlier for a high trajectory, later for a low one); and the effect of the temperature on the grease that will ease the friction of wooden axles in wooden bearings (unless our Muslim engineers decide to cast bronze-and-metal bearings, which have the remarkable property of wearing so smooth that they are, in effect, self-lubricating). It was Ismail's skill to know all this, and to approach but not overstep the limits of what was possible. And there were still things he could not have known before he arrived, like which timber to use for the lever arm, for all trees differ in their weight and strength, both of which vary again as they dry out.

Now consider the ammunition. Accuracy was crucial. It was no good roughly cutting any old rocks to make approximately 100 kilos, because small variations in weight and shape translate into the difference between hitting and missing a target. A tumbling irregular rock is in chaotic motion, its trajectory unpredictable. If we want to strike a battlement, a tower, or a particular piece of wall several times running, we need missiles of the same weight and of a regular shape, namely spherical. So we need a contingent of stonemasons, a local quarry and good transport.

Speed was vital. That June, 100 Song boats brought 3,000 soldiers downriver, entering the city after a running battle along 50–60 kilometres of river. The only loss, apparently, was the Song general, whose body was found a few days later, still clasping his bow, bobbing against the pontoon bridge across the river. Ismail and Ala ad-Din set their teams to work, felling suitable trees in nearby forests and hewing rocks. If Edward I's Warwolf trebuchet is anything to go by, the work would have taken a good three months: the trees felled and stripped, the timbers shaped for the frame, rocks chipped into spheres, 10 tonnes of ballast gathered for the counterweight, the whole thing being designed so that it could be dismantled by block-and-tackle lifting gear and moved.

Where was the best place to attack? The Mongol general Ariq-khaya decided on an indirect approach by assaulting Fancheng. In the words of his biography, 'He took the relation of Fancheng to Xiangyang to be like that of the lips to the teeth,' and asked Kublai's permission to switch the focus of the attack to the subsidiary city. Kublai approved. The first thing to do was to isolate Fancheng by destroying the pontoon bridge to prevent supplies being ferried across. Ariq-khaya's biography summarizes the story: 'At the same time, Ismail, a man from the west, had presented a new method of making catapults, and so Ariq-khaya took this man with him to the army. In the first moon [January–February 1273, though the *Yuan History* dates the assault at December 1272] they made catapults and stormed Fancheng.'

Now, if this was the first time Ismail had used his machine, he would have fine-tuned it like an artilleryman, shooting off a couple of ranging shots, then adapting the length of the sling or the setting of the sling-release hook to lob another ball clear over the wall. In artillery terms, he was bracketing. A final bit of fiddling – perhaps slipping a knot to give the lever-arm a few centimetres less of a sweep – and the third shot would have been dead on target. Fancheng's guardians would have watched the ball arc lazily towards them, then smash into the battlements in an explosion of stone that left a nasty hole in the top of the wall. As Ariq-khaya's biography says, Ismail's *hui-hui pao* (Muslim catapult) 'breached the walls . . . [since] the reinforcements from Xiangyang no longer reached the fortress, it was captured'.

Here was an interesting situation. Fancheng had resisted to the end, and everyone knew what happened to cities that did not surrender: the inhabitants were murdered en masse, primarily to terrify other cities into rapid submission. Kublai discouraged such tactics. But the problem of Xiangyang remained unresolved. From the Mongol point of view, Ariq-khaya and Aju agreed there really was no option. The city had to die, very publicly. In the Muslim campaigns, artisans, women and children had often been spared, because they could be enslaved. But there was no point keeping any of these people alive. No distinction was made between young and old, civilian and soldier, man, woman and child. Some 3,000 soldiers and an estimated 7,000 others had their throats cut like cattle, the bodies being piled up in a mound to make sure that the massacre was visible from Xiangyang. In Richard Davis's words, 'Nothing could demoralize Xiangyang's defenders like this grotesque sight and the terrifying message it so forcefully conveyed.'

Then Ismail was told to turn his siege engine on Xiangyang. This must have been quite an operation: dismantling it, dragging and floating and carrying it across the river, reassembling it within range of Xiangyang, 'at the south-east corner of the city', according to the *Yuan History*. Ismail, a master of his art, now knew his machine's abilities very precisely. By triangulation, he would have positioned it, I think, so that its distance from one of Xiangyang's watchtowers was the same as it had been at Fancheng. The missile, we are told, weighed 150 *catties*, which is just short of 100 kilos. The result was astonishing. In the words of Ariq-khaya's biography, 'The first shot hit the watchtower. The noise shook the whole city like a clap of thunder, and everything inside the city was in utter confusion.'

On the Mongol side, there then followed a debate among the generals about whether to follow through with an assault, which would, of course, end with another pile of bodies, but with rather less strategic purpose and with understandable revulsion from the Mongols' potential subjects downriver. Ariq-khaya had his own ideas. He went in person to the foot of the wall and called for the city's leader, Lü Wen-huan.

'You have held the city with an isolated army for many years,' he shouted (presumably through an interpreter). 'But now the approaches are cut off even from the birds of the air. My master the emperor greatly admires your loyalty and if you surrender he will give you an honourable post and a generous reward. You may be sure of this, and we certainly shall not kill you.'

Lü, 'suspicious as a fox', hesitated. Ariq-khaya had to snap an arrow and four times repeat a cross-my-heart-and-hope-to-die promise. Finally, Lü believed him, and surrendered the city on 17 March 1273. Ariq-khaya was as good as his word. Lü Wen-huan instantly made himself a traitor in Song eyes and accepted high office on Kublai's side. He would prove a valuable asset in the coming campaign.

It is hard to overstate the significance of this victory. If Song was a castle, Xiangyang was the drawbridge. Not only did it open the way militarily to Song's heartland, but it began to destroy the workings of government. In Hangzhou, the prime minister Jia Sidao – Kublai's old adversary from the Wuchang siege, the rich politician who liked crickets and their pugnacious ways – was in trouble. It was partly his own fault, because he had kept the truth from the Song emperor – or so people believed, which was as damaging to morale.

The story went like this:

In 1270, the emperor had asked Jia if it was true that the siege had been going on for three years.

'The northern troops have already retreated,' replied Jia. 'But who told Your Majesty this?'

'One of my concubines,' came the reply.

According to the Song official history, Jia found out who it was among the several hundred girls at court, accused her on some unrecorded charge – treason, perhaps – and forced her to commit suicide. Apparently, the emperor had not missed the poor girl, but courtiers took note of Jia's high-handedness and townspeople started to exchange jokes and make up derisory songs about him. After that, 'no-one dared speak of the affairs of the frontier', say the annals, which meant that the news of Xiangyang's fall struck the emperor and his court like a ball from a Muslim catapult.

A grateful Kublai awarded Ismail 250 taels of silver – 325 oz or just 9 kg, which would fetch a mere $2,000 today, but was then the equivalent of about ten years' income for an artisan, enough to buy an estate if he had had the time to do so. He didn't, first because he was also appointed the head of the local Muslim artillerymen, and second because the next year he fell ill and died. His work, though, lived on. His position and expertise were inherited by his son, Abu-Bakr, beginning a line of succession from generation to generation that would continue almost until the end of the Yuan dynasty. And from then on, his great creation was known not only as the Muslim (*hui-hui*) catapult, but as 'the Xiangyang catapult'.

* * *

This was one of the most famous sieges in Chinese history; so famous that Marco Polo heard its story and loved to tell it. The trouble was that by the time he came to dictate his adventures, he had apparently told the story so many times that he had written major roles for himself, his father and his uncle. His account of the siege of 'Saianfu' is, if you wish to be generous, garbled. To many scholars, it sounds like a flagrant bit of self-promotion. Let's be frank: it's a lie.

This is how Marco's ghost-writer, the romance author Rustichello, recorded in his pseudo-intimate way what Marco told him when the two were in prison in Genoa some 25 years after the event (the quote is from the Yule–Cordier edition of 1903, with its charming archaisms):

Now you must know that this city held out against the Great Kaan for three years after the rest of Manzi had surrendered [not true: Manzi – i.e. Song – fell in 1279, six years after the siege came to an end]. The Great Kaan's troops made incessant attempts to take it, but they could not succeed because of the great and deep waters that were round about it, so that they could approach from one side only, which was the north. [Northwards was the River Han. Hard to see how any approach could be made from that direction.] And I tell you they never would have taken it, but for a circumstance that I am going to relate.

You must know that when the Great Kaan's host had lain three years before the city without being able to take it, they were greatly chafed thereat. Then Messer Nicolo Polo and Messer Maffeo and Messer Marco said: 'We could find you a way of forcing the city to surrender speedily;' whereupon those of the army replied, that they should be right glad to know how that should be. All this took place in the presence of the Great Kaan ... Then spoke up the two brothers and Messer Marco, and said: 'Great Prince we have with us among our followers men who are able to construct mangonels which will cast such great stones that the garrison will never be able to stand them, but will surrender incontinently, as soon as the mangonels or trebuchets have shot into the town.'

The Kaan bade them with all his heart have such mangonels made as speedily as possible. Now Messer Nicolo and his brother and his son immediately caused timber to be brought, as much as they desired, and fit for the work in hand. And they had two men among their followers, a German and a Nestorian Christian, who were masters of that business, and these they directed to construct two or three mangonels capable of casting stones of 300 pounds weight. Accordingly they made three fine mangonels, each of which cast stones of 300 pounds weight or more. And when they were complete and ready for use, the Emperor and the others were greatly pleased to see them, and caused several stones to be shot in their presence; whereat they marvelled greatly and greatly praised their work. And the Kaan ordered that his engines should be carried to his army which was the leaguer of Saianfu.

And when the engines were got to the camp they were forthwith set up, to the great admiration of the Tartars. What shall I tell you? When the engines were set up and put in gear, a stone was shot from each of them into the town. These took effect among the buildings, crashing and smashing through everything with huge din and commotion. And when the townspeople witnessed this new and strange visitation they were so astonished and dismayed that they wist not what to do or say. They took counsel together, but no counsel could be suggested how to escape from these engines. They declared they were all dead men if they yielded not, so they determined to surrender . . .

. . . and all this came about through the exertions of Messer Nicolo, and Messer Maffeo, and Messer Marco; and it was no small matter.

It is a good story, but deeply flawed. Young Marco, aged just 21, did not reach Kublai Khan's court until 1275, two years after the great siege was over. There is absolutely no way he or his father and uncle could have had anything to do with devising a catapult, and really no excuse for Marco writing the Polos in and Ismail and Ala ad-Din out. The whole thing reeks of self-serving fantasy – no details of the trebuchets, unnamed 'followers' who never appear again, no mention of Fancheng, vague generalizations about Xiangyang.

Well, he (or his ghost-writer) liked to dramatize – witness the bare-faced claim concerning Yangzhou: 'and Messer Marco Polo himself, of whom this book speaks, did govern this city for three full years, by the order of the Great Kaan'. He didn't; all the governors are listed in the sources; he's not among them. All one can say is that it was not the first time, or the last, that truth (which predominates in Polo) has been pushed aside by a ghost-writer eager for hype: *Oh, come on, Marco! No-one will ever know.*

A couple of points need to be made in Marco's favour. First, many writers who skewer him for bending the truth seem to think that he claims to have been at the siege. He doesn't. The idea and the construction all take place with

Kublai in Xanadu, which is where, I guess, he first heard the story and made it his own. Second, the claim to have been governor of Yangzhou appears only in two of the five main editions of his work, all of which are corrupt versions of a lost original. So perhaps along the way Marco's conscience had been at work after all.

In Hangzhou, when the news of the fall of Xiangyang arrived, panic took hold. Suddenly, top people woke up to the threat to their comfortable and civilized ways, their literate discourses, their picnics by the West Lake, their time-honoured rituals, their glorious works of art. It was unthinkable: never before in China's history had barbarians threatened the southern heartland. The court instantly cancelled a state occasion and said the money saved would be spent on strengthening the defences on the Yangtze. To buttress morale, those held responsible for the debacle were not executed, merely demoted. Even the relatives of Lü Wen-huan, the man who had surrendered Xiangyang and joined the Mongols, were told their loyalty was not in doubt. These were, of course, more symptoms of the regime's weakness.

And then: catastrophe upon catastrophe. Without warning, the Emperor Duzong died, aged only 34. Next, the Mountain of Heavenly Visage, the beautiful volcanic range a day's ride west of Hangzhou, shook itself and released devastating landslides and floodwaters. In Chinese, a landslide and an imperial death are different meanings of the same character, *beng* (崩). For leaders, Song had Duzong's four-year-old heir, his ailing grandmother the Empress Dowager, and the discredited prime minister,

Jia. Disasters were linking up, like tears in old silk, and there was no-one to patch Song's tattered fabric. Heaven was withdrawing its mandate to rule. An age approached its end.

9

JUGGERNAUT

FOR THIS NEXT VAST AND VITAL CAMPAIGN, KUBLAI WANTED to leave no room for error. He retained Aju, the victor of the Xiangyang siege, but placed him under his dynamic and widely experienced statesman-general, Bayan.

A word about Bayan. By appointing him, Kublai was playing two royal cards, empire and family, for Bayan's ancestors had played leading roles in one of *The Secret History*'s more dramatic tales. It happened five years before Genghis became khan, when, still bearing the name Temujin, he was fighting to unify the Mongol clans. As a young man, Temujin/Genghis had been captured by a rival clan leader, an overweight character called Tarkutai ('Fatty') Kiriltuk. He had staged an escape, and then a revenge raid. Defeated and in hiding, Fatty Kiriltuk is captured by some of his subjects – a man and his two sons – and dumped in a cart because he is too fat to ride a horse. His three captors are off to deliver him to Genghis

KUBLAI'S NEW GUARDIAN, MAHAKALA THE TERRIBLE

Kublai found in Buddhism what he needed, spiritually and politically. It was an established religion that could counteract the influence of Confucianism and Taoism. It supported his belief that the Mongol sky-god, Tenger, had granted the world to the Mongols to rule. And its pantheon of deities included the fearsome Mahakala, who, if accorded proper respect, would scare off other spirits and help in the great task of conquering the southern Chinese empire of Song. Mahakala, staring from his shrine in Beijing's White Pagoda, displays his terrifying attributes: a black face, a snarl, a headdress of skulls, and three eyes.

THE CONQUEST OF SONG

The campaign to conquer Song depended crucially on seizing the town of Xiangyang, which guarded the Han, the main river leading south to the Yangtze. An assault across the Han river using a pontoon bridge (*far left*) was not enough. To crack its great walls, Kublai summoned Muslim catapult-builders, with expertise in building counterweight trebuchets, like the ones used in besieging Baghdad in 1258 (*below left*). Modern trebuchets, like the one in Caerphilly Castle, Wales (*below right*), operate in the same way, with a throwing arm and sling powered by a counterweight (*inset*).

Once Xiangyang fell in 1273, the way was open along the Yangtze to the Song capital of Hangzhou (*bottom*), 'without doubt the most noble city and the best in the world' according to Marco Polo.

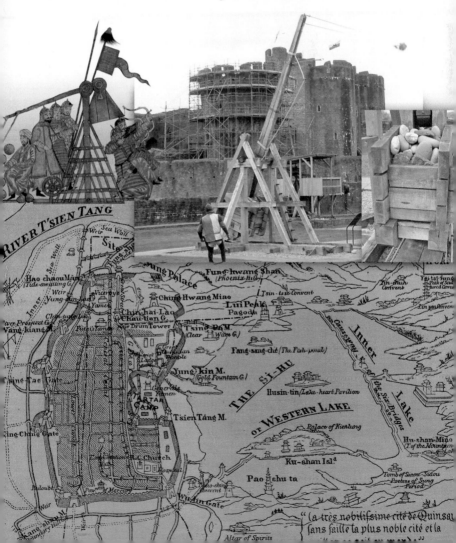

Clay model of medieval Chinese actor (*right*).

IN KUBLAI'S NEW CHINA, OLD TRADITIONS ENDURE

In theatre, painting, calligraphy and other arts, the Chinese continued to follow long-established traditions, generally ignoring the brutality and humiliation brought by the Mongol conquest. Street theatre, perhaps something like that which exists today (*above*) recycled old tales, like *The Romance of the Western Chamber* (*top right*). Potters turned out beautiful ceramics (*middle right*), now known by the dynastic name invented by Kublai – Yuan. Artists created superb paintings that, with rare exceptions, avoided any comment on their Mongol overlords. In his *Sheep and Goat* (*right*), Zhao Mengfu may – just possibly – be contrasting a fat and complacent pro-Mongol 'collaborator' with a scrawny but tough anti-Mongol 'rejectionist'.

HOW THE KHAN MADE HIS MARK

To rule his empire, Kublai built his Great Capital, Dadu, beside the Beihai, 'North Lake'. Much of his work was replaced by later rulers, but it can still be seen in the city's geography – like Beihai's island (*below*), with its curved marble bridge – and in details, like stele-bearing tortoises (*left*). Evidence of his administration – his laws, his economic reforms – exists mainly in museums and history books.

鈔寶行通明大

Kublai and his officials in a Persian view (*top*).

Strings of bronze coins (*left*) from the Song dynasty, superseded by Yuan banknotes (*above*).

A Yuan official – possibly a Muslim, if his beard is anything to go by – on a tour of duty, guarded by a Mongol.

when his sons gallop up to rescue him. The father, Shiregetu, leaps on his fat captive, holds a knife to his throat and yells Back off! And then, to Kiriltuk (to quote *The Secret History*): If they attack, 'at the very moment I die, I shall die taking you as my death-companion.' OK, shouts Fatty, do as he says; Temujin will spare me; after all, I didn't kill him when I had the chance. The sons retreat. The captors start to ponder. Temujin admires loyalty, doesn't he? Here we are betraying our khan. Surely, Temujin is more likely to kill us for disloyalty than reward us? So they let Kiriltuk waddle away, free. And when they get to Temujin, they are proved right: "Your thought that you could not do away with your rightful lord is correct." So saying, he showed favour.' That was one family's entrée to fame and fortune. Old man Shiregetu was immortalized in legend. On becoming khan in 1206, Genghis made the two sons, Naya and Alak, commanders of 1,000 men; and in addition Naya became one of his top three generals.

Now to the point: the man who held the knife to Kiriltuk's throat, Shiregetu, was Bayan's great-grandfather; Naya his great-uncle; Alak his grandfather, who went on to command in the campaign against Persia in 1219–20, and became a city governor there. Bayan's father was with Hulegu in 1256 and died in action when Bayan was about 20. Bayan himself stayed on working with Hulegu for a decade or so, then came to China to join Kublai as one of his top civilian administrators. In five years, he had won a reputation for calmness and clear thinking under pressure (and also brilliance: he had managed to learn Chinese). Kublai had then picked him in effect to run the Bureau of Military Affairs, under its nominal head, Kublai's eldest son. Now, at the age of only 34, Bayan found himself charged with the task of taking one more giant step towards the fulfilment of the divinely ordained destiny with which his family had been intimately involved for four generations.

This was to be an immense operation. The old days in which victory was all down to the Mongol cavalry were long gone. Cavalry was just one wing among three. The army that Bayan and Aju gathered around Xiangyang in summer 1274 numbered about 200,000 infantrymen, over half of them northern Chinese, backed by a river fleet of 800 newly built warships and another 5,000 smaller boats for transport, carrying 70,000 sailors, 14 per boat. This was a flexible, amphibious, multinational force. It needed to be, because Song still had 700,000 men at its disposal, and 1,000 warships on the Yangtze.

Victory, yes, of course that would come. But it should be victory with a longer-term purpose, as Kublai had first accepted in the Yunnan campaign. An adviser had urged restraint, and he had listened: 'What you told me about Cao Bin not killing people, that is something I can do.' Now he knew from experience that military victory must be matched by victory of another sort, over the hearts and minds of ordinary people. If the conquest of Song was to last, it would take good government; and that meant minimizing the suffering of civilians. He told Bayan: 'Emulate Cao Bin!'

Bayan's first task in the autumn of 1274 was to get his army down the Han river to the Yangtze, a distance of about 250 kilometres. But the Han was blocked by 100,000 men camped around two fortresses which were linked by a cross-river chain. To avoid another siege, Bayan ordered his troops to bypass this section of river. Shielded by two smaller 10,000-strong columns advancing in parallel a few dozen kilometres on either side, the main force carried the boats overland on bamboo poles, repulsing an attack along the way. No wonder it was a slow haul, averaging 20 kilometres a day. By spring 1275, Bayan and Aju had led their force out of the Han valley into the flood plains of the Yangtze.

Kublai would have been following this campaign with passionate interest, not only because the outcome of the war depended on continued success. He himself had crossed the Yangtze at this very point 15 years before, when Mönkhe's death and Ariq's rebellion had thrown his advance into reverse. He knew all too well the layout of the three cities that form today's Wuhan, the great fortress of Yang-lo downstream, the maze of shallow lakes and inlets, and the broad sweep of the Yangtze which he had crossed in his fruitless attempt to take Wuchang.

Bayan had somehow to overcome that apparently impregnable fortress Yang-lo, which was guarded by a fleet much larger than his own. His only chance of gaining an advantage lay in crossing the well-guarded river and establishing a base on the southern bank. A frontal assault might fail, so he tried a trick. He divided his force, and set one section to attack the fort, forcing the Chinese commander to draw reinforcements from upriver. Then, on a snowy January night, he sent Aju with the other half of his troops 20 kilometres upstream, carrying some of their boats with them. They waded into the icy river and occupied some sandbanks. Come the dawn, they built a pontoon bridge and, overcoming opposition from the depleted enemy forces, made a bridgehead on the south bank. Back downriver again, they took on the Song navy, and somehow – we have no details – won. The commander fled, the shattered Song fleet sailed away downriver, and the fortress surrendered.

The next month was a clear run downriver, much aided by the ex-commander of Xiangyang, Lü Wen-huan, who had also been the boss of many downriver garrisons. A word from him, and commanders surrendered, allowing the Mongol army to advance steadily.

Hangzhou was sliding into desperation. Bayan's reputation grew with every victory. They called him 'Hundred Eyes', because that's what *bai yan* means in Chinese. Jia's status, by contrast, diminished daily as the court officials and ordinary people reviled him for his love of luxury, his accumulated treasures, his wasteful parties. In an attempt to regain his authority, he decided to take command of the army himself. That February, he led a force over 100,000 strong out of the city, a vast throng 40 kilometres long heading westward to intercept Bayan's progress down the Yangtze. Suddenly, the capital was bare of troops, and more were needed.

At this point the emperor's widow, the formidable Dowager Xie, became her people's inspiration. She was no beauty, having an odd-looking dark skin and a cataract in one eye. But she had been a reassuring force for years, generous, restrained, never ambitious to extend her authority beyond the palace. Now she spoke out, urging ordinary people to join the war effort: 'In spite of my old age and decrepitude, I reluctantly took charge of state affairs,' ran her edict. 'How has it come to this present state that deviates from the constants of Heaven and Earth? Three hundred years of virtuous rule – surely this has made an impression on the people . . . Those worthy men with loyal livers and righteous galls [i.e. hearts], come forth and combat the forces that plague the throne and submit your skills.' It worked. By March 1275, all over the country, men were streaming to arms, as many as 200,000 of them.

A month and 250 kilometres later, Jia was in today's Anhui province, deploying his army near Tongling, aiming to block the river. Easier said than done: as Tongling's newish (1995) bridge across the turgid Yangtze shows, the river is 2.6 kilometres wide here, and the hills between which it winds its way are low and far off. Still, at Tongling a slight rise pushes the river in a wide curve, and a midstream island could act as a keystone. Joined by 2,500 warships, many from the bruising defeat at Yang-lo fortress, Jia awaited Bayan's arrival.

Bayan, though, was high on his previous successes, his naval force carrying well-tried contingents of every armed service – the Mongol cavalry (also scouting sideways and ahead), the Chinese infantry, a good supply of turncoat Song commanders full of helpful information about downriver defences, and terrific artillerymen, armed with devices including Ismail's 'Xiangyang catapult', the vast limbs of which did not even need to be carried; they could simply have floated, shepherded by barges.

What shall I tell you (as Marco might have said)? Not much, I'm afraid, because no-one recorded the details. Artillerymen set up the giant trebuchet, which would have a much greater range – several hundred metres – if throwing less weight. Stones rained on to boats, cavalry attacked on shore, infantry were landed on the island, and Jia's demoralized forces scattered, leaving 2,000 boats in Mongol hands.

Jia fled, defeated, humiliated, doomed. Enemies at court petitioned to have him executed, but Dowager Xie, toughened by half a century's experience, would not bend to such pressure. 'Jia Sidao has laboured untiringly through the successive reigns of three emperors,' she replied. 'How, for the failure of one morning, could one bear to abandon the proprieties due to a great official?' Instead, she stripped him of office and banished him to Zhangzhou, on the coast 800 kilometres south. But there was no escape. Along the way, the officer in command, a certain Jeng Hujen, ordered the bearers to taunt the captive with the insulting songs about him they had heard in Hangzhou; and then, when approaching their destination, Jeng killed him. In death, only his faults were remembered, and he was vilified as Song's 'Bad Last Ruler'.

Bayan, meanwhile, continued his victorious progress downriver. Wuwei, He Xian, the local capital of Nanjing all surrendered, inspiring half a dozen other civil leaders to bring their towns into the Mongol camp, and in two cases to commit suicide (the first of many, as we shall see). In Nanjing, Bayan recalled Kublai's long-term scheme of conquest: to hold and to govern, for ever. For four months he paused, setting up a local government for his 30 city conquests and his 2 million new subjects, secured by defences on both sides of the river. From here he opened negotiations with Hangzhou, an exchange hampered by the anti-Mongol antagonism of ordinary people and rank-and-file officials. This would prove to be an increasing problem, because outside the military and higher levels of government people were astonishingly loyal to their land and culture. Already there were the beginnings of guerrilla warfare, which briefly regained several towns for Song. In April, two of Bayan's envoys were murdered by locals before they entered Hangzhou. His next envoy met the same fate.

Now it was summer. The Mongols and northern Chinese wilted in the sticky heat. Bayan was all for pressing on, but was forced to delay because Kublai was faced with another rebellion at home – the subject of the next chapter – and wanted the benefit of Bayan's advice. The delay allowed Aju to fight off a renewed challenge from the Song and mop up other cities, notably Yangzhou and its nearby river-port Zhenjiang. Here, in another great battle, the Song blocked the river with unwieldy seagoing warships all chained together, which, when the little Mongol ships set a few ablaze, acted as a giant fuse that destroyed the lot: another military catastrophe, 10,000 dead, another 10,000 captives (with the usual caution that all the figures are guesstimates). Now the Mongol forces were within 225 kilometres of the Yangtze's mouth; round the nose of the Shanghai peninsula lay Hangzhou. Overland, it was also 225 kilometres. One last push would do it.

Back in the field in September, Bayan planned his final assault, a three-pronged attack by sea and by land. He would lead the central prong of this trident, following the Grand Canal. The main naval and land forces made fast progress. But Bayan's corps hit a problem, in the form of unexpected and dogged resistance from the ancient and prosperous town of Changzhou, noted for its scholars – a key to the southern section of the Grand Canal, and now newly reinforced by 5,000 Song soldiers. Bayan gave them a chance to surrender, firing a message wrapped around arrows: 'If you persist in this senseless and staunch resistance, then not even children will survive the piled corpses and bloodletting. You should reconsider your position promptly, so as not to regret things later.' They did not reconsider, and did not live long enough for regrets. For the second time in this campaign, the Mongols committed urbicide. Bayan stormed the place, took it in two days and had everyone slaughtered: the surviving troops, the civilians, the lot, perhaps 10,000 people in all. Again, as at Fancheng, a vast mound of bodies arose, covering half an acre near the city's eastern gate. Later covered with earth, it survived for over 600 years until well into the last century, with bones sometimes emerging from it.

This massacre, so close to the capital, was intended to encourage immediate capitulation. Its first effect was to spread panic and paranoia. Soldiers mutinied, deserters fled, a senior officer was bludgeoned to death by Jia's replacement. The Empress Dowager did her best to delay the inevitable, with a passionate and self-deprecating plea for mass support. 'The empire's progression toward impending peril is entirely, I regret, due to the in-substantiality of Our moral virtue.' People should recall over 300 years of moral and charitable rule, and come to the capital to 'engage the enemy of their prince'. This second plea for a *levée en masse* also worked, in a sense. They came, by the ten thousand, from the nearby hills and plains; but loyalty was nothing without direction. The newcomers were simply a motley collection of small militias that merely added to the confusion and panic.

For six weeks Dowager Xie sent out envoy after envoy, seeking some sort of settlement. Despite the brash opposition of Jia's replacement, she offered tribute, she offered to divide the country, she offered to honour Kublai as the uncle of the Song's young emperor. Bayan, settling in around Hangzhou, refused to discuss terms. It was total capitulation, or continuing war. But there was no vindictiveness. He gave his assurance that capitulation would buy peace for the people and security for the royal family. He even sent a copy of Kublai's edict to that effect. Some in court advised fighting to the last man, others wanted to abandon the capital altogether, but Dowager Xie decided otherwise. Really, there was no choice. Bayan's naval and land forces met up. The capital was all but surrounded, and weakening daily as soldiers and civilians fled south.

The end, at least of this chapter, came quickly. The new prime minister, Chen Yizhong, scuttled for safety. On 26 January 1276 the Empress Dowager sent a note to Bayan in his HQ 20 kilometres north of the city acknowledging Kublai's overlordship: 'I respectfully bow a hundred times to Your Majesty, the Benevolent, Brilliant, Spiritual and Martial Emperor of the Great Yuan.' A week later, the city's prefect, representing the court, handed over the Song dynastic seal and a memorandum stating the emperor's willingness to give up his title to Kublai and hand over all his territories. Bayan made a triumphal entry into the city, with his commanders and contingents in full array. Hundreds of pretty courtesans trembled at the thought of what might happen to them, and one hundred of them, waiting to be tied up with eunuchs and musicians for the long march north, drowned themselves to avoid finding out. And finally, on 21 February, came the final, formal ceremony of submission, when the five-year-old Emperor Zhao Xian himself led his officials into Bayan's presence and bowed in obeisance towards the north, the direction in which Kublai resided.

Bayan was as good as his word, and Kublai's. When the Mongols had taken Beijing, the Jin capital, in 1215, they had gone on an orgy of destruction and killing. The seizure of this capital was very different: a peaceful handover, a strict ban on unauthorized troops entering the city, the safety of the royal family guaranteed, the royal mausoleum protected, no attempt made to upset the currency or even the style of dress. Mongol-Chinese officers made inventories of troops, civilians, cash and food supplies before removing the treasures for transport northward. Militias were disbanded, regulars incorporated into Bayan's armies. Officials, of course, were all replaced with Mongols, northern Chinese and several Song turncoats; but in other respects, as Bayan reported proudly to Kublai, 'the market places of the nine thoroughfares were not moved and the splendours of a whole era remained as of old'.

An edict from Kublai told everyone to continue their lives as normal. Officials would not be punished; famous sites would be protected; widows, orphans and the poor would be assisted from public funds.

On 26 February the first of two great entourages left Hangzhou for Beijing – 300 officials, 3,000 wagons of booty, the seals of office, the surrender itself. A month later, Bayan, his task completed, left Hangzhou – indeed all of southern China – in the hands of subordinates, and headed north with the second entourage, the royal family: the boy ex-emperor, his mother, the princesses, the concubines, the relatives, leaving the ailing Dowager Xie behind until she was fit enough to travel.

Three months later, in June, this immense throng arrived in the capital, to be welcomed by a Kublai whose joy was such that he had no praise high enough for Bayan. He conferred upon him 20 sets of 'garments of a single colour' – to receive just one being a high honour – and reconfirmed him as co-director of the Bureau of Military Affairs. 'Hundred Eyes' was the empire's hero, genius, saviour: Subedei reborn.

The Empress Dowager and her grandson were then settled in Beijing, where they were given tax-free property. Kublai's wife Chabi took a personal interest in their well-being. The old lady lived out her life with a small official stipend and attendants, and died six years later. And so, officially, the Song dynasty ended not in a bang of destruction, but in a whimper of peace and compassion.

But there was another end, an end as different as you can imagine: a messy end, an end of despair and suffering and heartbreak. It made 'a drama of unthinkable intensity', in the words of Richard Davis's powerful study of the conquest of Song.[1] Its prologue came just before the final capitulation, when the Song court sent away the two remaining young princes – Zhao Xia (4) and Zhao Bing (3), brothers of the young Zhao Xian, soon to be on his way to Xanadu – to safety in the far south. With them went a spirit very different from that which marked the ceremonies of capitulation: a spirit of outraged and uncompromising resistance to alien domination. There was heroism here, something redolent of Horatius' words in Macaulay's *Lays of Ancient Rome*:

> And how can man die better
> Than facing fearful odds,
> For the ashes of his fathers
> And the temples of his Gods?

But there was also a tragedy being played out, as a great

[1] Richard L. Davis, *Wind Against the Mountain: The Crisis of Politics and Culture in 13th-Century China*.

culture blocked its ears and closed its eyes and chose death when denial was no longer possible.

As the princes fled, the Mongols advanced, and death filled the air: not just imposed death but self-selected death, whether in action or by suicide. Richard Davis, in his evocation of this terrible time, lists 110 named male suicides of prominent, albeit not of the highest rank. There were many hundreds of others at lower levels of government, and many thousands of ordinary people of both sexes and all classes. To take one extreme example: in January 1276, Ariq-khaya met stiff resistance from Tanzhou (now Changsha), 750 kilometres inland in Hunan province. Resistance was, of course, overcome. The town's leader, Li Fu, made careful arrangements for the mass suicide of his family and household. All made themselves drunk; all were put to the sword by Li Fu's assistant, who then killed his wife and slit his own throat. A military adviser drowned himself with his wife and concubine. A local scholar burned his house, himself, his brother, two sons and some 40 servants. All around the town, so the *Song History* says, people 'annihilated their entire family. No wells in the city were empty of human corpses, while strangled bodies hung in dense clusters from trees.' The Xiang river became thick with the dead. Was this an exaggeration? Were many of those deaths in fact from the assault? Possibly; but when the town fell, Ariq-khaya saw there was no need for further punishment, because the city had in effect committed suicide.

What, meanwhile, of the two small princes and their entourage? They had been taken south, picking up recruits to their cause on the way – not a problem, for their entourage had with them immense amounts of cash. They had then taken to ships, hopping from port to port down the coast, heading for Vietnam. This was no small band of loyalists, but an army of 200,000 carried by a navy of 1,000 ships. There was a terrible storm. The elder of the little princes, Zhao Xia, almost died, and then died anyway on an island not far from Vietnam. By now, the Mongols had overtaken them on land. With the remaining prince, Zhao Bing, the fleet slowly backtracked along the coast to the bay where the Pearl River (Chu Chiang) broadens out west of Hong Kong. Here a dense cluster of islands offered protection.

So all was not yet lost. They found a good island base from which to stage a comeback. To the north were shallows that seemed to exclude enemy warships. At the southern end hills fell sharply into the sea, from which the island took its name: Yaishan, Cliff Hill. It was here, in the summer of 1278, that the six-year-old prince and his loyal followers – his stepmother the Dowager Consort Yang Juliang, his real mother, a low-level concubine, chief counsellor Lu Xiufu – made their stand, with many of their followers living in warships, many others ashore, racing to throw together simple houses and fortifications.

The Mongol forces were 80 kilometres upriver, in the city that used to be called Canton and is now Guangzhou. In late February 1279 the Song navy's 1,000 ships, well stocked with food and water, prepared for battle. They struck an eye-witness as impressive, the sides of their ships covered with mud-encrusted matting against flaming arrows and incendiary bombs, protected with staves to ward off fire-ships. With the young prince on the flagship the fleet was, according to one account, chained together in preparation for an imminent onslaught.

The Mongol fleet, of only around 300 ships, approached from downriver, round the coast. With their inferior numbers, they were in no hurry to attack. Their commander sent a message giving the Song a chance to surrender. No deal. Now the Mongols discovered they had the advantage of mobility over their chained and anchored enemy. They set a blockade between the Song vessels and the shore, cutting off their water supply, and settled down to await the moment to strike. For two weeks they sat there, trying the occasional raid, but content to observe the tides and weather, while the Song ran out of water.

Then, on the rainy morning of 9 March, one half of the fleet rode the outgoing tide into the flanks of the demoralized and weakened Song; and six hours later the other half struck from the other direction with the rising tide.

The result was a catastrophe for the Song. Accounts speak of the sea turned red by blood, and of 100,000 dead. Scholars agree this is a huge exaggeration, but even the real figure was horrific enough – perhaps 30,000–40,000. The only witness who recorded the details was the loyalist Wen Tianxiang, who was a hostage in one of the Mongol ships. He later captured the horrors he had seen in verse:

> Suddenly this morning the sky darkened;
> wind and rain manifested evil;
> catapults and thunder flashed; arrows descended.
> . . .
> human corpses are scattered like fibres of hemp.
> Foul smelling waves pound my heart to bits.

When they saw what was happening, many – hundreds, perhaps thousands – committed suicide by leaping into the water with weights attached to them. One among them was Lu Xiufu, the adviser to the boy-emperor. And on his back when he jumped he bore the six-year-old prince, the last of his line, the thirteenth generation of Song rulers, still in his gown of royal yellow, with the imperial golden seals strapped around his waist.

So ended the very last of the Song. For Wen Tianxiang, nothing could have better captured the despair of defeat, or better symbolized what was best in Song culture – loyalty that could embrace the ultimate sacrifice. Such high ideals were surely immortal.

> A mountain refuge exchanged for a grave at sea,
> Without empire is to be without family.
> For men with wills of a thousand years,
> Our lives have no limits.

Wen Tianxiang has a significance beyond his presence as an eye-witness of the end of the Song. He was the exemplar of those loyalists who absolutely refused to accept the new regime. From a brief summary of events, you would think that Kublai, once victorious, had an easy time of it. Not so. There was a Song resistance at all levels, finding expression in many ways: by withdrawal, by guerrilla warfare, by assassination and – most strikingly – in suicide.

First see what Wen's high ideals – or rigidity, depending on your point of view – meant in practice. Rich, a brilliant scholar, a noted poet and famously good-looking, he had been a senior figure at court, even involved in negotiations with Bayan. But he was too inflexible to be a great politician – passionate, intolerant, arrogant and a complete pain to work with. Even before the final battle, while the family were fleeing the Mongols as they advanced south, his unwavering loyalty had caused the deaths of his mother and three children. His wife, two concubines and three other children were captured. His wife would be in detention for 30 years. One of the children died; two would remain in permanent exile – 'Young swallows without nests, shivering in the autumn chill,' in their father's mournful words.

After the battle, Wen spent four years in captivity, from which Kublai himself offered to free him if only he would join the Mongol side. He refused, despite the agonizing consequences for his family – his daughters dead, and he unable to collect their bones; his mother dead, and he, unable to perform the funeral rituals, a traitor to Confucian ideals of filial piety. Yet he would not bend – 'The loyal subject cannot serve two masters,' he said – an attitude that proved, in effect, suicidal. He sought death, as martyrs have throughout history, to justify his ideals. In January 1283 a cart carried him to Beijing's firewood market, where he was executed before a huge crowd.

Wen became the epitome of the loyal servant, Song's martyr and an example of how the true loyalist should behave: never mind the bonds of family; loyalty to a master, a cause, was above all. 'When life is exchanged for a cause,' he wrote, 'it is not lived in vain.' For those of a more accommodating temperament, this self-denial is masochistic. To the true believer, it is glorious.

There were many others – many thousands – who chose to die rather than submit; many by killing themselves. This is one of the most astonishing things about the early days of Kublai's rule. Suicide was a well-established response to defeat among honour-bound military men, but among civilians as well as the armed forces there had never been anything like what happened after the Mongol victory over Song. Nothing could more searingly state the strength and depth of Song culture. For 300 years people at all levels of society had lived in relative stability and growing prosperity, governed by officials who, whatever their faults, operated within a framework of dedication to the idea of service and high-minded behaviour. Three hundred years! For such stability, cultural unity, growing wealth and intellectual sophistication, westerners must look back to the Roman empire. The effect on the minds of ordinary people survived the growing weakness of the Song government, symbolized by Hangzhou's corrupting luxuries. All that was merely another sign of impending catastrophe, the main one being the war, which over the previous 45 years had killed millions and displaced millions more in the north, and which was now devastating the south. Intriguingly, where the wars had been worst, in the north, there was no habit of suicide, perhaps because suffering at barbarian hands was routine for Jin's inhabitants, perhaps because they could always flee south. Yet in the south, in Song, many of its bereft inhabitants derived life's very meaning from their culture. With nowhere left to flee to, there was, for these thousands, only one way to assert their free will: by choosing what they considered an honourable death over a life empty of meaning and honour.

There remained one member of the Song royal family: the Dowager's grandson, Zhao Xian, who as a five-year-old had formally surrendered to Kublai. As he grew to manhood, he became an increasing embarrassment to Kublai. Sources usually say no more than that he was eventually sent away to Tibet to become a monk, and that he died in 1323.

I heard a rather more interesting account of his fate in the Giant Buddha Temple in Zhangye, Gansu province, one of the traditional gateways to Tibet. Director Wu told me the story:

One day, Kublai Khan had a dream. In his dream, a dragon flew up from a certain spot in the palace. Next day, Zhao Xian came to see him. Unfortunately, Kublai found that the lad was standing on the exact spot from which the dragon had ascended. This caused Kublai to realize that Zhao was a danger to the state, and would one day try to overthrow the Yuan dynasty. It was for this reason that he had Zhao sent away to become a monk, right here in the Great Buddha Temple, the burial place of Kublai's mother. Here he remained for many years, until, at the age of 53, he committed suicide.

If true, it is a strange footnote to the end of the Song: the last emperor locked away in a distant monastery, forgotten by the outside world for decades, long outliving the man who had displaced him, until he, like so many of his subjects, escaped despair by choosing death.

III

AUTUMN

10

BURNED BY THE RISING SUN

ON THE VERGE OF ACHIEVING ACTUAL OR NOMINAL dominion over much of Eurasia, having seen his commanders build and sail warships down the Yangtze, and already making preparations to pursue the remnants of Song resistance down 1,500 kilometres of coastline, Kublai was in a position to look outwards across the ocean, to Japan.

Officially, Japan had had remarkably little to do with China for 400 years, ever since China had persecuted Buddhists in the middle of the ninth century. The two had no running disputes, no cause for war; indeed, the opposite, because there were long-established private trading contacts. In Japan, Chinese fashions were all the rage among the ruling classes. Gold, lacquer ware, swords and timber flowed in from Japan, in exchange for silk, porcelain, perfumes and copper coins. Monks arriving in Japan in response to an upsurge in Zen Buddhism brought with them tea, made a fashionable part of Zen studies by a celebrated monk, Eisai, around 1200. None of this reflected official policy. But it was happening under Song rule, and the Song were about to be targeted by Kublai. It didn't take much imagination for strategists in Xanadu to foresee the Japanese sending aid to the Song. Better take them out fast.

Like other imperialists at other times, Kublai saw an overriding reason to do this: because it seemed possible. A Korean monk who had become an interpreter at Kublai's court told him Japan would be a pushover: ruled by a figurehead emperor and rival warlords and samurai warriors more interested in their own chivalric codes than in their decrepit coastal defences, it had no large field army nor any experienced commanders to match the Mongols. Kublai not only had well-tried armies and commanders with unrivalled experience – he had a new navy; and he had a springboard in the form of Korea, whose southern coast is a mere 200 kilometres from Japan.

The Mongols had had experience of Korea since their first invasion in 1231. At that time Korea had proved a tough nut, in the hands of a military clique which had seized power from the king 60 years before in order to fight off barbarians from Manchuria. While the king remained a figurehead for 30 more years, the generals fought the Mongols, much helped by their naval skills, which allowed them to hole up in an offshore island and supply themselves with food by sea, in effect thumbing their noses at the Mongol cavalry. In response, the Mongols turned to arson, slaughter and theft, all on a vast scale. In their 1254 invasion they had taken some 200,000 captives and devastated much of the country. In 1258 the king and his officials staged a counter-coup, assassinated the military boss and sued for peace, the crown prince himself travelling to China to submit – directly to Kublai, as it happened, because Mönkhe was campaigning far away to the west. It all worked out neatly: both the Korean king and Mönkhe died, and Kublai was left with a new vassal, the former crown prince and now king, Wonjong. In 1271 a joint Korean–Mongol force re-established Wonjong in the old capital, Kaesong, and blotted up what remained of the military opposition. So Kublai had firm enemies in ordinary Koreans and an unwilling vassal in Wonjong. He gave a daughter to Wonjong's son in marriage, so that eventually his grandson would inherit the throne. The two swapped presents, Kublai sending a jade belt and medicines, Wonjong responding with annual missions of tribute – falcons for the imperial hunting grounds and fish skins to be made into soft shoes for Kublai's gouty feet. Korea became a Mongol-Chinese colony, with resident commissioners watched over by Mongol-Chinese troops and served by a corps of Mongolian-speaking interpreters. Kublai was not loved; but he was the power behind the throne. He needed ships; and ships began to roll from Korea's shipyards, first for the conquest of Song, and then to transport a Mongol-Chinese army across to Japan.

By the early 1270s Kublai had engineered a justification for war. In 1266 – with Ariq's rebellion newly crushed, the campaign against Song still being planned – he had sent his first embassy off to Japan, with a demand that the king of this 'little country' submit instantly. The message was rushed through from its point of entry in southern Japan, Hakata (present-day Fukuoka) on Kyushu, 800 kilometres north-east to Kamakura, HQ (or *bakufu*) for

Japan's military ruler, the shogun, then halfway back again to the shogun's nominal overlord, the emperor in Kyoto. It caused quite a stir, outrage – 'little country', indeed! – mixed with terror. The emperor drafted a letter offering negotiation, an idea instantly vetoed by the shogun who, after six months, ordered the envoys to leave for home with no answer at all. This was playing for time, with fingers crossed. The court, useless in every practical way, devoted itself to prayer.

Silence seemed to work, because nothing more was heard from Kublai for several years. Kublai's forces were otherwise engaged, embarking on the siege of Xiangyang that would hold the key to the conquest of the south. It was not until September 1271 that another Korean envoy arrived, officially bearing a request to submit, unofficially warning the Japanese to prepare for an attack. Again, there was no official reply, but now vassals were ordered back to their fiefs, and constables and stewards set about strengthening the 30 decrepit coastal castles. At court, prayers became even more fervent. So when in 1272 a Mongol ambassador landed, demanding that his letters be forwarded to the emperor at once, Japanese martial spirit had revived. The shogun, latest in line of the ruling Hojo family, was a feisty 22-year-old called Tokimune; he sent the ambassador packing – a gross insult to Kublai, and nothing less than an invitation to invade.

Kublai was soon ready. In 1273 Xiangyang fell, releasing reserves for action elsewhere; Korea was at last at peace; and there were ships enough around in Korean and Song harbours for the assault. In late October or November 1274 (again, sources vary), some 300 warships and 400–500 smaller craft, with crews of 15,000 and a fighting force of anything up to 40,000 (again, sources vary) left Masan on the south Korean coast to cross the 50 kilometres of sea to the islands of Tsushima, the prehistoric and historic stepping-stone from the mainland to Japan.

On the shore, locals put up a spectacular but hopeless defence which became the stuff of legends, full of Japanese chivalry and Mongol barbarism, of lone warriors issuing dignified challenges, of poisoned Mongol arrows flying like raindrops in spring, of the sea made crimson by blood, of the governor's honourable suicide. Stories tell of 6,000 dead and the Mongols carrying 1,000 heads back to their ships to embark for the next stepping-stone, Iki, 50 kilometres away.

Hearing news of the Mongol advance, Iki's governor sent off to the mainland for help, before the overwhelming assault, the brave but futile defence, the deeds that burned themselves into folk memory – the governor's daughter spirited away by boat only to die at sea in a hail of Mongol arrows; the noble governor and his family accepting death in their burning palace; prisoners nailed by their palms along the prows of Mongol warships.

To invaders, Kyushu's coast is a problem. It has delightful, inviting sandy beaches, but inland is a tangle of steep forested hills which preclude a fast advance. There is only one good harbour, Hakata bay, protected by islands that make natural breakwaters and two headlands that reach westward as if to welcome ships from all mainland Asia to its shallow waters, gentle sandy shores and low-lying hinterland. Japanese warlords advanced from the local administrative centre of Dazaifu, on hills 10 kilometres south-east of present-day Fukuoka, and set up a base nearer the coast. The Mongols first made a tentative landing at Hakata's western end, perhaps thinking to head up a river, then changed their minds and set their army ashore right in the middle of the bay. There, they easily cut through the few disorganized Japanese. As one Japanese account put it, the grandson of the Japanese general fired whistling arrows as the signal for action to start, 'but the Mongols all laughed. Incessantly beating their drums and gongs, they drove the Japanese horses leaping mad with fear. Their mounts uncontrollable, none thought about facing the Mongols.'

Rapidly, the Mongols advanced a kilometre inland to seize a strategic sandstone hillock with steep sides which gave them a good view. The hill, Mount Sohara, is now a park, with rough paths leading up its soft yellow flanks, and the view from its summit is blocked by new buildings. But that summer afternoon, Mongol scouts would have been able to see their own ships riding at anchor in the bay, Dazaifu looming to the south-east, and 5 kilometres to the east the Japanese camp, from which, within a couple of hours, horsemen approached at the gallop.

Among the Japanese defenders that day was a young warrior named Takezaki Suenaga, from Higo province, a *gokenin* (direct vassal of the shogun) who later acquired enough wealth to commission a series of paintings that were then pasted together to form two scrolls illustrating this and the later invasion of 1281. The scrolls were probably created some time after 1293, by which time Suenaga had become a landowner and guardian of several shrines and temples. He had had something of a struggle to get his deeds of valour officially recognized after the invasions, so it seems likely that he wished to record his own role in the battle and at the same time honour the man who backed him for the official commendation on which his later wealth and influence depended. The Invasion Scrolls passed through various hands, surviving as much by luck as by care – they were once dropped in the sea, which dissolved the glue holding the panels together, leaving the precise sequence in doubt. In the late eighteenth century they were stuck back together, restored and copied, with several much-analysed additions. The scrolls have since become famous as a unique and vivid portrayal of the invasions – and, most scholars agree, an authentic one. They were accompanied by 69 documents – letters, prayers, edicts, battle reports – which have recently been translated and analysed by Thomas Conlan of Bowdoin College, Brunswick, Maine, in an extraordinary book printed back to front, so that the pages of text read backwards and illustrations run from right to left, as the scrolls themselves do. To read it is to be immersed in events by something that is a cross between a comic and a novel.

The section of the scroll depicting the 1274 invasion shows the young Suenaga (aged 29), sporting a trim moustache and goatee beard, advancing through pines with five followers. They carry extraordinarily long bows (by Mongol standards), which they wield with great skill, firing at the gallop, quivers on their backs, protected from head to toe by lamellar armour, made of overlapping metal scales.

Suenaga is a headstrong character. Coming upon one of the Mongol forces, perhaps the one advancing from Mount Sohara, he cannot wait to fight. The text takes over from the pictures:

Shouting a battle cry, I charged. As I was about to attack, my retainer Togenda Sukemutsu said: 'More of our men are coming. Wait for reinforcements, get a witness, then attack!'

I replied: 'The way of the bow and arrow is to do what is worthy of reward. Charge!' . . .

My bannerman was first. His horse was shot and he was thrown down. I Suenaga and my three retainers were wounded. Just after my horse was shot and I was thrown off, Michiyasu, a *gokenin* from Hizen province, attacked with a formidable squad of horsemen and the Mongols retreated . . . I would have died had it not been for him. Against all odds, Michiyasu survived as well, and so we each agreed to be a witness for the other.

A picture shows Suenaga thrown from his wounded horse, which spouts blood, while a Mongol shell explodes nearby. This shell has been the source of controversy. Though Conlan thinks the image is an eighteenth-century addition to increase the drama, other scholars believe the content is authentic. Either – or, indeed, both – could be the case. As we have seen, the Mongols had long known about explosives, having acquired them after they seized Beijing in 1215. What is shown exploding near Suenaga is a 'thundercrash bomb', a ceramic shell with an explosive core. These were first recorded in 1221, when the Jin of north China, still only partially conquered by Genghis, were besieging the city of Qizhou on the Yangtze. So this could well have been Japan's first experience of explosive weapons.

Delivered how, exactly? Not with counterweight trebuchets, which demanded tonnes of ballast and throwing arms as big as masts – not the sort of thing you would put on a ship. Anyway, the Mongols were not planning to batter down castle walls. Thundercrash bombs were anti-personnel devices, weighing only 3–4 kilos. They could be cast by traction trebuchets, which had been in common use for two centuries. We know the Mongols had thundercrash bombs with them, because several have been found in the remains of one of the Korean/Mongol ships (I'll get to the details later). So whether this particular example was added to the scroll later or not, it captures a truth. With a traction trebuchet, half a dozen men on a ship's prow could easily lob a thundercrash bomb 100 metres as part of an assault to clear the beach.

So far, so brave. It is clear even from this little incident that Suenaga, like any good samurai, is obsessed with individual glory, and not at all concerned at the lack of centralized command. In these circumstances, such tactics had some effect. Good archers were in their element. One warrior, Yamada, made a name for himself by organizing a team of powerful bowmen to fire long range at isolated Mongols, killing three of them, raising laughter and cheers from the Japanese. Another shot a Mongol commander in the face and captured his horse. But individual bravery was not enough. Some of the Mongols galloping back and forth between the beach-head and Mount Sohara managed to burn the local town of Hakata.

As the day died, the Japanese took refuge away from the beach, barricading themselves into Dazaifu. Backed by a hill, it had a rampart of earth and a moat that can still be seen today. It was hardly enough to stop a Mongol army that had become expert in siege warfare. But the Mongols had never mounted an amphibious landing before. They would need food and supplies, in particular more arrows. They had no heavy catapults with them. A siege would take time. And, to cap it all, a storm was brewing. It would be a miserable night for all, worse for the Mongols and Koreans if their boats were caught in the shallows and the troops were trapped on the beach with no means of retreat. Captains urged the troops to retire to the ships to ride out the bad weather at sea, away from the breaking waves. The next day would surely allow another landing, another breakthrough, and victory.

It would not be that easy. In the worsening weather, a flotilla of 300 Japanese open boats crept up the coast towards the Mongol fleet, some bearing a dozen soldiers with bows and swords, some loaded with dry hay to act as fire-ships. These little ships infiltrated the ranks of their massive targets, moving too fast to be caught by the bombs launched by trebuchets or heavy shafts from crossbows, and then in close beneath the outward-curving hulls. Many of Kublai's ships were already on fire as the wind picked up and the Japanese oarsmen headed for the bays and beaches they knew so well, leaving much of the Mongol fleet to the mercy of storm and flames.

The dawn revealed sights both dire (for Mongols) and uplifting (for Japanese): ships scattered by the wind, hulks smouldering, the flotsam of a broken army left behind as the survivors limped for safety in Korea. Korean records claim that 13,000 were drowned.

Kublai did not take this defeat to heart. It had all been down to the weather, nothing to do with Japanese *élan*. Next time, surely – and there would be a next time – the Mongols' natural superiority would tell. Why could not the Japanese see the obvious? He sent another message, another demand for submission.

Neither the Hojo shogun, Tokimune, nor the emperor in Kyoto had any doubts about what had to be done. A Japanese courtier noted in his diary that the bad weather, though nothing worse than a 'reverse wind', 'must have arisen as a result of the protection of the gods. Most wonderful! We should praise the gods without ceasing. This great protection could only have happened because of the many prayers and offerings to the various shrines ... throughout the realm.' The emperor prayed, and urged all to do likewise, inspiring an upsurge in both Shintoism and Buddhism.

But the gods would only help those who helped themselves. Tokimune ordered Kyushu's coastal provinces to build a wall, and man it, avoidance of military duty being made a criminal offence. Whether this was Tokimune's idea or one of his advisers, it was brilliant and original, for the Japanese had not previously built many military installations, certainly not many that compelled Japan's divided clans and rival provincial governors to collaborate.

The spirit of resistance hardened. When more envoys came from Kublai in May 1275, they were taken to Kamakura and four months later executed (you can see the tomb of their unlucky leader, Du Shizong, in a temple in Fujisawa, close to Kamakura). The shogun might as well have slapped Kublai's face. Court and civil leaders economized, so that the national wealth could be poured into defences. There was even thought of a pre-emptive strike: new ships were built and crews trained. In the end, the military leaders opted for defence, focusing on the building of small, easily manoeuvrable boats that would run rings round the mighty Korean warships. All around Hakata bay clans gathered to build the wall. Since there was no telling when Kublai might strike again, they were in a hurry. But, with no tradition either of co-operation or of large-scale building to guide them, they had to make it up as they went along. Hakata bay's shoreline is almost all sand, backed by dunes and pines, no good at all for building. The wall would have to be of stone.

The result, or some of it, is still visible today, the bits forming several tourist attractions: Genko Borui, the Yuan Invasion Defensive Wall. Fukuoka has filled in the coastal inlets here and there, but standing on the beach away from the port you can easily imagine yourself in Suenaga's saddle. There are the same sweep of sand, the same mountains at either end, similar dunes and pines. Of course, sand gathered over the centuries and stones were snatched for buildings. But along one 50-metre stretch the sand has been dug away, and other sections have been rebuilt, so you can still see how the inexperienced locals responded to the challenge. At least you can if, like me, you look through the expert eyes of archaeologist Sumitaka Yanagida, a diminutive, wiry Indiana Jones figure with flyaway white hair and a jutting jaw. Having been involved with the wall for 40 years, he supervised its rise to fame as a symbol of Japanese independence and courage.

Symbolically it's great, yes; but it's no Great Wall. Its main purpose was to pin horses back on the beach, so it needed to be no more than 2 metres high. Then there was the problem of technique. To make stone walls you need good masons, experts in dry-stone walling and/or cement. The Japanese lacked all three, and never agreed on a standard blueprint for construction. There were stones aplenty: granite from one end, sandstone from the other, some hacked from the mountains, others collected from the beaches at either end where the sand runs out. Each clan was given a length of wall to construct, depending on the clan's wealth – 3 metres here, 10 metres there. It seems that each clan collected its own rocks, dressed them and set them in place, each section coming to an abrupt end with stones stacked vertically rather than overlapping in proper bricklaying fashion. You can almost hear a clan leader snorting disdainfully, 'And take care you don't build any of *their* section!' This is a wall that would have fallen apart with one ball from a Muslim catapult. At one point, the wall is a double wall, because at the first attempt the foundations had given way: rather than start again, the clan responsible had simply piled on more rocks. Here the wall is backed by a platform for defenders to stand on; in a second spot it has a walkway protected by a secondary wall; in a third the wall is not solid but hollow, two faces packed with earth. Imagine these variations being repeated along the whole 20-kilometre stretch, imagine the arguments about design, technique and materials – but also imagine the overriding sense of urgency that forced rivals to swallow their disagreements, and in six months build something that would be impossible for cavalry to take in a frontal assault.

By late 1276, they were ready, with, as it happened, five years to spare.

11

CHALLENGE FROM THE HEARTLAND

AS A GLANCE AT THE MAP TELLS YOU, CHINA TODAY stretches halfway across Asia. Its western limits are almost on the same longitude as India's western edge. This is surprising, because it is so far beyond the traditional Chinese heartland as defined by its old northern limits, the first Great Wall established by the 'First Emperor' in the third century BC. That wall ended deep in Central Asia; but today's border is as far again beyond. How come China is so big?

The reason for China's size – a major theme of this book – is that Genghis and Kublai made it so. But this leads on to another problem: Kublai's empire stretched way beyond today's borders. This suggests the question should be flipped: how come China is so *small*? Why does it not reach even further into Central Asia?

The answer is that Kublai was limited by the amount of force he could bring to bear on his independent-minded relatives. One reason for this was that they had ready access to horses, which made them as hard to catch as quicksilver. There was nothing much to be done about the more distant parts of the empire – Persia, the Golden Horde of southern Russia – but Central Asia, though far from China's heartland, was on Mongolia's doorstep. In one sense, all of Kazakhstan and a good deal of the other 'stans' to the south were part of Genghis's inheritance and therefore part of Kublai's, and therefore might well have remained in the Chinese sphere. But in this direction Kublai reached his limit. He had moved from beyond the Wall to inside the Wall, and was now constrained by distance and by his own, or rather his troops', inability to pin down his mercurial opponents.

This takes us into a murky backwater of history – the rivalry between Kublai and a distant relative; but it is important because the outcome explains much about the shape of China today. The opposition Kublai met at this time dictated how far he could go. That he went thus far and no further presented an idea of China's western boundary that endured through a time of retreat under the successor dynasty, the Manchus, when these remote regions were ruled again by Mongols. It re-emerged in the eighteenth century with the 'New Kingdom' – Xinjiang (Sinkiang, as it used to be spelled) – when the Manchus regained control, extending the borders once again to the limits defined by Kublai.

This vast and varied region – running from the deserts of Uzbekistan and the grasslands of southern Kazakhstan into the heights of the Tien Shan and the wastes of western China – has no historical unity, but it exerts a strange power to spread trouble. In part this is because it was increasingly Islamic, even in Kublai's day; in part because it is hard for either Islamic realms or China to win permanent control over it. For the same reasons, trouble is brewing again today, with disaffected Islamists wanting to carve out a new state that will suck in China's Islamic far west. It is worth taking a closer look at the great-grand-daddy of this idea, and at how Kublai failed to resolve it.

It was in Central Asia that the real threat to Kublai lay – real because it came from his own family, from the descendants of Genghis's chosen heir, Ogedei, whose line had been pushed aside by Tolui's powerful widow, Kublai's mother Sorkaktani, in favour of her children; real because it came from Kublai's original homeland, and because opposition here would block the westward flow of goods from China to India, the Islamic world and Europe. If it were allowed to fester, Kublai would be cut off from the wealth that underpinned his power, and would then be as vulnerable as any emperor of old to barbarian hordes sweeping in across the Gobi. Perhaps one day Mongol emperor would fall to Mongol barbarian, some remote cousin with as good a – no, a better – claim to the throne than Kublai himself.

The cousin in question was Kaidu, Ogedei's grandson. This is his story. It is a peculiar one, in that it was played out over Kaidu's rather long life, and over a good deal of Kublai's. For some 40 years, the two ill-matched contestants engaged in a sort of long-distance boxing match, Kaidu the lightweight throwing punches from the northern and western frontiers, occasionally attracting the gaze of his heavyweight opponent, who always had other claims on his attention.

Kaidu never had a hope of actually winning, but his successes highlight another theme, common to many great-power rulers: conquest (if it can be managed at all) is simple, however hard-fought; administration is complicated. Conquest unites subordinates in a great adventure; administration allows free play to character, ambition, the formation of rival groups. Things fall apart, especially at the edges, which in this case was an area 3,000 kilometres from headquarters. It took as long for an official to reach Kaidu as it took an English official to reach America in the 1780s. By the time he got there, who knew what might have happened in the meantime?

Born in about 1235, Kaidu had been too young to be caught up in the purges unleashed by Mönkhe against the supporters of Ogedei in 1251, but not too young to be given his own estate when Mönkhe made peace with the survivors the following year. At 16, Kaidu was master of a territory some 2,000 kilometres to the west of Karakorum, a land running down from the Tien Shan into desert, but divided by the lush valley of the Ili river, one of the main routes linking China and the west. This, Asia's geographical dead centre, was his base, where he grew to manhood, far from the ever-more-Chinese world of Kublai. Here he started empire-building on his own account, the new kid on the block elbowing his way into the scrum.

From now on, the story does not come easily, because it means making sense of obscure events, teasing significance from odd references in shadowy sources about petty squabbles. Marco Polo faced the same problem, which he solved, as he often did, by riding roughshod over history and going for a good yarn. In this case, it was not a bad idea, because the gossip he picked up captures something

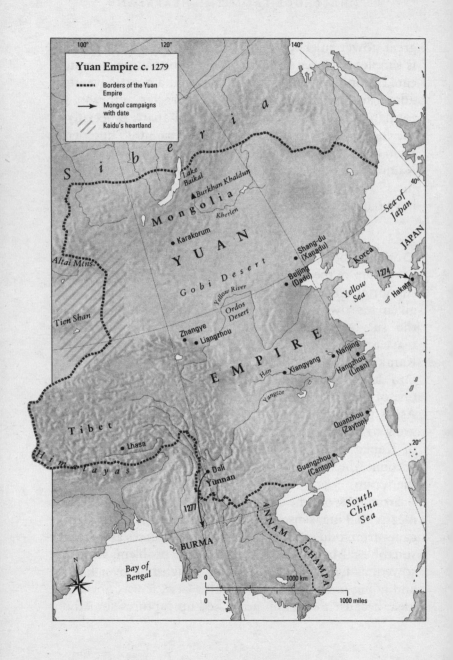

Yuan Empire c. 1279

- **▪▪▪▪▪▪** Borders of the Yuan Empire
- **→** Mongol campaigns with date
- **▨▨▨** Kaidu's heartland

100° 120° 140°

S i b e r i a

40°

Lake Baikal

▲Burkhan Khaldun

Mongolia

Kherlen

Karakorum

Y U A N

Altai Mtns

Gobi Desert

Shang-du (Xanadu)

Beijing (Dadu)

Korea

Sea of Japan

JAPAN

1274

Hakata

Yellow Sea

Yellow River

Tien Shan

Ordos Desert

Zhangye

Liangzhou

E M P I R E

Han Xiangyang

Nanjing

Hangzhou (Linan)

Yangtze

Tibet

Lhasa

H i m a l a y a s

Dali

Yunnan

1277

Quanzhou (Zaytoni)

Guangzhou (Canton)

20°

South China Sea

ANNAM

CHAMPA

BURMA

N

Bay of Bengal

0   1000 km

0   1000 miles

essential about Kaidu and the nature of his rebellion.

Marco remembered Kaidu because of his daughter, Kutulun, another one of those formidable women who stamp their mark on Mongolia's history. Kutulun was famous not for her political skills but for her fighting ability and independent spirit. 'This damsel was very beautiful,' Marco begins, as if opening a fairytale, 'but also so strong and brave that in all her father's realm there was no man who could outdo her in feats of strength . . . so tall and muscular, so stout and shapely withal, that she was almost like a giantess.' Kaidu doted on his Amazonian daughter and wanted to give her in marriage, but she always refused, saying she would only marry a man who could beat her in a wrestling match. Her rule was that a challenger had to put up 100 horses. After 100 bouts and 100 wins, Kutulun had 10,000 horses. Now, as in all good fairytales, a noble prince appears, the son of a rich and powerful king, both father and son being suspiciously anonymous. So confident is he that he puts up 1,000 horses. Kaidu, eager for a wealthy son-in-law, begs her to lose the fight on purpose. Never, she says: he'll have to beat me fair and square. Everyone gathers to watch the match, which after this great build-up ends in anti-climax. They 'grappled each other by the arms and wrestled this way and that', without either gaining an advantage, until suddenly Kutulun throws her opponent. Shamed, he heads for home, wherever that is, leaving his 1,000 horses behind. Her father swallows his anger at the loss of a good match and proudly takes her on campaigns. She proves a great warrior, sometimes dashing into the enemy ranks to seize some man 'as deftly as a hawk pounces on a bird, and carry him to her father'.

Are we to believe this? Well, some of it. Yes, she existed,

because Rashid mentions her; but only in passing, with a rather more jaundiced explanation for her failure to marry. He says the refusal came from her father, 'and people suspected that there was some kind of relationship between him and his daughter'. And Polo's story is rather too reminiscent of others – like the Amazons, or Brünnhilde in the *Nibelungenlied* – to be convincing. What is convincing is the light it throws on Kaidu and the virtues he admired: the traditional pastoral-nomadic virtues of pride, bravery, strength, fighting spirit, independence. He was no lover of scholars, artists or administrators. As Morris Rossabi says, a man with such attitudes would naturally come into conflict with Kublai.

How, then, did things stand with the empire in the early 1260s?

It was no longer a unified empire, but the battleground on which a great family fought over its inheritance. In Central Asia, three Mongol powers battled to increase their own shares: the Golden Horde in today's southern Russia, the Il-Khans in Persia, and Chaghadai's heirs between the Aral Sea and western China. (Actually, there were three-and-a-half powers: there was also a White Horde, ruled by Golden Horde relatives eager to create their own separate estate.) Into this mêlée Kaidu was now elbowing himself, making space in the borderlands where Chaghadai's lands, the Golden Horde and Kublai's China met. All the contestants, of course, acknowledged that they were family, created by Genghis. But who was best suited to wear the mantle of their great forefather? Everything was under strain, pulled by forces over which successive claimants had little control. In the west, Islam drew Mongol rulers; some resisted, some converted, the converts looking to an old enemy, Egypt, for support. In the centre were some who held to traditional nomadic virtues, despising the very cities and cultures they needed for their incomes. In the east, Kublai ruled, for some their nominal overlord, to others a traitor for choosing to be so Chinese.

Kaidu – intelligent, competent and cunning, in Rashid's words – moved steadily into rebellion. In his twenties, he supported Ariq in opposition to Kublai and refused Kublai's summons to his coronation in 1260, with the weak excuse that the pastures were too scanty for his horses. Soon after, all three Central Asian Mongol leaders died – Hulegu in Persia, Alghu in Chaghadai's territory and Berke in the Golden Horde – leaving a power vacuum across all Central Asia. Kaidu grabbed more land, reaching west towards Persia and east into present-day China, relying on the Golden Horde's new ruler as an ally. Kublai tried to bring order to his squabbling family by sending a representative, Baraq, who placed himself in charge of Chaghadai's estate. Baraq and Kaidu fought on the banks of the Syrdar'ya. Kaidu won a great victory, then proposed peace in the name of Genghis.

In 1269 there was a peace conference in Taraz, on the border of Kazakhstan and Kyrgyzstan, to which the new rulers of all three established Inner Asian Mongol 'nations' came, with Kaidu making a fourth. Three of them – the Golden Horde leaders having no interest in this local matter – divided Transoxania between them, with Baraq and Kaidu, the dominant participants, somehow agreeing to share the trade from Samarkand and Bukhara. The two confirmed their treaty with the great oath that made them *anda* – blood brothers – and by 'drinking gold', as the saying went, which meant exchanging golden cups and toasting each other.

Notice what is happening. Baraq, originally sent by Kublai, and the upstart Kaidu are operating as independent monarchs. No-one checks back with his nominal overlord, Kublai, except (according to an unsourced quotation in the *Yuan History*) to send a rather rude message: 'The old customs of our dynasty are not those of the Han laws. Today, when you remain in the Han territory, build a capital and construct cities, learn a method of reading and writing, and use the Han laws, what will happen to the old customs?' In other words, they were declaring themselves independent of Kublai, because he had turned from the ways of Genghis.

It quickly emerged that the peace conference was a sham. No-one trusted anyone else. Everyone prepared for more fighting. The Golden Horde ruler, Mönkhe Temür, stayed out of it, leaving the other three to scrap, in a vicious round of assaults, alliances and deceptions that we can summarize at speed. Abaqa, Hulegu's successor as Il-Khan, defeated Baraq; Kaidu sent an army to 'help' Baraq, intending to take advantage of his defeat; Baraq died; his commanders defected to Kaidu, along with 30,000 soldiers. As a result of these developments, in late summer 1271 Kaidu was crowned in Taraz, becoming khan of a state 2,500 kilometres from side to side, encompassing today's southern Kazakhstan, most of Uzbekistan and almost all of Kyrgyzstan. This area has no name: Marco Polo refers to it as 'Great Turkey'; others call it Turkestan (despite its Mongol elements) or Chaghadai's nation, a shifting entity that was never an exact fit with Kaidu's realm. Roughly speaking, it ran from the River Amudar'ya in the west into Xinjiang in the east, from Lake Balkhash in the north down to the Tien Shan – 1.25 million square kilometres in all, which is the size of France, Germany and Italy combined.

This was no mean achievement. Kaidu had proved himself smart enough to exploit his opponents' weaknesses and Kublai's move into the Chinese heartland. He was a commander in the tradition of Genghis himself: tough, austere – he didn't touch alcohol – tolerant of religions other than his own shamanism, and also careful to preserve his tax base, the great Silk Road cities such as Samarkand and Bukhara. Through an efficient chancellor, he introduced his own currency (coins with a high silver content have been found in a dozen cities). He is even credited with building Andizhan, which in the 1280s became a crossroads for trade in the rich Fergana valley. Traditionalist he may have been, but he also took after Genghis in his awareness of the need for administrative skills. He created regiments of cavalry, using the decimal command structure introduced by Genghis to reform units based on established tribal loyalties. In this way, he was able to incorporate many, often rival, Mongol and Turkish tribes. The horsemen, armed with bows and arrows, also used swords and lances. They were reinforced by units of infantry and 'naphtha throwers' – teams expert in the use of trebuchets and other siege engines. How strong were his armies? The sources toss around the figure of 100,000, probably an exaggeration, as almost all such estimates are, though even this is rather smaller than rival forces in Persia, the Golden Horde and Kublai's China. But what they lacked in quantity they made up for in quality. They were terrific at raids: quick advances, hard strikes, rapid retreats.

But economic revival did not last long, and dreams of wider empire were soon shattered. In the very year of Kaidu's coronation, Kublai took action to bring him to heel. He sent a delegation of six princes led by his fourth son, Nomukhan, to Almaligh, well inside Kaidu's territory, with the aim of persuading him to come to court in Xanadu or Beijing. This must have seemed a good way to force the royal cousins to work together. If so, it backfired disastrously. Kaidu took no notice, keeping his army out of harm's way, securing his western borders. Nomukhan did not have enough cavalry to mount an offensive – his top general told him it would take 110,000 horses to hunt down Kaidu.

This goes to the heart of the problem for Kublai. China did not normally produce horses on this scale. Yuan records show that from Ogedei onwards imperial rulers issued a steady stream of edicts about how horses should be requisitioned.[1] 'As for the people's horses, there is a percentage system,' says one. 'When the number reaches 100, one is taken.' Another, from Kublai in 1293, could apply to Nomukhan's predicament in the mid-1270s: 'Because the rebellious princes [i.e. Kaidu et al.] have not submitted, the time has now come for military operations. Collect 100,000 horses from all the provinces and give the price accordingly.' Herds began to flow from China via the Gansu Corridor, but there was no real chance of sending enough. And anyway, it would surely take Nomukhan time to train his army to use them. Meanwhile, he built up a court and turned himself into yet another warlord.

This stand-off lasted for five useless years, time enough for resentments to grow among the entourage of cousins. The focal point was Tokh-Temür, the son of Tolui's ninth son, famous for his bravery and his skill as an archer. He

[1] Sechin Jagchid and C. R. Bawden, 'Some Notes on the Horse-Policy of the Yüan Dynasty'.

rode a grey horse because he said blood – 'the adornment and decoration of men' – showed up well on it. He was also a hothead. As Rashid puts it, 'Because of his great bravery his brain was full of rebellion.' Tokh-Temür persuaded another cousin, Mönkhe's son Shiregi, that he had a better claim to the throne than Kublai. One night, they captured both Nomukhan and his senior general, sending the prince off as a prisoner to the Golden Horde as a gift and the general to Kaidu, with a message saying, 'We must not think ill of each other, but unite to drive off the enemy.' But, as often with hotheads, Tokh-Temür and Shiregi themselves destroyed the unity they sought. Their army turned into a robber band; the two men squabbled about the succession and fought each other; they suffered various defections; eventually they struck eastward into Mongolia, where they occupied Karakorum. Kublai sent troops to drive them out, after which this rebellion petered out. But imposing his will on his unruly family was a task beyond Kublai's reach. He was totally involved in the war against Song, which would last until 1279, and simply gave up trying to control Kaidu's distant realm.

(And what of the unfortunate Nomukhan? He survived the long journey to Crimea as a prisoner to find himself – of course – among cousins. Presumably thinking he might be useful as a pawn, they kept him for ten years. When he was returned to China in 1284, he was given a job as head of the department looking after the northern frontier, but no longer in line for the succession. He died the following year.)

All this was good news for Kaidu. After reoccupying Almaligh, he was free to deal with constant cross-border raids from Persia and several uprisings from disenchanted members of Chaghadai's family. Sitting squarely over the old Silk Road, he presided over a shaky revival. Silver coins underpinned economic stability. Over the next few years, a strategy would become clear. He would build a network of support all around the fringes of the empire, reaching out southward into Tibet and at the same time eastward to Manchuria. From Almaligh, he would build an arc of yes-men and allies hemming in Kublai's Chinese empire. With Baraq's son Duwa as his right-hand man, he would make good his claim to be the true heir of his grandfather Ogedei, Genghis's appointed successor.

One day, there would have to be a final showdown. It would not come for over 20 years; not in Kublai's lifetime. But for the rest of his days, Kublai's hold on Central Asia remained purely nominal.

12

THE KHAN'S NEW CHINA

KUBLAI HAD INHERITED ASTONISHING MANAGERIAL SKILLS. HE was no intellectual genius, but he had talents that made him one of the greatest CEOs of all time: he was a superb judge of character, entirely without personal prejudice, and had the knack of hiring people who were smarter than he was. Like his grandfather, he was happy to employ anyone with talent. His advisers formed an international team. Muslim traders were headhunted to become financial administrators. He employed 66 Uighur Turks, 21 of whom were resident commissioners or local officials running Chinese districts, while several others tutored princes of the royal family. Also like his grandfather Genghis, he could spot organizational problems – totally unprecedented ones caused by the novelty of unfolding events – and then, out of the blue, devise solutions that actually worked. Genghis had taken tribes, broken their structure and forged a nation, then started to do the same thing with different cultures to forge an empire. Kublai took the process further. His mission was conquest, then government, for which his people were doubly unprepared, first because they had had no government before Genghis and second because, although previous non-Chinese conquerors had taken on north China, none had taken on the whole lot, north and south. Can you think of any precedents in history of such small numbers taking on so much and so many, and succeeding?

Kublai's main fault, as we shall see later, was that he could not be content. How could he be, if he was to be true to his grandfather's mission – to set the bounds of empire wider still and wider, until all the world acknowledged the fact of Mongol supremacy?

At home, by comparison, he was a rock. That, too, was a consequence of his mission. Having seen that China was the key to imperial rule, he needed China to be stable and prosperous, for that would be his foundation for the world rule ordained by Heaven.

To present himself to his subjects as a Chinese ruler, it would not do to go on about the Mongols' divine right. Nor was it enough to be a Buddhist. He also had to be, or at least claim to be, a Confucian. Confucians had always honoured their ancestors. This Kublai did in 1277 by commissioning a Great Ancestral Temple that would prove to his subjects north and south of the Gobi that he was both a good Mongol and a good Chinese. Rising on the south-eastern edge of his new Da-du, the temple's eight chambers were local versions of the Eight White Tents that were already established as travelling shrines to Genghis back in Mongolia, and which centuries later reached their final resting place, Edsen Khoroo, the Lord's Enclosure, south of Dongsheng, Inner Mongolia; in the

1950s, they were replaced by a new shrine, the temple known as the Mausoleum of Genghis Khan. Kublai's original eight-chambered Great Temple commemorated his great-grandparents; Genghis himself; and Genghis's sons, including Kublai's ruling predecessors. Genghis also acquired a Chinese title, T'ai-tsu – the same one given posthumously to the founders of several other dynasties: Song, Liao, Jin and Ming. It was Kublai, therefore, who gave Genghis his Chinese credentials, and thus founded the belief widespread among Chinese today that Genghis was 'really' Chinese – and thus that all Mongols and Mongolia itself are Chinese.

World rule it was to be then, with China as the foundation stone. From this astonishing ambition came something just as remarkable: not a grim dictatorship, but a revival of much that had vanished from Chinese society during the turmoil of the previous century. For a brief moment, about two decades, all of China underwent something of a renaissance. Kublai, as a foreigner, would never be truly accepted; but he was indisputably the boss; and it is arguable that the changes he brought about improved the lot of his new subjects. Certainly, there were those who were ready to admit that unity with peace under the Mongols was better than disunity with civil war. An epitaph of Kublai might say: He tried to be good.

This is a judgement which conflicts sharply with commonly held opinions about Mongol rule, which is often seen as nothing but a catalogue of abuses, along the following lincs.

Almost all the top positions were held by Mongols. They lorded it over the population as the new landowners, the new elite, the new aristocracy. A new class system brought new humiliations: Mongols at the top; then, those from the Muslim lands – Persians, Arabs, Uighurs, Turks – who knew about business and trade; then the 40 million northern Chinese, along with other fringe minorities, like Tatars, Khitans and Koreans; and finally, at the bottom of the heap, the new subjects, the 70 million southern Chinese, who at a stroke were turned from heirs to the richest and most sophisticated culture on earth to subjects and servants. Many were actually enslaved, and a slave trade sprang up. If a Mongol murdered, he was exiled; a Chinese murderer was executed. A Mongol could beat a Chinese with impunity, while the Chinese was forbidden to return the blow. The Chinese were banned from carrying weapons, hunting, military training, raising horses, praying in groups, holding fairs. Curfews were imposed, lights forbidden. The examination system, by which scholar-officials acquired office, was no more. In the ten grades into which Mongols categorized their Chinese subjects, Confucian scholars ranked ninth, below prostitutes, above only the lowest of the low, the beggars.

All this is true. But it is not the whole truth. The scholars, aristocrats and officials represented only a tiny part of Chinese society. Most were peasant farmers and ordinary town-dwellers earning their living by agricultural work, low-level trading and performing the myriad humble jobs that are vital in any large, complex, urbanized society. With such a vast population, with such teeming cities, with such a thin upper crust of Mongols, no changes permeated from top to bottom. For ordinary people, the routines of everyday life hardly changed . . .

. . . or actually improved. Stability depended on more than the raw exercise of power. Kublai was the most powerful man of his day, one of the most powerful of all time; yet, as his actions showed, he knew that his power depended only in part on a flow of authority from the top downwards, from him through the court and his army of officials to the masses. It also depended on support flowing from the bottom upwards. Ordinary people had to feel happy and secure, or unrest would fester and spread from below. North China was sick enough as it was, recovering from the half-century of warfare initiated by Genghis back in 1211; the south was seething from his own campaign of conquest; all needed healing.

The foundation of stability was the vast mass of peasant farmers, on whom all depended for food. To look after their interests, Kublai set up a new Office for the Stimulation of Agriculture, with eight officials and a team of experts who organized aid, built 58 granaries that could store almost 9,000 tonnes of grain, arranged tax remissions and banned Mongols from grazing their wandering herds on farmland. Local councils, each covering 50 households, helped with production, irrigation – and even schools, an idea that proved too revolutionary to work, but did at least show that the emperor was no mere barbarian nomad. Taxes now flowed not directly to the landowner, who in the north was probably a Mongol, but to the government, which then divided the revenue between itself and the landowner. The peasant farmer still paid, but at least Kublai tried to curb abuses. He also insisted that forced labour, which remained vital for large-scale public projects like canals and the postal system, was rather less forced than previously.

Let's see how he ruled. He had had a good start, under the aegis of Genghis's Khitan adviser, the great Yeh-lü Chu-tsai, who successfully set up a decent working bureaucracy,

despite opposition from some dyed-in-the-wool traditionalist factions. But Kublai faced a much vaster problem:
namely, how to combine steppeland with town and farmland, nomadism with settled cultures, the few with the
many. He was not ready simply to abandon the one (from
which he derived his core values) and adopt the other.
Besides, he also had to take into account his Muslim
subjects, a vital component of the empire: his brother
Hulegu ruled a good chunk of Islam, and Muslims were
important as governors, tax-gatherers, financial advisers
and business partners. His response to this many-sided
challenge was to make it up as he went along, sometimes
finding solutions in the practices of previous dynasties,
sometimes devising his own. Over 30 years he created a
form of government that was predominantly Chinese, but
also uniquely complex and cosmopolitan.

He had one supreme advantage: he was not bound by
precedent. Previous emperors had governed through
several executive agencies. Kublai saw that this would be
a recipe for disaster. He had just one, the Central Secretariat,
with him at the top, ranging down through chief councillors
(usually two or three, occasionally up to five), privy
councillors, assistants, some 200 officials and hundreds of
clerical staff, in 18 levels, the status of each minutely defined
in terms of precedence, title, salary and perks.[1]

The Secretariat controlled six ministries: Personnel,
Revenues, Rites, War, Punishments and Works, each of
which had dozens of departments. The Ministry of Works,
for instance, had 53 of them, including agencies that
handled Buddhist icons, lost-wax casting, a bronze foundry,

[1] This section is mostly based on F. W. Mote, *Imperial China
900–1800*.

agate and jade workers, masonry, woodworking, paint, weaving, dyeing, carpets, tents, kilns and leatherworking. Checking up on all ministries and their departments was a Censorate, a sort of National Audit Office, with three national headquarters.

Entirely separate from the civil administration was the Bureau of Military Affairs, the Ministry of War being merely its link to the civil service. This had been established by Kublai after Li Tan's Shandong rebellion in 1262 as the guarantor of his power. The Bureau was hard-core Mongol territory, top secret, staffed by Mongols, with all Chinese excluded to prevent their knowing anything of troop strengths, dispositions or armaments. It controlled all the armed forces, including the appointment of officers, the training of Chinese and Central Asian units, kept the records and conducted all its own auditing procedures. This was perhaps Kublai's greatest stroke of administrative genius. Genghis had created a non-tribal system owing personal loyalty to himself. Kublai had realized that such a huge and enduring establishment as his would be far removed from him as an individual. Its personnel – most of them pen-pushers, not generals – needed to be made loyal to a different entity: not a here-today-gone-tomorrow emperor, but the state.

Then there was the court. Specialized staff took care of the rituals, the protocol, the kitchens, granaries, warehouses, clothing and special food. Teams of artisans supplied gold, silver, porcelain, gems, textiles. There were departments for the hunting facilities and the stud farms. This was a universe unto itself of servants, managers, entertainment specialists, historians, translators, interpreters, astronomers, doctors, librarians, shrine-keepers, musicians and architects.

Other institutions were not under the direct control of any of the above. Three academies were devoted to Mongol studies; a Muslim Bureau of Astronomy gave Muslims their own research facilities; the Commission for Tibetan and Buddhist Affairs – Phags-pa's private empire – acted as a sort of Tibetan government-at-a-distance, supervising the Pacification Bureau in Tibet and the ever-growing Buddhist interests across China: temples, monasteries, other properties.

It was the job of the Bureau of Military Affairs to handle the changeover from conquest to a permanent military administration. The repercussions of this shift would store up trouble for the future. Under Genghis, the Mongol system had drawn every family into its military machine. Families had to be supported with rather more than a salary (which in any case was not a concept that existed in the early days of empire). At first the rewards were booty, then, as territory fell, lands. That was how commanders of 'hundreds' or 'thousands' were supposed to support their troops. Hence the system which gave estates – appanages – to princes and commanders. But with an empire to manage, the appanage system did not work. Few Mongols had the ambition or talent to administer farms. Most were absentee landlords, abandoning their estates to the care of servants who were little more than slaves with no interest in doing a good job. The system tended to collapse of its own accord, leaving the estates ruined, their people destitute. So Kublai stopped awarding appanages. Mongol landowners sold up and found themselves cast adrift, outside the military system, with no skills, no education, no place back in their homeland, yet still supposedly part of an elite. They were the empire's equivalent of poor whites in the American

South. Later, this would be part of the sickness that ate at the soul of Kublai's heirs.

The provinces were another of Kublai's creations. As the tide of Mongol conquest flowed outwards, newly conquered regions were given their own mini versions of the Central Secretariat, and these remained as branches of government in the eleven provinces, which then acquired branches of all the other departments. They were not provincial governments – Kublai wanted his officials governed from the centre, to avoid local empire-building – but they formed the essence of the provincial administrative system set up in succession by the Qing and then by the Communists in 1949. Yunnan, Shaanxi, Sichuan and Gansu all owe their existence to Kublai. The administrations reach right down to the roots. Provinces were sub-divided into prefectures, sub-prefectures and counties, each divided into two classes depending on size, each with its own set of ranked officials, from 3A for the largest prefectures (over 100,000 households) down to 7B for the smallest counties (under 10,000 households).

As CEO, Kublai was committed to Mongolia Inc., which rode high on the wheels of commerce. Craftsmen were favoured with rations of food, clothing and salt, and were exempted from forced labour. Merchants had previously been seen as parasites; now they were encouraged. Trade, mainly with Muslim lands, boomed. Chinese textiles, ceramics and lacquer ware flowed out through the ports; medicines, incense, spices and carpets flowed in.

In some ways, Kublai was the ideal patron of the arts. He had no pretensions to being an expert himself, but he knew art was tremendously important, and since he wished to appeal to all his subjects, he encouraged artists without distinction of race or creed. He was thus, almost by default, a force for change. Remember the Nepalese architect Arniko, Phags-pa's friend and designer of the White Pagoda? He proved such a hit that he became head of all artisans nationwide, ending up with a mansion and a rich wife found for him by Kublai's wife Chabi. As a result, some Yuan buildings had Tibetan and Nepalese designs.

Or take ceramics, for which China had been famous, having established ten main kilns in the north and fourteen in the south. The war had largely destroyed ceramic production in the north, and when Kublai came to power he showed no interest in tableware, which you might think would put a damper on the trade as a whole. Exactly the opposite. Southern kilns continued to fill wagons rolling into the great southern port of Quanzhou, the place Marco Polo calls by its Arabic name, Zayton. It was, he says,

> frequented by all the ships of India [i.e. Asia], which bring thither spicery and all other kinds of costly wares. It is the port also that is frequented by all the merchants of Manzi [southern China], for hither is imported the most astonishing quantity of goods and of precious stones and pearls, and from this they are distributed all over Manzi. And I assure you that for one shipload of pepper that goes to Alexandria or elsewhere, destined for Christendom, there come a hundred such, aye, and more too.

In exchange for these imports, ceramics flowed into the holds of ships bound for South-East Asia, India and the world of Islam – half of which, remember, was ruled by

Mongols, who quickly adopted the refined tastes of their subjects. Indeed, Quanzhou/Zayton, from which most goods were exported, was under the thumbs of Persian merchants. With Kublai standing back, the southern kilns could focus on exports, and on experiments to give their customers what they wanted, namely high quality. As a result, as one expert, Margaret Medley, puts it: 'The Yuan marks the beginning of the change-over from stone wares, that is wares fired at high temperatures with bodies varying in colour, to the fine white porcelains, hard, vitrified and translucent, that we now automatically associate with the name of China.' There was more to the revolution. In the Middle East cobalt, an extraordinarily rare metallic element, had long been used to give a blue tinge to statuettes and necklace-beads. It seems someone brought it to Chinese porcelain-makers to see what they could do with it. They made it work: cobalt blue ceramics became famous, exports boomed, and taxes – on kilns, craftsmen and production – rolled into Kublai's coffers. It is a minor irony that Kublai's own indifference led to the creation of techniques and products – the white wares of Fujian, the grey-green celadons of Zhejiang, underglaze blue – which strengthened his economy and for any one example of which a modern collector will pay thousands of dollars.

Working in groups to make use of their wealth, merchants became bankers, lending at 36 per cent annual interest. They and Kublai's government were partners: laws forced merchants to convert their metal coins into paper currency on entry, which gave the government a reserve in metals, which was used to back loans at around 10 per cent annual interest back to the merchant groups, who became, in effect, government-sanctioned loan sharks. From trade, everyone profited. Even the peasants?

Why, yes. No doubt Kublai, with a financial adviser at his shoulder, would have argued that merchant wealth translated into government wealth, which financed public works and allowed tax relief to be granted to the needy. Naturally, if peasants chose to get into debt with a loan shark, that was their fault. The government could not be responsible for every merchant banker who sent in the bailiffs to twist the arms of those who had fallen behind on their monthly payments. The majority would benefit. This was trickle-down economics before its time.

Kublai's big success in economics was to extend the use of paper money. Paper money is a great invention, for practical reasons, as the Chinese had discovered almost 300 years before when the Song unified the country and revolutionized it with a booming economy. As we saw in chapter 3, unification, wealth and stability had opened the way to a single currency based on copper coins, which came in cumbersome strings of 1,000. Since rich merchants with nationwide businesses did not like handling such a weight of cash, local governments issued certificates of deposit – so-called 'flying money' – that could be redeemed in other cities. The elements had been in place for centuries, principally paper (AD 105 being the traditional date of its invention), which came to be made from the beaten inner bark of mulberry trees, and printing with carved wood-blocks (eighth century, from Japan). In 1023 the state printed the first banknotes, without taking account of basic economics. One inescapable truth about paper currency is that it is not worth the paper it is printed on. It's all a matter of confidence, based on whatever backs the bills – the economy as a whole, or gold, or in this case coins. By the early twelfth century, 70 million paper 'strings' were in circulation. This was far in excess of anything that could be backed by coins, leading to the first inflation in history. Another problem was forgery, which can be countered by making the designs so elaborate that only authorized institutions can print them – and, of course, by executing the counterfeiters.

Kublai, with the right advice, had both problems under control in an economy of which a modern finance minister would be proud. Four economic pillars – national unity, internal stability, high confidence, good growth – allowed for a far more effective system of paper money than the Song had had. He tried three systems, one backed by reserves of silk, the other two by silver, the last of which became universal, to the astonishment and admiration of Marco Polo. It was the oddest notion – that a whole society should place value on the solidified slurry made from the underbark of mulberry trees – so he goes into it in some detail. He describes the manufacture of the paper, its reduction to notes, the application of an official vermilion stamp, and their introduction into circulation. 'Everybody takes them readily, for wheresoever a person may go through the Great Kaan's dominions he shall find these pieces of paper current, and shall be able to transact all sales and purchases of goods by means of them just as well as if they were coins of pure gold.' Kublai naturally used his own notes to buy wares from foreign traders. 'He buys such a quantity of those precious things every year that his treasure is endless, whilst all the time the money he pays away costs him nothing at all ... You might say he hath the Secret of Alchemy in perfection.'

Polo could not understand how Kublai created wealth out of paper. In a sense, simply by avoiding what had not worked and doing what did, Kublai almost stumbled on the economic principles of John Maynard Keynes, who asserted that a government can stimulate an economy by borrowing from itself and investing its own money to create the surpluses that allow it to pay itself back. Nothing so sophisticated as borrowing was needed in thirteenth-century China. It was enough that the emperor ensured stability, and preserved confidence in his own currency. This he did by always allowing a free exchange with silver on demand, and by not making the mistake the Song had made: that of printing too much currency, thereby sparking inflation. It is a neat trick, which later dynasties (and many modern governments) could not match. Soon after the Yuan fell in 1368, paper money fell out of use for 400 years.

Another element in Kublai's revolution was a new legal system.[2] Basically, since he had come from outside, all preceding codes, with legal traditions dating back 2,000 years, were suddenly null and void until reinstated. Genghis's legal system, a list of statutes recorded by his adopted kinsman Shigi, did not have the sophistication necessary for a vast and complex society like China's. Advisers quickly began afresh, combining elements of the two systems. How they did it exactly is not known, because only fragments of the texts have survived, but, as one expert wrote in a memorandum in 1266, it would take 30 years to generate all the correct procedures, decrees and precedents. Even then, there would be no unified code applying equally to Mongols, Muslims and Chinese. Draft codes came and went. Meanwhile, day-to-day justice depended, as it had for over 700 years of Chinese history, on the Five Punishments: death by

[2] This section is based on Paul Heng-chao Chen, *Chinese Legal Tradition Under the Mongols*.

strangulation or decapitation; exile for life to three distances – 1,000, 1,250, or 1,500 kilometres – depending on the seriousness of the crime; penal servitude for up to three years; beating with a heavy stick, from 60 to 100 blows; and beating with a light stick, from 10 to 50 blows. Under Kublai, various adaptations were introduced. The khan's officials had doubts about using strangulation, which did not involve the shedding of blood and was reserved in Mongol tradition for high-born criminals. For the most serious crime – treachery – he revived a seldom-used precedent: death by slow slicing, from which comes the sadistic notion of 'death by a thousand cuts'. Not a thousand, actually, but eight initially – face, hands (2), feet (2), breast, stomach, head – to be increased in stages – 24, 36, 120 – depending on the pain to be inflicted. Mere exile was not considered an adequate sanction, either, mainly because, for a nomad of no fixed abode, being sent somewhere else was no great punishment. So exile was replaced by hard labour in salt mines or iron works or some distant military base, backed up by blows with a stick, from one year plus 67 blows to three years plus 107 blows. Beatings were delivered in six degrees of punishment with a light stick (7, 17, 27, 37, 47 and 57 blows), and five degrees with a heavy stick (67–107 blows). 'And many of them', as Marco Polo records, 'die of this beating.'

This sounds grim, but in fact the Yuan code was noted for its leniency. The Song code had listed 293 offences punishable by death. The Yuan had only 135, which contradicts the common view that the Mongols used extreme brutality against all criminals. Indeed, the successor dynasty, the Ming, pushed the number back up again, one official complaining about

Kublai's wimpishness. Moreover, the actual number of executions was remarkably low. Between 1260 and 1307, 2,743 criminals were executed (though nine years are missing from the records). An average of 72 executions per year out of a population of 100 million is about half that carried out in the United States when it had an equivalent population in about 1930, since when attitudes have shifted somewhat. Death Row executions in 2002–4 averaged about 60 a year, which, given the size of the population, is half the rate under Kublai Khan. Some things improve with time.

A criminal was also expected to pay compensation to his victims. This practice derived from the Mongolian tradition of paying your way out of trouble. In the Mongolian code, for instance, one statute stipulated that, in a murder case, the perpetrators could escape death 'by paying fines which were: for a Muslim – 40 gold coins; and for a Chinese – one donkey'. Under Kublai, too, certain people could simply pay up: specifically, men over 70 or boys under 15 (unless the crime was a sexual offence against a girl of 10 or under). But in most cases, punishment and compensation went together. If a man beat his sister-in-law to death, for example, he would receive 107 blows with a heavy stick and have to pay for the dead woman's funeral.

Traditionally, officials got off lightly. Not under Kublai. 'Any official who commits an unsuccessful act of rape against the wife of his subordinate shall be punished by 107 blows with a heavy stick and be dismissed from the civil service.'

In other respects, Kublai favoured leniency. Certain criminals received the equivalent of control orders. For first-time robbery-with-violence, the convicted individual was punished, and in addition tattooed on the right arm with the words 'robbery or theft once' and ordered to register with local authorities wherever he went and to serve as an auxiliary policeman for five years: a combination of punishment and community service, of discrimination and surveillance, that reinforced the bonds of society.

How come the world's most powerful man, the head of a regime noted for its iron control, ruled a regime of such relative leniency? Because his people did as they were told, and Kublai knew that justice was justice, and that harshness was counter-productive. In 1287 some 190 people were condemned to death. Kublai ordered reprieves. 'Prisoners are not a mere flock of sheep. How can they be suddenly executed? It is proper that they be instead enslaved and assigned to pan gold with a sieve.' There speaks a man who knew how to get the best from his assets.

So, a conqueror ambitious for ever wider empire, whose troops had been responsible for the death of millions of Chinese, may still come over as a man whose intentions and actions were not all bad. Even from the Chinese point of view, we must grant him some virtues. And this, for those Chinese subjects who had any freedom of choice in the matter, which was not many of them, was a problem, the age-old problem of conquered peoples: whether to oppose the invaders for ever, until death, as the hundreds of known and uncounted unknown suicides would have demanded; or to embrace *disloyalty* – the accusation marked the accused like a plague-spot – accept, kow-tow, collaborate, live and prosper?

There is no easy answer, of course. The passage of time helps. Today's intransigence will seem pig-headed tomorrow; this year's disloyalty will seem like next year's good sense. But still there will be no lasting solution. Even though Kublai proclaimed a Chinese dynasty, even though China accepted and still accepts that fact, the conquest injected a virus of bitterness that would in the end infect and overwhelm Kublai's inadequate heirs.

Let's see how one man struggled to find a way through this moral maze. He is not typical, because he was a master painter, some say a genius, but then who is typical, when everyone with the freedom to do so must make their own choices?

His name was Zhao Mengfu (Chao Meng-fu in the old transliteration). Zhao, a distant relative of the Song royal family, was starting a career as a minor official, aged 25, when his world was shattered by the Mongol invasion. Like many other scholar-officials, he was appalled by the new regime, its boorishness, its crude class structure which put southerners at the bottom of the heap, and by their own helplessness. Without the examinations which offered the educated the chance of a career, they had no hope. He became one of the *yi-min*, the 'leftovers', the rejectionists, who preferred obscurity to collaboration, and retreated to his home town, then Wuxing, now Huzhou, which then and now was famous for its glorious countryside – the huge Taihu lake to the north, the bamboo forests of the Tianmu mountains to the west. In a country retreat, the Gull-Wave Pavilion, he buried himself in classical studies, and discovered prodigious talents. He wasn't the only one. Wuxing's lake and green mountains inspired a loose confederation of masters, the Eight Talents of Wuxing as they became known. In the course of the next seven years, he won fame as a master of three genres, painting, calligraphy and poetry (later to become, many think, the greatest of his age in all three). In 1286 an imperial official arrived in Wuxing, scouting for talent in the name of Kublai. He heard of the Eight, sought them out, and made them all offers of employment in the imperial service.

Zhao accepted. One account says it was his mother who persuaded him, ambitious for him to achieve high office while still young. Some who refused turned against him – a descendant of the first Song emperor serving the Mongols! – and from then the reek of disloyalty hung about him. It was no easy decision, and there was no escape from its consequences. Zhao achieved eminence, in government – as an official in the Ministry of War and provincial administrator – as a scholar, as an artist. But regret for his lost world of lakes and mountains, where he had been his own master, gnawed at him for the rest of his life. As he wrote in one poem:

> Unfortunately I have fallen into the dusty world
> My movements being restricted.
> Before I was as a seagull,
> Now I am a bird inside a cage,
> No one cares about my sad weeping,
> My feathers are falling off every day.

His distress also permeates a painting of a sleek sheep and a miserable-looking goat: simple enough at first glance, less so the deeper you look. In traditional fashion, it includes some of Zhao's beautiful calligraphy, which hints at hidden meanings. 'I have often painted horses, but never before painted sheep or goats,' he notes, as if to say he had painted subjects dear to his horse-loving masters, but not those closer to the people they ruled. 'I did this playfully from life. Although it may not approach the old masters, it does capture something of their spirit.' One commentator, Li Chu-tsing, has argued that there is more here than a reference to ancient artistic traditions. The sheep and the goat are two generals of the Han dynasty (206 BC–AD 220) who were both captured by the Xiongnu, the barbarian empire that lay north of the Great Wall. (The Xiongnu – Hunnu in Mongolian – may have been ancestors of the Huns.) Both generals had a chance to collaborate. One, Su Wu, refused, and was forced to be a shepherd for 20 years. There he is as the haughty sheep, with its fatuous expression and bloated look, ripe for the pot. The other, Li Ling, accepted, and returned home – the scraggy goat, dejected, but at least alive to fight another day.

There's a paradox about Kublai and the arts. He encouraged artists, yet, like many other patrons, could never be a part of China's brilliant artistic tradition. In the eyes of China's artists, the Mongols were and would remain barbarians. But there they were, these great artists, serving the new regime. The inner conflict might have destroyed them. In fact, it stimulated them. Whether collaborators or rejectionists, they might have retreated into traditionalism. In fact, they took the traditions forward.

One reason for this was that, for the first time in 150 years, there was free movement between south and north. Artists from the south, imbued with the pretty, trivial stuff that the southern Song had liked, discovered a tradition of sturdier, freer styles that had dominated the north before the old Song empire had been cut in half by the Mongols' equally 'barbarian' predecessors, the Liao, in 1125.

In his most famous painting, Zhao wraps all this, and more, up together. He combines two artistic traditions, draws on his own experience and emotions, makes a touching gesture to an old friend and reveals something of the pain imposed by the political situation. For six years, his job was Assistant Civil Administrator of Jinan, in Shandong province, just north of the old north–south frontier. Back in his home town in 1295, he rediscovered a friend, Zhou Mi, whose ancestors, three or four generations back, had fled from the Jinan area when it fell to the Jin. He still considered Jinan his home, and dreamed of returning one day. With the country reunified by the Mongols, it was a dream he might have realized – except that he was one of the *yi-min*, the rejectionists who had withdrawn from public life in protest against Mongol rule. Zhao described to his old friend the place of his dreams, as he relates in the inscription. 'I told him about the mountains and rivers of Qi [near Jinan]. Among them, Mount Hua-fu-zhu is the most famous . . . its shape is lofty and precipitous, rising isolated in a most unusual way. So I painted this picture for him, setting Mount Jiao on the east, which is why I call it *Autumn Colours on the Jiao and Hua Mountains*.' It's a deceptively simple scene: marshy land stretching to the horizon, clumps of trees, two contrasting mountains – one a stark double triangle, the other an Ayers Rock lump in the distance – a couple of houses, a tiny fisherman almost lost in the landscape, all washed by a mood of autumnal melancholy. It is not a scene of traditional beauty: there are no towering cliffs and misty forests. Nor is it true to life, for the two mountains are actually far apart. It's more as if, by showing a bleak version of his friend's unseen homeland, he is saying: Don't let's pretend that life is a pretty thing. It's not.

It's a tough business. Anyway, what in the end does it all matter, the Mongols, our own petty agonies and divisions? These things pass. Here, in my picture, is what endures: stark mountains, gnarled trees, and hard work.

Autumn Colours is one of the most admired of Chinese paintings, one of many that, in the words of one scholar, James Cahill, 'exhibit an astonishing inventiveness and creativity, offering major stylistic innovations that would change the course of Chinese landscape painting'. Without Kublai, they would not exist. We may question the initial conditions, the brutality of the conquest. But, given those, the outcome could have been worse.

Here's an odd thing. The Mongols loved the theatre. They loved it mainly because it was a total novelty. 'There is no evidence of any form of dramatic productions being presented in Mongolian society prior to or during the early empire period,' say two experts on Mongol society, Sechin Jagchid and Paul Hyer, adding wrily, 'It is difficult to develop institutionalised drama in a nomadic society.'

No-one recorded the first performance attended by Mongols – some street show, perhaps, in a town that had the good sense to surrender when Genghis first invaded north China in 1211. I imagine the scene as something like the one I saw in Guyuan, Gansu, one of China's poorest areas in 2002, when a travelling theatre visited: a ragged crowd of two or three hundred sitting on the ground in the main square a good hour before dusk and show time, the curtained stage, the actors behind putting the final touches to their garish make-up. Now we flash back 800 years and see a contingent of Mongols in the background, still on their horses. They have been on campaign for months, and are eager for some light relief. Mongol officers in their lamellar armour and leather helmets dismount and come forward, grim but curious. They are ushered to the front row by trembling townsfolk; there they wait in puzzled silence, until darkness falls. With a rush of fabric, the curtain opens, and footlight candles reveal a fierce-looking man. Mao, for that is his name, speaks directly to the audience:

Mao: I, Mao Yen-shou, am travelling all over the country with the emperor's order to search out beautiful maidens for the palace.
[After a couple of minutes in this vein, a girl named Zhaoqun comes on, incredibly, untouchably, magically beautiful in silk and perfect make-up. Gasps from the armoured front row.]

Zhaoqun: I am Wang Qian, also called Zhaoqun, a native of Zikui in Zhengdu. My father, the Elder Wang, has worked the land all his life. Before I was born . . .
[She explains her circumstances: poor family, chosen to be a royal concubine at 18, gives offence, is hidden away. She's never seen the emperor, and she's sad.]
. . . Now at night in my solitude, I shall try to play a song to while away the time.
[Plays the lute. The Emperor enters.][3]

The Mongols may not get all the references, but their

---

[3] A little authorial licence here. These quotes are actually from a Yuan play, Ma Zhi-yuan's *Autumn in the Han Palace*, but the story is much older. It is not impossible that a version was in existence in Song times.

interpreter is working hard; they are smitten by the beauty of the girl, they are spellbound by her singing, they hate the villain, they know all about the emperor, their enemy, and they are gripped by the story, which, as they will soon learn, is famous in China. (Still is, actually: the best hotel in Hohhot, the capital of Inner Mongolia, is named after its heroine.) Everyone knows of how pretty little Zhaoqun is sent off across the Great Wall to be the wife of the khan of the Xiongnu in distant Mongolia. She mourns, she wishes she were a gold swan flying home, she weeps: it's heartrending.

Something like this must have happened. In 1214–16 Genghis's great general Muqali swept across Manchuria while Genghis himself was besieging Beijing. Two towns had the temerity to hold out. As usual in these circumstances, Muqali said, 'If we let these rebellious bandits live, there will be nothing with which to admonish later generations.' He slaughtered them all, except for artisans, craftsmen – and *actors*.

The traditions were certainly rich enough to seduce the Mongols. The Chinese had been watching dance shows, musicals, recitations, storytellings, pageants and variety shows for centuries; divergent traditions emerged in north and south, with a boom in drama under the Song. Archaeological evidence confirms that this was more than street entertainment. Tenth-century tomb-tiles unearthed in Henan in 1958 show actors in traditional dramatic roles, and in Shanxi excavations around 1970 revealed the remains of a brick-and-tile provincial theatre. Even in distant Manchuria, there were a company and a play and music and a leading girl to entertain the invaders.

Once in power, Kublai the arts patron made sure his people had theatre, lots of it. But he didn't want just the old stuff. He wanted new writing, designed to appeal to the Mongols and his very international court. That meant it would have to be easy to follow, because Kublai himself did not speak very good Chinese and was unfamiliar with high-flown Song literary traditions. This caused something of a revolution among the Song literati. They had contradictory attitudes towards the theatre, as did Restoration audiences in England. They loved it for its entertainment value, but plays were written in common language, actors were held in low regard and actresses were whores. In brief, from any point of view other than their own, the Song literati were appalling snobs. To create new drama would be prostituting their poetic skills. No-one thought of plays as literature; no-one thought of preserving them. As a result, very little survives from pre-Yuan times.

All this changed under Kublai. At court, there were two bureaux, one responsible for music and acting, the other for staging court rituals and plays. The customer called the tune, and, by comparison with his subjects, the customer had simple tastes. As one of the first translators of Yuan drama, Henry Hart, put it in slightly non-PC terms in 1936: 'Ignorant of literature and of the amenities of civilised life, philosophy and poetry, dainty dancing and soft music had no allure for them. Nurtured on the windswept deserts, exulting in battle and rapine . . . they preferred drama written and acted in the everyday language of common people.'

It was this demand that reinvigorated Chinese drama. Starting in and around Da-du, Kublai's newly built Beijing, a new breed of playwright emerged. Many of them were scholars frustrated by the ending of the examination system, and eager to supplement their meagre clerks' incomes, to win recognition and to find an outlet for their literary skills. They created (as one historian of Chinese drama, Chung-wen Shih, has written) a 'body of works qualitatively and quantitatively unequalled before or after in the Chinese theatre, and making Yuan drama one of the most brilliant genres in Chinese literary history'. This rich field has one disadvantage for the historian. The authors were still embarrassed to have their names associated with their products, so very little is known about them. Fortunately one playwright, Zhong Su-cheng, gathered biographical notes about Yuan writers in *A Register of Ghosts*, its very title a comment on the invisibility of its subjects. Of the 152 listed, 111 are dramatists.

Thousands of plays must have been written, of which some 700 are known by name and 150 have survived, perhaps because they are the best. They are of a type known as 'variety plays', or 'mixed entertainment' – what we would call musicals, except that, with the involvement of fine writers, they are much more than that. They examine contemporary concerns: oppression, injustice, corruption, struggles with authority. They do so in their own terms, of course, not in western ones. Set in a carefully ordered universe, the plays do not display the internal agonies and destructive passions common in western drama from Shakespeare onwards. Some flee the real world for timeless romance, like *The Romance of the Western Chamber*, which derives from a story first written down around 800. A student rescues a beautiful girl from rebels; he woos her; her fierce mother objects; a clever maid helps them; the mother is won round; happy ending. Rewritten several times, the story was turned into a famous drama by Wang Shifu, and has remained popular ever since. I bought a novelized version in Beijing in 2004.

As in Shakespeare, the themes are explored in historical contexts. They could not be set in the present, for fear of giving offence (though mild criticism was OK, if veiled, as one description of a royal command performance reveals: 'If there is any criticism . . . the actors cloak the case in a story to criticise with hidden import; thus no displeasure shadows the emperor's face'). This means that the plays are not time-bound. They try to do what drama should do, which is turn current concerns into timeless themes and present them as entertainments that now and then claim the literary high ground as well.

Let Guan Hanqing (Kuan Han-ch'ing) stand for all, because he was the most prolific of Yuan playwrights. Practically everything about his life is vague. Born by about 1240, he lived to a great age, dying some time before 1330. He wrote 63 or 64 musical plays (the authorship of one is disputed), of which 14 or 18 (another dispute) survive. Most of them are about love, its joys and agonies: love between courtesans and scholars, emperors and concubines, lovers of high and low status. Heroines were his forte. Eleven of the 14 extant plays have at their core strong, brave, determined women, none more so than the star of his best play, *The Injustice to Dou E*. She's a simple village girl, a young widow of 18. A coarse suitor wrongly accuses her of murder. She is dragged into court and beaten by a corrupt magistrate. When she refuses to confess, he threatens to beat her mother-in-law. To save her, Dou E makes a false confession and is condemned to death. On the eve of her execution, she makes three wishes, one of which is that the area should suffer with three years of drought. All her wishes come true, proving that Heaven has heard her prayers. The drought attracts the attention of her father, a high official, who reopens the case. Dou E reappears as a ghost to accuse her accusers. Justice is done, the universe rebalanced.

It was not the plot that made the play a classic, but its poetic language, which gave it an epic grandeur. Dou E is no ordinary girl. Chaste, obedient, self sacrificing, she is a Joan of Arc figure, a symbol of the suffering nation. When she is abused – as the Mongols abused China – the laws of heaven are overturned, corruption and stupidity rule. 'The good suffer poverty and short life,' she sings. 'The wicked enjoy wealth, nobility and long life.' But virtue cannot for ever be despised. Her death spurs Heaven to action, returning justice to an unjust world – great themes that have ensured the play's survival in several later versions, including one performed by the Peking Opera today.

Kublai brought to China a measure of stability and security unknown for centuries. Bearable levels of taxation, the rule of law, a positive, or at worst neutral, policy towards the arts, public works to aid the common good – you might say that he brought a level of happiness to his people. A tiny percentage, the elite – top Mongols, top Chinese officials, Muslim merchants – would have agreed. Would the 100 million less well off? We cannot possibly know, because happiness as we understand it only came to the fore in the eighteenth century. Recently it has emerged as a subject in its own right; now, on the basis of surveys, statistics and analyses, we can look back and argue a case. As Richard Layard points out in *Happiness: Lessons from a New Science*, one definition of happiness is the feeling that today is a little better than yesterday. The vast mass of people in thirteenth-century China started from a pretty low base. They would surely still have feared famine, disease and flood, the tax-man, the loan-shark, the official looking to press-gang men into forced labour; but they also knew that in the previous two generations millions had died and millions more had been driven from their homes, while at least from 1276 onwards they were at peace. They could work with more hope than previously that it would not all go to waste. No-one in medieval China argued that the purpose of government was to increase the sum of human happiness, but somehow Kublai and his officials, working to create stability, continuity and national wealth, managed to achieve, if not the greatest happiness for the greatest number, at least, for 25 or 30 years, a decrease in unhappiness.

IV

WINTER

13

KAMIKAZE

IN 1280, AFTER THE CONQUEST OF THE SOUTH, KUBLAI COULD turn again on Japan. He was now 65, and time was snapping at his heels. But it was more than his age that drove him. He acted like a man obsessed, both with the need to fulfil his grandfather's ambitions for world conquest and with the need to punish this 'little country' for its temerity in resisting him. For an emperor as raw as ever on the subject of his own legitimacy, he was, as always, determined to prove himself, as fast as possible.

Accounts of this campaign have, until recently, been dominated by the Japanese point of view, because they were the victors, and history belongs more to winners than to losers. The story has been often told: how the mighty Chinese fleet was about to crush the hapless, outmoded Japanese samurai when the heavens themselves came to the aid of the Japanese by unleashing a typhoon that swept Kublai's fleet to oblivion. Soon thereafter, the

Japanese called the storm the Divine Wind, the *kamikaze* (*kami* also having the sense of 'god', 'spirit' and 'superior'), referring to it as proof that Japan was under the protection of Heaven. This suited the ruling elite, whose power depended in part on faith in their ability to perform the correct religious rituals. It was to evoke the idea of heavenly protection that the suicide pilots of the Second World War were called *kamikazes*: they were a new Divine Wind that would ensure protection against foreign invasion. Until Japan's defeat in 1945, it was a comforting idea. Yet research since 2001 has revealed it to be a myth. After almost 800 years, it turns out that the Japanese were far more capable than they themselves believed. It was not the Divine Wind that saved them, but Mongol incompetence and Japanese fighting strength.

There was a bad smell about this operation from the beginning. Kublai was out of touch with reality. Like Hitler during the battle for Stalingrad, he seemed to believe that the mere decision to attack would inevitably lead to victory, as if will alone decided military matters. He overrated himself, underrated the opposition, made impossible demands, ignored logistical and command problems, and took no account of the weather, despite what had happened six years before.

To guarantee success, Kublai needed a bigger fleet than before to carry more land forces; and for that he needed the compliance of Korea, his unwilling vassal. But Korea had borne the brunt of the 1274 débâcle. Its grain had been commandeered and its young men drafted as shipbuilders and warriors, leaving only the old and the very young to till the fields. There was no harvest, and no

DISASTER IN JAPAN, 1

The Mongol force that invaded Japan in 1274 made landfall in Hakata bay, deploying explosive shells like the one below. It is shown exploding over Takezaki Suenaga and his wounded horse, an incident in the Invasion Scrolls commissioned by Suenaga to commemorate his role in defending his homeland. The scrolls also portray Suenaga in other acts of bravado, before a storm ended Kublai's first attempt at invasion.

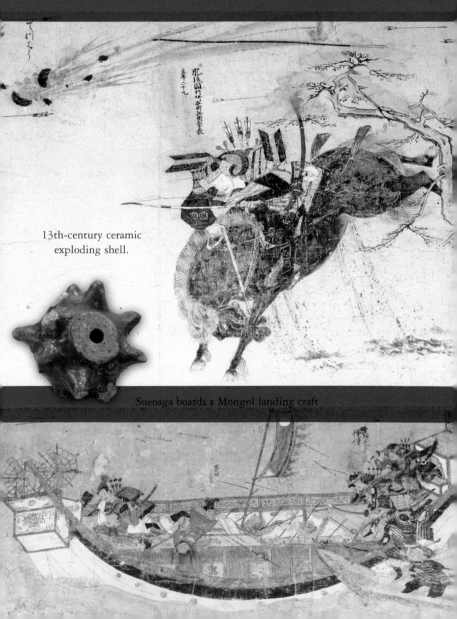

13th-century ceramic exploding shell.

Suenaga boards a Mongol landing craft

Disaster in Japan, 2

By 1281, when Kublai launched his second invasion, the Japanese had built a wall round Hakata bay, as the Invasion Scrolls show (*above*), and as visitors to Fukuoka can see for themselves today (*above left*).

Kozaki bay (*below*), Takashima Island, where the anchor-stock and seal were found.

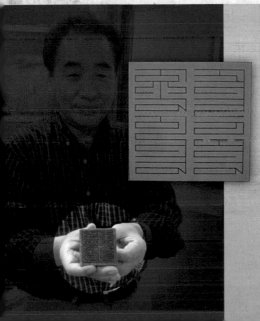

The wall was never tested. The fleets' rendezvous was off Takashima island, where a typhoon struck. The difficult work of raising and cataloguing the detritus of shattered ships is led by Kenzo Hayashida (*left*). He is holding a copy of a famous seal in the script devised by Phags-pa (*inset*), the first hard evidence that the fleets' remains lie scattered on the ocean bed off Takashima. It reads in Chinese: 'Seal of Army Commander.' His thousands of finds include the granite crosspiece, or 'stock' of an anchor which, when restored (*far left*), weighs a tonne.

THE WORLD'S MOST POWERFUL MAN GROWS OLD – AND FAT

In a contemporary portrait of Kublai out hunting, the bulky 65-year-old khan, swathed in ermine, looks off-screen at something pointed out by a courtier. His wife Chabi is beside him. The artist, Liu Kuan-tao, was a court painter famous for his realistic and intimate images – unlike the anonymous artist who painted the khan's portrait (*below*) a few years earlier in the bland style favoured by the Song court. He also portrayed Chabi (*right*), giving her the wooden-framed headdress, or *bogt*, worn by upper-class Mongol married women.

In the West, Legends of Wealth and Cruelty

Kublai became known in Europe mainly thanks to Marco Polo. Kublai helped him return by giving him a passport (*above*), or *paiza* (*inset*). The *paiza* is almost true to life, but Kublai and his minister are shown in western dress, with Kublai wearing a hat in the style of a Byzantine emperor. But his reputation for wealth and pomp was at odds with that of the Mongols themselves, whose invasion of Europe in 1236–41 turned them into murderous barbarians in western eyes (*below*). Possibly, some hint of Phags-pa's script indirectly influenced Giotto's design on the hem of a Roman cloak (*top right*).

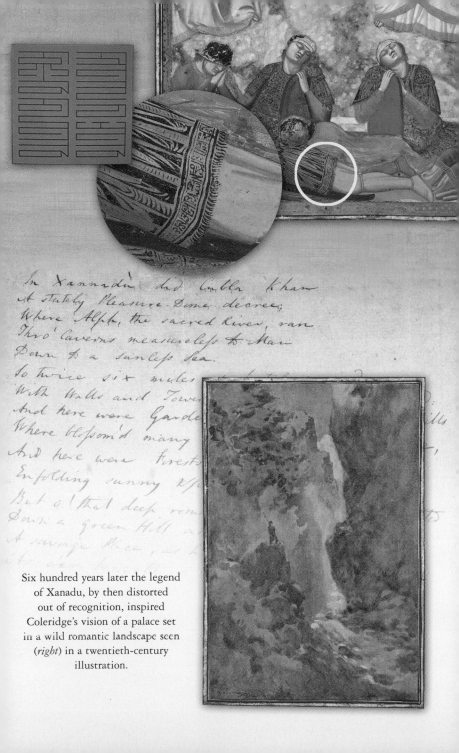

In Xannadu did Cubla Khan
A stately Pleasure-Dome decree;
Where Alph, the sacred River, ran
Thro' Caverns measureless to Man
Down to a sunless Sea.
So twice six miles
With Walls and Towers
And here were Garde
Where blossom'd many
And here were Forests
Enfolding sunny
But o! that deep rom
Down a green Hill
A savage Place,

Six hundred years later the legend
of Xanadu, by then distorted
out of recognition, inspired
Coleridge's vision of a palace set
in a wild romantic landscape seen
(*right*) in a twentieth-century
illustration.

A Secret Burial on a Sacred Mountain

Kublai is buried near his grandfather, Genghis, somewhere on the flanks of Burkhan Khaldun (Khan Khenti), the great ridge in the Khenti Mountains, some 200km east of the Mongolian capital Ulaanbaatar. Though the only way into this remote region is a track along the Kherlen and Bogd rivers, the sacred mountain draws pilgrims who build shrines (*ovoos*) of firs or stones, drape silk scarves (*khatags*), hang prayer flags and leave offerings. One place of worship on the way to the summit is a flat area where Kublai's grandson Kamala built a temple, which has now vanished (*bottom left*). Another, higher up, is a rocky plateau (*bottom right*) with a stunning view over the Bogd river.

manpower. For five years, Kublai had had to send food aid to keep Korea alive; it was in no condition to provide all the necessary ships. Most would have to come from the south, from the former Song empire and its unwilling inhabitants.

It would be simple, of course, if only Japan would acknowledge his overlordship. In 1279 yet another embassy arrived in Japan, with instructions to be extremely polite, in order to avoid the fate of their predecessors. Unfortunately, they arrived just at the moment when rumours were spreading fear across the land. A local beauty had vanished in mysterious circumstances, supposedly abducted by a band of Mongol spies who had made a base on an uninhabited rocky islet. It was said their chief had fallen in love with the girl. A Japanese force had invaded to rescue her. The chief had dragged her to a cliff-top and threatened to kill her, but she had cast herself into the sea and had swum to shore, while all the Japanese were murdered by the Mongol spies. She alone had survived to tell this dramatic tale. So the story went. It may or may not have been true; in any event, the government in Kamakura believed that the three-man delegation from Kublai was part of the same plot. It didn't help the envoys' case that Kublai had sent as a gift a golden cockerel engraved with the insulting words: 'To Hojo Tokimune: I will appoint thee King of Japan,' implying he would be happy to usurp the emperor. The three were beheaded, and resolve strengthened. Foot soldiers and cavalry massed on Kyushu. The barrier around Hakata bay grew longer and higher, and defences arose at other possible landing sites – Nagato on the southern tip of the main island; Harima and Tsuruga, 400 kilometres up the same coast. Japan braced itself for an assault that was now seen as inevitable.

Kublai ordered that the fleet should be ready to invade in little more than a year. If the figures are to be believed, it would be the biggest fleet ever to set sail, and would remain the biggest for over 700 years, until exceeded by the Allied invasion of Normandy on 6 June (D-Day) 1944. It would combine two forces, one from Korea with a Korean admiral and the other from south China under a turncoat Chinese, Fan Wen-hu – one of those who had defected to the Mongols during their advance down the Yangtze in 1275 – with a Mongol co-leader, Xin-du. They led a force of about 140,000. According to the *Yuan History*, the Koreans supplied 900 boats, with another 3,500 supposedly coming from the south. The pressure was too much for one area, Fukien (now Fujian), whose trade superintendent had been told to build 200 ships: this, he said, was impossible, and provided 50. The plan was for the troops to be transported in two fleets, 40,000 in the 900 ships from Korea, 100,000 in the 3,500 vessels from Quanzhou in Fukien. The two would link up at the island of Iki, 30 kilometres off the Japanese coast, and then invade the mainland together.

That was the plan. But there's something significant about these figures, which reveals that this plan was highly optimistic. Consider the number: 4,400 is an awful lot of ships, especially if they were warships, as accounts usually suggest. In fact, a little long division shows that this invasion was very unlike the Spanish Armada of 1588, which consisted of 130 massive warships, carrying 27,000 men, about 200 per ship. Kublai's fleet was more comparable to the Allied force that invaded Normandy in 1944: some 156,000 men in around 5,000 vessels (most of which were landing craft), which is 31 per vessel . . .

At which point we should pause and ask: are the figures about Kublai's fleet true? No-one has any idea, because there are no statistics other than the official sources. All estimates should be treated with extreme scepticism. But in this case they are not incredible. Kublai had access to huge numbers of ships that had been massed for the assault on Song down the Yangtze. Only a few years before, the official sources were speaking of a fleet of 3,000, and that was on the Yangtze alone. Since then, all Song, and all its remaining ships, had fallen to the Mongols. Look at it from another angle: Spain in 1588 could muster 27,000 men from a population of about 7 million: a proportion of 1 man-at-arms per 260 civilians. The population of thirteenth-century China was about 50 million. Proportionally, China could have raised a naval force of 189,000, more than enough to justify the official figures.

If we accept that the southern force was indeed something like 140,000, the implication is clear. Except for a few massive warships, mainly from Korea, what we are dealing with here is a fleet of small landing craft. Now, Portsmouth to Normandy is a mere 170 kilometres, a six-hour crossing by engine-driven ships. When bad weather struck on 2 June, Eisenhower could afford to postpone the invasion by one day, and then order Go! in a 24-hour lull. Kublai would be relying on wind power and oars to propel his 900-strong Korean fleet over 200 kilometres and the 3,500 much smaller vessels from the south over a forbidding 1,400 kilometres. Even with a good wind in the right direction, it would take them six days to reach the rendezvous.

Obviously, Kublai and his commanders aimed to get the conquest over, and have the troops well inland, before the typhoon season started in August. But any experienced sailor would have known in his heart of hearts that it was crazy to plan on a fixed schedule of operations. Kublai, the supreme commander, knew a lot about warfare in large, open spaces, and was perfectly at home wheeling across the Inland Sea, as the Chinese called the gravel and grass of Inner Asia. But he had hardly ever glimpsed the real sea, let alone sailed it, let alone seen what a typhoon could do. Blinded by desperation and isolated by power, he was taking a fearful risk, and there was no-one to tell him the truth.

There were those who sensed trouble ahead. When Yuan officials learned that the Japanese emperor had prayed that the country be saved in exchange for his own life, they reported omens: Mongol soldiers waiting to make the crossing 'saw a great serpent appearing on the surface of the water, and the water smelled of sulphur'. But in Kublai's presence, mouths were buttoned.

Things went wrong from the start. The Korean fleet reached Iki as planned around the end of May, and waited . . . and waited. The southern fleet gathered in Quanzhou could not even start on time. A commander fell ill, and had to be replaced. Food rotted in the heat. Epidemics spread. Even when it did finally put to sea, contrary winds drove many ships into ports along the coast.

Eventually, on 10 June, the commander of the Korean fleet occupied Iki anyway; then, after waiting another two weeks, he crossed the small gap and made a landing just north of the Japanese wall at Munakata, only to be forced back to an island in the middle of the bay. He therefore had ample opportunity to recce Hakata bay and confirm the reports he would surely have had from other sources about the defensive wall; after all, it had been there for the past five years. He would have seen the difficulty of fighting his way off the beach, and seen a solution. The wall covered the beach, not the mountains at either end. Genghis had gone over mountains when he took the pass leading to Beijing in 1213. These mountains were nothing by comparison. The Mongols would simply force their way round the edge of the wall, and take it from the rear – the only problem being that they would be highly visible, and strongly opposed. They needed more troops. The Korean fleet could not do the job on its own.

Meanwhile the southern fleet, now a month behind schedule, went straight for the mainland, missing out on Iki and the rendezvous at sea, settling instead for the hilly little island of Takashima in Imari bay, 100 kilometres west of Hakata, the other side of a peninsula. Here they intended to regroup, replenish stores and mount the invasion proper. Now, Takashima will play an important role in this story, so let me introduce it. Takashima – Kite Island – is a pretty place, warm, fertile, famous for its blowfish: *fugu*, a delicacy that has to be carefully prepared because bits of it are deadly poisonous. Though most of its irregular coast offers only steep slopes and rocky bottoms, it has one small harbour where the sea-floor is muddy and shallow – good for holding the wood-and-stone Mongol anchors, with their granite cross-pieces and wooden flukes. Takashima had a few hundred inhabitants, peaceful farmers and fisherfolk utterly unable to resist the Mongol invasion. In a few days, all were slaughtered, right down (so the story goes) to the last family, whose hiding place was revealed by their cockerels. The sole survivor was one old lady who lived to tell the tale. Even today, I was assured, the people of Takashima do not keep cockerels.

It was not a good plan. Takashima is only a kilometre offshore, but the coast here is steep and backed by forested mountains, ideal for guerrilla warfare. Away from Hakata bay, landing places were few, and at every undefended place Japanese cavalry soon arrived to isolate the soldiers and force the ships back out to sea; all they could do was set up a few useless camps on outlying islands. The Japanese also took the fight out from the shore, rowing nimble little skiffs out at night to cut cables, sneak aboard, cut throats and start fires. True, from the larger ships, siege bows acted like artillery, firing massive arrows that could splinter a Japanese dinghy. But the traction trebuchets which might have been effective inshore against land forces were useless when trying to hit moving targets from moving decks. Kublai's generals bickered in three languages and the greater part of their troops – the Chinese and Koreans – had no heart to fight for their new Mongol masters. The Japanese, with a unified command and years of preparation on home territory behind them, had well-fortified positions from which to stave off assaults and mount counter-attacks.

From the Mongol point of view, the Japanese were everywhere, in huge numbers, well able to cover the 20-kilometre length of the wall and beyond, galloping back and forth to congregate wherever a landing threatened. One Yuan source later claimed there were 102,000 of them. But Mongol and Chinese officials were recording a catastrophic defeat and had every reason to exaggerate the strength of the opposition to provide an excuse for failure. Besides, numbers of troops were always, notoriously, exaggerated, sometimes by a factor of ten. A twelfth-century courtier had his servants count an army estimated at 10,000, and found the true number of troops to be 1,080.[1] In this case, historians have made estimates based on duty reports and other documents, which have survived in considerable numbers. The result of two such surveys overlap, with lows of 2,300 and 3,600, highs of 5,700 and 6,000. Now, these figures are based on surviving written sources; many others must have gone missing, and the estimates must be too low. From a population of something like 5 million, the Japanese commanders would surely have been able to muster men in the same proportion as the Spanish in 1588 or indeed their current Mongol and Chinese enemies, which would suggest a force in the order of 20,000 – making about one defender per metre of wall.

There were enough, in any event, to hold back the Mongols, Chinese and Koreans, whose huge superiority in numbers was negated by the difficulty of mounting a joint sea-and-land operation so far from home and by their being hopelessly scattered.

For almost two months, from 23 June to 14 August, the two sides skirmished, reaching no conclusion. The wall was never even tested in battle. The sight of it was enough to put off the Korean fleet, and the joint force never had a chance to approach.

* * *

[1] William Wayne Farris, *Heavenly Warriors: The Evolution of Japan's Military, 500–1300*, quoted in Thomas D. Conlan (trans. and interpretive essay), *In Little Need of Divine Intervention: Scrolls of the Mongol Invasions of Japan*.

Among those eager to fight was Takezaki Suenaga, whose story continues in the Invasion Scrolls. Suenaga arrives on his horse in full regalia as warriors take up position behind the wall (which appears in one of the illustrations, looking much as its restored sections do today). The enemy are all out at sea. He's desperate to get at them.

'I cannot fight them during this crisis without a ship!'

Gota Goro, his commander, replies: 'If you don't have a ship there's nothing to be done.'

But another *gokenin*, from Hizen – 'I forget his name' – says: 'Let's find a good ship among the damaged craft in the harbour and drive off the pirates!'

'That's right,' Suenaga replies. 'Those troops would be infantry and their boats would be seaworthy craft. I want to cut down at least one of the enemy!'

Suenaga and two companions search for a boat. No luck. As they are on the point of giving up hope, a Japanese war-boat comes by. These war-boats are not impressive: about 8 metres long, riding low in the water, holding no more than ten or eleven people, half of whom are rowers. They are handy for use in the bay, but would be hopeless on the open sea. Gota Goro recognizes this one as belonging to Adachi Yasumori, a senior official, and sends Suenaga and his friends off as messengers. They board a messenger's skiff and row out to the larger vessel. Standing precariously at the bow, Suenaga yells that he has orders to get on board the next boat and fight. Then, without waiting for permission, he jumps aboard.

The captain, Kotabe, is outraged. 'This is the summoned boat [of Adachi]! Only members of his forces can board it! Stay off this boat!'

Suenaga argues. 'In this vital matter I want to aid my

lord. Since I just got on the boat, I am not going to get off and wait for another that may never arrive.'

He makes no impression on the captain. 'It is an outrage for you not to leave a boat when you have been ordered to disembark.'

Suenaga unhappily climbs back into his skiff, and he and his companions row onwards. Another war-boat comes by, this one belonging to an official called Takamasa. Suenaga brings his skiff alongside, though the effort makes him remove his helmet, which gets lost in the chaos. This time Suenaga takes no chances. He comes out with a barefaced lie.

'I am acting on secret orders. Let me on the boat.'

Shouts come from Takamasa's boat: 'You have no orders! Get out of here! There's no room for all of you!'

Suenaga is utterly shameless. Now he tries another tack. 'Since I am a warrior of considerable stature,' he boasts, 'let me alone get on your boat.'

That does the trick. 'We are heading off for battle,' comes the exasperated reply. 'Why must you make such a fuss to Takamasa? Get on!'

He does so, grabbing the shin-guards of one of his companions as a make-shift helmet. Shouts of complaint from the skiff below. But Suenaga ignores them. 'The way of the bow and arrow is to do what is worthy of reward,' he says in the commentary. 'Without even a single follower I set off to engage the enemy.'

He starts to offer advice to Takamasa himself. 'The enemy won't give up until we board them. We have to use grappling-hooks. Once we have them hooked, stab them by impaling them where there is a joint in their armour.' But Takamasa's crew are not properly armed. Nor, come to think of it, is Suenaga. He spots a retainer who has just taken off his helmet, a nice one, braided with yellow and white cords decorated with small cherry blossoms.

'Give me your helmet,' Suenaga says, rather abruptly.

'Sorry. I have a wife and children. What of them if I get killed because of you?'

'Give it to me!'

'Sorry, no. Only I or my lord wears this helmet.'

Suenaga accepts, with pretty bad grace, and prepares for action, making do with his shin-guard helmet and throwing away some of his arrows to lighten his load.

Now the pictures take over. Somehow, Suenaga and five companions have found another punt-like skiff and attacked a Mongol ship, one of the small vessels, only about 10 metres long, with seven Mongol crew and a couple of Chinese officers – hardly the sort of boat to cross a few hundred kilometres of open ocean. Suenaga is first on board, in the bow already. One officer lies dead, his throat cut, and our hero is busy slitting the other's, gripping him by his pigtail, even as his companions are storming the stern. Shortly the boat will be theirs, because a later illustration shows Suenaga with his two heads.

That's the action he wishes to record. Somehow, he returns to shore with his trophy-heads. He reports his deeds to his commander, Gota Goro, whose disapproval at Suenaga's wilfulness is overwhelmed by admiration. 'Without your own boat, you repeatedly lied in order to join the fray. You really are the *baddest* man around!'

On 15 August nature stepped in, with rather more than the 'reverse wind' of 1274. The first typhoon of the season approached, earlier than usual. Nowadays, when tropical cyclones – hurricanes in the Atlantic, typhoons in the

Pacific – are named and tracked, their destructive power is a commonplace of news programmes. But to see news footage is not the same as feeling the force. There's no telling whether this particular typhoon ranked as a mere No. 1 on the Saffir–Simpson Scale ('74–95 mph/119–153 kph. Damage limited to foliage, signage, unanchored boats and mobile homes') or a No. 5 super-typhoon ('winds of over 150 mph/249 kph. Complete roof failure . . . catastrophic storm surge damage'). To sailors in small boats, it wouldn't make much difference.

Joseph Conrad, a China hand in his youth, lived through one of these storms, and there is no better evocation of what it is like than his *Typhoon*. Here the storm strikes the *Nan-Shan*, with the stolid Macwhirr as captain, and young Jukes as first mate:

> A faint burst of lightning quivered all round, as if flashed into a cavern – into a black and secret chamber of the sea, with a floor of foaming crests.
>
> It unveiled for a sinister, fluttering moment a ragged mass of clouds hanging low, the lurch of the long outlines of the ship, the black figures of men caught on the bridge, heads forward, as if petrified in the act of butting. The darkness palpitated down upon all this, and then the real thing came at last.
>
> It was something formidable and swift, like the sudden smashing of a vial of wrath. It seemed to explode all round the ship with an overpowering concussion and a rush of great waters, as if an immense dam had been blown up to windward. In an instant the men lost touch of each other. This is the disintegrating power of a great wind: it isolates one from one's kind. An earthquake, a landslip, an avalanche, overtake a man incidentally, as it were –

without passion. A furious gale attacks him like a personal enemy, tries to grasp his limbs, fastens upon his mind, seeks to rout his very spirit out of him.

Jukes was driven away from his commander ... The rain poured on him, flowed, drove in sheets. He breathed in gasps; and sometimes the water he swallowed was fresh and sometimes it was salt. For the most part he kept his eyes shut tight, as if suspecting his sight might be destroyed in the immense flurry of the elements ... After a crushing thump on his back he found himself suddenly afloat and borne upwards. His first irresistible notion was that the whole China Sea had climbed on the bridge. Then, more sanely, he concluded himself gone overboard. All the time he was being tossed, flung, and rolled in great volumes of water, he kept on repeating mentally, with the utmost precipitation, the words: 'My God! My God! My God! My God!' ...

The motion of the ship was extravagant. Her lurches had an appalling helplessness: she pitched as if taking a header into a void, and seemed to find a wall to hit every time. When she rolled she fell on her side headlong, and she would be righted back by such a demolishing blow that Jukes felt her reeling as a clubbed man reels before he collapses. The gale howled and scuffled about gigantically in the darkness, as though the entire world were one black gully. At certain moments the air streamed against the ship as if sucked through a tunnel with a concentrated solid force of impact that seemed to lift her clean out of the water and keep her up for an instant with only a quiver running through her from end to end. And then she would begin her tumbling again as if dropped back into a boiling cauldron ...

The sea, flattened down in the heavier gusts, would

uprise and overwhelm both ends of the *Nan-Shan* in snowy rushes of foam, expanding wide, beyond both rails, into the night. And on this dazzling sheet, spread under the blackness of the clouds and emitting a bluish glow, Captain MacWhirr could catch a desolate glimpse of a few tiny specks black as ebony, the tops of the hatches, the battened companions, the heads of the covered winches, the foot of a mast. This was all he could see of his ship. Her middle structure, covered by the bridge which bore him, his mate, the closed wheelhouse where a man was steering shut up with the fear of being swept overboard together with the whole thing in one great crash – her middle structure was like a half-tide rock awash upon a coast. It was like an outlying rock with the water boiling up, streaming over, pouring off, beating round – like a rock in the surf to which shipwrecked people cling before they let go – only it rose, it sank, it rolled continuously, without respite and rest, like a rock that should have miraculously struck adrift from a coast and gone wallowing upon the sea.

The *Nan-Shan* was being looted by the storm with a senseless, destructive fury: trysails torn out of the extra gaskets, double-lashed awnings blown away, bridge swept clean, weather-cloths burst, rails twisted, light-screens smashed – and two of the boats had gone already. They had gone unheard and unseen, melting, as it were, in the shock and smother of the wave.

Now imagine that striking wooden sailing ships: not just the warships, which would have been built for storms, but the 3,000 or more little 20- or 30-man craft that came from the south. The Korean sailors knew what was coming. Their admiral ordered his fleet out to sea to avoid being dashed on the rocks. Those who could boarded in order not to be stranded ashore. Many were still clambering aboard or struggling through the shallows when the storm struck. Some 15,000 of the northern force and 50,000 of the southerners died at sea, while hundreds of others perished at Japanese hands, or were tossed to their deaths in the small boats that had remained near the rocky shore.

It was a catastrophe never matched in scale on a single day at sea before or since, and never on land either until the atom bomb destroyed Hiroshima, killing 75,000 at a single blow, in 1945.

No wonder the Japanese soon saw it as an act of the gods, and adopted the idea of divine protection from then on. Both court and military authorities prayed assiduously to keep foreigners at bay. Temples and shrines flourished. Even Suenaga, whose élan had been so evident, ascribed his success as 'a man of the bow and arrow' to the gods. Not that prayer was the only defence, for the wall was maintained and manned constantly for the next 30 years, as a result of which some of it has lasted pretty well to the present day. But the idea of divine intervention became rooted in Japanese culture. Few questioned the conclusion: that Japan had been saved by a divinely ordained typhoon.

Yet there is growing evidence that this was not so; that in reality Japan's salvation was down to the Japanese themselves. It is there in Suenaga's story. Look at his fighting spirit. He's brave, eager to take a risk, but well in control of himself. Although the epitome of the Japanese warrior, he's one among many. There's a terrific sense of common purpose. And it works. He's on the winning side.

There's the usual chaos of war, no overall strategy, but all these unco-ordinated actions by individuals are enough to hold back the enemy and take the action to them, out in the bay. Crucially, there is no mention of the typhoon at all. In the Invasion Scrolls, success is down to the Japanese fighters. Suenaga shows respect to the gods with prayers, but there is no hint in either the written account or the pictures that Heaven actually intervenes during or after the action.

Text and pictures together show that, as Conlan puts it, 'the notion of the "divine winds" represented a function of the medieval mindset, which emphasised otherworldly causality, rather than a caustic commentary on the ineptitude of the Japanese defenders, as has commonly been assumed'. He concludes: 'The warriors of Japan were capable of fighting the Mongols to a standstill.' Suenaga and his fellow-fighters were, in the words of Conlan's title, in little need of divine intervention.

Further support comes from marine archaeologists as they try to answer the question: What happened to the armada? Understandably, this is not a subject on which the Chinese records have much to say. The flagship, bearing the admiral, Fan Wen-hu, and a general, Chang Xi, was wrecked on Takashima. The two mustered other survivors, a couple of thousand of them, who raided the houses and farms of the slaughtered locals for food and repaired one of the wrecks, in which the admiral limped home. The others were mopped up by Japanese, some 1,500 being taken away into slavery. Three were allowed to return, to tell Kublai of the fate of his great armada and its all-conquering army. As for the rest of the fleet, it seemed to have vanished from history and into the belly of the ocean.

Not quite. The story of the victory over the Mongols became part of the Japanese nationalist revival in the 1930s; that was when restoration work first started on the wall around Hakata bay. After the war, a Tokyo University archaeologist, Torao Mozai, began wondering about Kublai's fleet. In the bay, fishermen had found a few anchor-stocks – the great stone cross-pieces that weighed down the anchors and twisted them into the correct position – but these might have come from any one of uncounted ships that had sunk over the centuries. In 1980 he decided to focus on Takashima, where the southern fleet had set up a base, and where it may therefore have sought anchorage to ride out the typhoon. Fishermen showed Mozai a few enigmatic bits of pottery they had found over the years.

Then, suddenly, hard evidence. In 1974 a fisherman, alerted by Mozai's interest, produced something he had dragged up with his clams off the pretty little south-facing harbour of Kazaki: a small square of bronze with a handle on the back and writing engraved on the front in the script devised by Kublai's Tibetan mentor, Phags-pa. It was in Chinese, and it read: 'Seal of Commander of One Thousand'. A Chinese character on the top indicated it was made in 1277. No doubt about it: the remains of one of Kublai's senior officers lay in these murky shallows – and so, probably, did those of his ship. (This little object has since become an iconic symbol of the event and the archaeological research, reproduced in brochures and replicas. The original is in Fukuoka's Kyushu National Museum, which opened in October 2005.)

Inspired, Mozai established a research programme, surveying the sea-bed with sonar and sending down divers. In the mud they found swords, spearheads, stone hand-mills for grinding rice, more anchor-stocks and round stone catapult balls: direct proof that the Mongols had catapults on board.

But Mozai was operating on a shoe-string. His finds were dramatic enough to win backing from the *National Geographic* magazine (see bibliography), but the research needed to be put on a sound, long-term, professional basis. Enter Kenzo Hayashida, newly returned from doing an MA in archaeology – bronze age Greece, of all things – at the University of Pennsylvania. There was no opening in southern Japan for a specialist in Greek archaeology; but there, right on his doorstep, was the possibility of solving one of the great mysteries of Japanese and Chinese history. He joined Mozai in 1981, inherited his role and committed himself to Takashima's silty waters, underpinning his research by working with the local education board and Fukuoka's university. In 1986 he founded the Kyushu and Okinawa Society of Underwater Archaeology, which reports annually on the findings made by him and his team of a dozen volunteer divers.

With a gentle voice and restrained manner, Hayashida has an aura of wisdom. From his half-closed eyelids and rapid blink, I thought at first he was just sleepy. Not so. First impressions gave way before his obvious intelligence and dedication. In English, through which he felt his way with care, as if along a track overgrown after 25 years back in Japan, he guided me through his work, his laboratory on Takashima and the island itself.

Everything about his researches has its problems. First – inexplicably for an island nation – Japan has no tradition, and no single university department, of marine archaeology. Funding is tight. A research project of this significance, now with its own museum, should attract an income from tourists. But – and this is the second problem – Takashima is remote, served by a charming ferry which takes 10 minutes to make the crossing. Though it will soon have a bridge, now half-completed, the island will always be out on a limb, off any tourist route. Third, conditions down in Imari bay are appalling. The bottom is several metres of mud, which swirls up at every touch, quickly reducing vision to zero, forcing a retreat until the waters clear. This is tough, expensive work.

Much of what Hayashida has on Takashima – the museum and his laboratory – he owes to a dramatic find made in 1994, 50 metres or so out from shore: first, two huge granite anchor-stocks, each 1.5 metres long and 300 kilos in weight; then the wooden anchor itself, making a massive 7-metre object weighing a tonne. Even more significant were its ropes: they were made from bamboo, they were intact, and they lay due north across the ocean floor. Further research showed that the granite came from southern China; and carbon-14 dating revealed that the anchor's oak had been cut some time before the 1281 invasion. It was not much of a leap to conclude that this was the anchor of a large Mongol vessel, some 300–400 tonnes, that had been forced northward by the typhoon and sunk, along (presumably) with its commander and his bronze seal of office. But where was the ship itself? And where were all the others?

Tantalizing finds emerged from the gloop, including massive, worm-eaten bits of bulkheads, the cross-pieces that divide large ships into watertight compartments. One of these is 7 metres long, which means the mother-ship was at least that much across – at least, because there is no way of telling which part of the bulkhead it came from, whether at the top or halfway down in the ship's hold.

Anyway, this was a big ship: at least 70 metres long, dwarfing anything else in the world. European sailing ships would not approach anything like this size until the nineteenth century. Henry V's *Grace Dieu*, the largest ship of the early fifteenth century, was paltry by comparison: 38 metres from stem to stern. Nelson's flagship *Victory* was 57 metres long, slightly exceeded by her Spanish and French equivalents. Only as the age of steam approached did the last western sailing ships exceed the dimensions of these Chinese and Korean men-o'-war.

But size was no defence against the typhoon. Perhaps the doomed commander had anchored here, in the lee of a southerly shore, in the hope that the typhoon, swirling anti-clockwise, would head past over land, delivering a glancing blow from the north. In the event, as the mooring-rope revealed, the eye of the typhoon was out at sea, and the blow came from the south, head-on across Imari bay.

Other finds followed, by the hundred, and all of them were brought to Hayashida's laboratory for cleaning. One of the most significant are six of the thundercrash bombs – *tetsahu*, 'iron bombs', as they are known in Japanese, despite the fact that they are ceramic, not iron. Some were even nastier than they looked: one, when X-rayed, was found to be filled with over a dozen metal fragments that would have made extremely effective shrapnel – direct proof that Suenaga and his friends could indeed have been bombarded with thundercrash bombs in 1274. I was the only person in Hayashida's museum that day, so an assistant opened a cupboard and handed me a couple of *tetsahus*. They made me nervous. I had been wondering about Suenaga and his narrow escape from death for months, and here I was holding the breakable, barnacle-encrusted, melon-sized devices that proved the account of the incident was true. What if, for some unfathomable reason, I dropped them? I was happy to hold them, happier to return them.

Next door, in the lab, Hayashida's staff of four minister to almost 4,000 bits, most of them lying in hundreds of tupperware containers of fresh water, where they stay for months and sometimes years until clear of all sea-water. Big tanks hold the bulkheads, little ones bits of pottery, scraps of metal, slivers of wood, bowls, even bones. On one side lie anchor-stocks, some so small they would have held mere dinghies. The prize, the one-tonne giant, is in a sealed container the job of which is to impregnate it with a preservative, polyethylene glycol (PEG). It's a painfully slow process that will take a year or two more.

The curator, Akiko Matsu, a round, bustling, enthusiastic woman, showed off some of her favourite finds: a fine celadon bowl, a helmet, a sword, a bundle of arrow-shafts, bits of a bow and a crossbow – and then, carefully packed in cotton-wool, human skulls.

'This one belonged to a young man,' said Hayashida. 'You see how the sea-water erodes the calcium. But we know from its development that he was about 20. And here, this is from an older man. Look at his teeth. These are the molars. He was in good shape, no cavities at all.'

It is too early to make sense of these finds. They are just a few pieces in a giant jigsaw created by the typhoon, and every typhoon since. What happened then and since has been like tossing 4,000 eggs into a giant blender, then scattering them over mud, then pouring more mud on the top, then trying to make sense of the mess. Four thousand ships! That's millions of bits, most of them scattered –

presumably – across the floor of Imari bay. And only 100 or so are ready for display. Hayashida is still right at the beginning, hoping for some other find that will inspire in others a passion to match his own, and allow the research to continue.

Yet it is not too early to point to some tentative conclusions. Of the pots, almost all are Chinese, not Korean, many of them from the long-established kilns at Yixing in Jiangsu. Indeed, of all the objects, a mere 20 or so are Korean – convincing evidence that the Chinese fleet bore the brunt of the damage.

How come?

What really matters for ocean-going vessels is construction. And here, it seems, there was a good deal of corner-cutting. One of Hayashida's associates, Randall Sasaki, of Texas A&M University, College Station, who has made a study of the 500 or so timber fragments, was surprised to find nail-holes that were suspiciously close together, grouped as if the builders were re-using old timbers.

There's more, from Hayashida. He showed me a square piece of timber with two holes in it. 'It's a mast-step, the bit of wood on which the mast stood, strengthened by two supports which went in these holes. But look: the holes are off-centre. This mast-step was made by someone who didn't know what he was doing.' And, as a final thought, he added: 'You know what is really odd, I think? So far, we have found no evidence of sea-going, V-shaped keels.'

These pieces of evidence, combined with the catastrophic loss of at least one large vessel that should have been able to ride out a typhoon, suggest a startling but logical conclusion: in response to Kublai's insane demands for mass building at high speed, his naval craftsmen improvised.

They took any ships available, seaworthy or not. The good ones they put into service; the poor ones they refashioned with the same materials. Except for the new ones built by the Koreans – none of which have yet been found – the vast majority of the invaders' vessels were keel-less river-boats, utterly unsuited to the high seas. Hayashida also wonders about another possibility suggested by the use of bad timbers and poor construction: was opposition to Kublai's plan so strong that workers actually engaged in sabotage? In any event, Kublai's ambitions led inexorably to a massive failure of quality control. I can almost hear the specious words of overseers by the dozen, all proudly stating that orders had been fulfilled, that the boats were all ready. No-one told the emperor that if things got rough, these boats would be death-traps.

Only about 0.5 per cent of the 1.5-square-kilometre site off Takashima has been searched, let alone the rest of Imari bay. There's surely a lot more still to find, and I would take a bet the finds will reveal more evidence of Mongol-Chinese inadequacy, backing Conlan's point that the Japanese had no need of divine intervention.

True, it was the storm that finally did for the Mongol fleet. True, the ships were poorly built, the strategy flawed. But it was Japanese resistance that denied the Mongols a beach-head. What Kublai needed was a D-Day-style landing: 100,000 troops ashore, then all the equipment – horses, catapults, siege bows and more horses – and a push inland. Instead, the spirited Japanese response delayed landings, while some, like Suenaga, took the battle to the enemy out in the bay, forcing a stalemate which the Mongols showed no sign of breaking.

Was this a campaign Kublai could have won? Frankly, I

doubt it. At best, with both fleets acting together, the result was always going to be a close-run thing. Certainly, once the southern fleet got behind schedule, the Mongols were on their way to defeat, victims of the complexity and size of the operation, internal opposition, incompetence and the fog of war. They were a long way from any base, with no back-up. As days stretched into weeks, they would have been running low on food, water and ammunition. Death or dishonourable retreat would have been the only options. The typhoon did not turn the course of the battle; it substituted a quick end for a long-drawn-out collapse. Kublai, with his insane ambitions, had in effect scuppered his own fleet before it set out.

14

MONEY, MADNESS AND A MURDER

THERE'S NOTHING LIKE A MURDER TO REVEAL HIDDEN emotions. There's nothing like an assassination to reveal a government's faults.

This story shows the beating heart of Kublai's administration. He had created a monster with a prodigious appetite for men, materials and money, and it had to be kept fed. One man seemed to have the secret, and for Kublai that was a good enough reason to ignore the hatred that spread like a plague around his power-obsessed and deeply repellent minister. For 20 years he allowed disaster to ferment, until it cooked up a melodrama more sensational than any fictional thriller, involving a suicidal fanatic, a mad monk, a farcical plot and the murder of the man at the centre of the seething brew. No wonder Marco Polo jumped on the story. But he didn't know the half of it.

*　*　*

The villain of the piece was Ahmad, an Uzbek (as we would now call him) from Banakat, a few kilometres south-west of Tashkent on the Syrdar'ya. The town was taken by Genghis at the start of his invasion of the Muslim world in 1220, the Mongols slaughtering the garrison and carrying off 'the artisans and a body of youths for siege works'.[1] That must have been about the time he was born. Perhaps his mother was captured along with the young men, because as a boy Ahmad was in the entourage of Chabi; after her marriage in 1239 to Kublai, then a prince of 24, he graduated to Kublai's household, helping with finances and military expenditures, and in this milieu he developed, in the words of his biographer Herbert Franke, a 'relentless craving for total control over government finances'.

When Kublai was enthroned in 1260, Ahmad became responsible for requisitioning provisions for the court. Driven by ambition, he rose fast. The next year he had two jobs, a senior position in the Secretariat and another as transport commissioner. He hated supervision – always a bad sign in an administrator – and asked to be made directly answerable to Kublai himself. His Chinese boss, one of the scholars who had joined Kublai when Jin fell in 1234, was a stickler for doing things through the proper channels. He objected and Kublai agreed, giving his son and heir Zhenjin (Jingim in another spelling) jurisdiction over the Secretariat. It was the first of many such attempts by Ahmad to gain ever more power, the first of many

---

[1] W. Barthold, *Turkestan Down to the Mongol Invasion*. The rest of this chapter is based on Franke's biography in Igor de Rachewiltz et al., *In the Service of the Khan: Eminent Personalities of the Early Mongol–Yüan Era (1200–1300)*.

confrontations with his colleagues, and the start of a long-running feud with Zhenjin.

Ahmad's job within the Secretariat was to increase government income, and he was never short of ideas. What if the production of iron tools in government-owned smelting works could be raised, so that the tools could be given to farmers in exchange for grain? That would increase grain reserves. What about a sales tax on silver transactions? Then merchants coming into the capital would have to produce a tax receipt. If they couldn't, they would be prosecuted for tax evasion, and have to pay a fine. What about cancelling tax exemptions for monks? And penalizing the salt-producers of Shanxi, whose cheap, low-quality stuff undercut the government's salt?

Kublai loved the result, and Ahmad prospered with a portfolio of jobs. His growing power was matched by his arrogance, and his arrogance by his unpopularity. When his bodyguards started a brawl, one of Kublai's Uighur advisers, Lien Xixian, had him prosecuted and actually beaten. It was not exactly routine, but in a world of rough-and-ready justice it was soon forgotten, and it didn't stop him. What did it matter to him if he was unpopular? Most foreign officials were, as Marco Polo recorded: 'For you should know that all Cathayans [northern Chinese] detested the Great Kaan's rule because he set over them governors who were Tartars, Saracens, or Christians who were attached to his household and devoted to his service, and were foreigners in Cathay.'

In 1266, Ahmad struck gold as head of a new Office for Regulating State Expenditure. To squeeze the last drop out of every available resource, he complained about the quality of linen here, or gold ingots there. He examined schemes for making non-flammable cloth from asbestos, and for exploiting a new silver mine better by smelting some tin from its ore. He wondered how to improve the grain supply to the troops fighting Ariq. He made sure that the empire's tax base was sound: in 1261 north China had 1.4 million tax-paying households; by 1274 it had almost two million.

Disputes around him continued: over his attempt to establish another government department to outflank the Secretariat, and over his objections to the new auditing office, the Censorate. 'Why should we have a Censorate?' he said. 'There's no reason as long as the money and grain come in!' He lost both battles, but shrugged off the outcomes as temporary setbacks. In 1270 he got his department – of State Affairs, the fourth of the great pillars of government, along with the Secretariat, the Bureau of Military Affairs and the Censorate – and also the directorship of political affairs in the Secretariat: both against the advice of senior officials, but in Kublai's eyes he had the magic touch and could do no wrong.

Then, inevitably, came another battle. Ahmad wanted the sole right to appoint his own people, undercutting the role of the Ministry of Personnel, which was controlled by the Secretariat. He appealed to Kublai, who changed the rules for him. But there was no satisfying him. Now he proposed disbanding the Secretariat itself. When two members of his own staff opposed this, he had one demoted, the other fired. In 1272 he succeeded in merging the two councils, with himself as number one, making him Kublai's top official. He had his eldest son Husain made mayor of Beijing. All complaints – there were several attempts to impeach him – were sidelined by Kublai, because nothing was allowed to get in the way of mobilizing resources to fight the Song.

When victory over Song seemed assured, Ahmad was part of the team summoned to advise on how best to exploit the new conquest. One point at issue was whether Song paper currency should be replaced by the Yuan currency. Bayan, the much-lionized commander of the southern forces, had promised there would be no change. Half Kublai's advisers agreed, arguing that such a change would undermine the new regime's credibility among the common people. The others disagreed, probably on the say-so of Ahmad, who saw profit in making the changeover. Kublai had the casting vote and went with Ahmad. The unfortunate southerners were offered a derisory exchange rate: one Yuan note for 50 Song ones.

Now Ahmad was almost supreme, having raised himself above the carefully balanced and frustrating system of Chinese government and made himself into a Middle Eastern vizier. Luckily for him, around this time several of Kublai's eminent advisers from before his enthronement died of natural causes, among them Liu Bingzhong and Yao Shu. He declared state monopolies on salt, medicinal herbs, copper tools and the sale of iron, which enabled him to manipulate their prices, on which he was able to capitalize. Another of his sons became governor of the southern capital, Hangzhou. He set up transport bureaux in each of the eleven provinces, nominating Muslims to head five of them – a slap in the face for his Chinese colleagues. He had his greatest rival, the Grand Councillor Hantum, sent off with Kublai's son Nomukhan to help put down Kaidu's rebellion in Central Asia, where both vanished for ten years as prisoners of the Golden Horde. Other critics were demoted or thrown into prison, where many died or were executed; some simply vanished, disposed of in sadistic ways, as a grisly find made after his death would suggest.

Ahmad might have got away with ruthlessness, even brutality. Corruption was another matter. He was eternally, fatally acquisitive, proposing through his associates that a property here, a jewel there, or a beautiful horse for his stud would oil the way to this or that appointment. He had a particular eye for women. In Polo's words, 'Whenever he knew of any one who had a pretty daughter, certain ruffians of his would go to the father and say, "What say you? Here is this pretty daughter of yours; give her in marriage [to Ahmad], and we will arrange for his giving such a government or such an office."' All told, according to the Persian historian Rashid ad-Din, he acquired 40 wives and 400 concubines. After his death, when his possessions were listed, he was found to have 3,758 horses, camels, oxen, sheep and donkeys.

Ahmad even took against the great Bayan, old Hundred Eyes, the conqueror of the south. When Bayan arrived to celebrate victory in Beijing, Ahmad made sure he was the first to greet him. Bayan gave him as a personal gift a jade belt-buckle, jade being Heaven's own stone, a symbol of nobility, beauty and purity. He pointed out that it was all he had, because he would not take anything from the Song treasures. This Ahmad took as a veiled criticism of his own sharp practices. He denounced Bayan to Kublai, once for stealing a jade cup, a second time for slaughtering some soldiers who had surrendered. After an examination – grossly humiliating to so eminent a general – both charges were found to be groundless.

Still Kublai remained in thrall to Ahmad's financial acumen, drive, self-confidence and plausibility. Actually, Kublai's behaviour is exactly what you would expect from a political leader. Any prime minister or president today, when confronted by scandal swirling around one of his ministers, will at once declare his full confidence in the minister concerned. On no account must anything be said publicly to give the impression of weakness or poor judgement. Only when meltdown is imminent does the leader accept the inevitable. Kublai clearly thought that he had a grip on events, that he could go on ignoring Ahmad's vices while profiting from his financial wizardry, what with the invasions of Japan and other upcoming foreign adventures to pay for.

In fact, events were about to explode out of anyone's control. A groundswell of opposition was gaining momentum. One former military officer named Zui Pin, a distinguished veteran of the Song campaign and now a senior provincial official, wrote a memo complaining that Ahmad had been empire-building by setting up 200 unnecessary government offices and appointing friends and relatives – some 700 of them, as it later emerged – to posts across the empire. Reluctantly, Kublai authorized action, and relatives were dismissed; but only to be quietly reinstated, Ahmad's Husain among them. Ahmad had his revenge, accusing Zui Pin and two colleagues of stealing grain and making unauthorized bronze seals. All three were executed in 1280.

But Ahmad had one enemy who was not so easy to handle. Kublai's son and heir Zhenjin absolutely loathed him, his existing antipathy only exacerbated by his admiration for Zui Pin: he had sent officers to save him from execution, but they arrived too late. In Ahmad's presence he tended to lose his temper. Once he punched Ahmad in the face so hard the minister couldn't open his mouth. When Kublai asked what the matter was, Ahmad muttered through clenched teeth that he had fallen off his horse. Another time, he lashed out at Ahmad in the emperor's presence, an outburst that Kublai simply ignored. Ahmad tried to gain some degree of control by proposing he set up a high court of justice that would have authority over all the princes. This was too much even for Kublai. He issued a mild rebuke, saying that he had never heard of anyone trying to censure the imperial clan.

In 1281, more scandals brought matters to a head. Two of Ahmad's protégés almost tripled the taxes in a district in Shaanxi province, from 950,000 to 2,700,000 strings of cash. An old member of the Imperial Guard wrote yet another letter condemning Ahmad for corruption and bribery, for which Ahmad had him sent off to run a provincial iron foundry. Accused of failing to fulfil his quota, he was demoted to the level of clerk; finally his property was confiscated and he was thrown in prison.

And still Kublai trusted him. Indeed, the next spring the emperor promoted him to the rank of Left Chancellor, leaving only the Right Chancellor above him in the official government hierarchy. The dreadful possibility arose that if he were not stopped he and Kublai would end up running the empire together.

Now, at last, a plot was hatched. There were two conspirators, both highly unstable characters. The driving force was Wang Zhu, a hard military man, a regimental commander so obsessed by his hatred of Ahmad that he had acquired a big brass club with which to kill him. His accomplice was a shady Buddhist monk named Gao, who claimed to be a magician. The two had met on a campaign, when Gao had cast spells that hadn't worked, then killed a man and used the corpse to fake his own suicide. He was now on the run.

In the spring of 1282 Kublai was based in Xanadu, as was usual at this season. Beijing was left to Ahmad, who, in the words of one version in the official history, 'devoted his whole energy to his avarice and his dissipation in a way which the people loathed and resented'. The plotters seized their chance, as the official history relates – in four different and often contradictory versions, which conflict again with Rashid ad-Din and Marco Polo. What follows is my attempt to make sense of the story.

The two plotters hatched a lunatic scheme, involving a crowd of a hundred or so, who would turn up at the city gates purporting to be the entourage accompanying Zhenjin, the heir apparent, who had suddenly decided to return to Beijing for a religious ceremony. It would be night-time, too dark for a quick check of who these people were. The idea was that Ahmad, galvanized by the approach of the one man he feared other than the emperor himself, would lead the way out to greet them, and that would be the moment to strike.

On 26 April Wang Zhu and Gao put the first stage of their complicated scheme into effect. They sent two Tibetan monks to the city council to announce the 'news' and tell the councillors to buy the right equipment for the ceremony. The council members were puzzled. They checked with the guards: no, no orders had been received. So where exactly was the heir apparent? The monks looked embarrassed and could not answer. Suspecting that foul play was afoot, the commander of the guard arrested them.

Next Wang Zhu put his back-up plan into action, sending a forged letter purporting to be from the heir apparent to the vice-commissioner of the Bureau of Military Affairs telling him, in effect, to go 'to my residence for further orders'. That worked. With the main guards out of the way at Zhenjin's palace, Wang Zhu hurried off to Ahmad, urging him to get all his Secretariat colleagues together to greet the 'prince'. That worked too, but only just. Ahmad sent out a small advance guard to meet the mock-prince and Wang's rent-a-crowd of horsemen, a meeting that took place some 5 kilometres out of town. The guards, of course, saw at once that the whole thing was a scam. The rebels had no alternative: they killed the guards, and proceeded.

At about 10 p.m. they gained entry to one of the city's north gates, and made their way to the west door of the prince's palace.

Here they struck a problem. The guard was ready, and highly suspicious. Where were the prince's usual out-riders? they asked. 'We beg first to see these two men, then we will open the gates.'

A pause.

The rebels backed off, worked their way around the palace in the darkness, and tried again, this time at the south door. There had been no time to rush a message across town to warn the guards. The gates opened, and the guards, fooled by another forged note from the 'prince', rushed out to act as his escort.

Now Ahmad and his entourage came out. All the new strangers dismounted, leaving the lone shadowy figure of the mock-prince on his horse. The figure called out to Ahmad. Ahmad stepped forward. Wang and a few followers were right behind him. They led him further forward, then away into the shadows, out of sight. Wang drew from his sleeve his brass club, with which he struck Ahmad a single, fatal blow.

Ahmad's number two was called next, and was killed in the same way.

Now Ahmad's retainers realized something was amiss, and yelled for help. All was sudden chaos, with guards and rebels mixed up in the dark. Gao the counterfeit prince galloped off into the darkness, arrows flew and the crowd scattered, leaving Wang begging to be arrested, certain that the nobility of his act would be recognized.

No such luck. The monk Gao was found two days later. On 1 May, both were condemned to death, along with the commander of the city guard.

Before the axe fell, Wang cried out: 'I, Wang Zhu, now die for having rid the world of a pest! Another day someone will certainly write my story!' The three were beheaded and quartered, a bloody end to an episode that cast doubt on Kublai's ability to judge character or control events.

It was the commander of the Beijing guard who brought the news personally to Kublai, covering some 500 kilometres in a non-stop gallop, changing horses along the post road. It took him two days to reach the emperor in a temporary camp at Tsagaan Nur (White Lake), about 170 kilometres north of Xanadu, where, as Marco Polo says, he was enjoying spring on the grasslands, 'a-hawking with his gerfalcons' for cranes, partridges and pheasants. Kublai at once ordered a return to Xanadu, from where he sent his Vice-Commissioner for Military Affairs, Bolad, to investigate and to ensure that Ahmad had a proper state burial.

Ten days later, Bolad was back with the truth about Ahmad. Kublai flew into a rage, and turned everything upside down: 'Wang Zhu was perfectly right to kill him!' He ordered the arrest of all Ahmad's clan members and associates, right across the empire. Everything he had done was undone; everything he owned was seized.

In a cupboard investigators made a puzzling discovery: two tanned human skins 'with both ears remaining', suggesting that Ahmad had done extremely nasty things to some of his victims, followed by some weird practices. When the investigators questioned the domestic eunuch in charge of the key to the cupboard, he said he didn't know what they were for; but, he added cryptically, 'If they placed the spirit-throne on them when they practised incantations, the answer was very swift.' Whatever Ahmad had been up to, it was nothing to do with Islam. The investigators suspected some sort of cult practice, and their suspicions hardened when they found two silk scrolls painted with images of horsemen surrounding a tent brandishing their swords and aiming their bows as if attacking someone inside. What did it all mean? No-one knew. But the artist was identified and executed, just in case. These disturbing details inspired much talk of magic, which accounts for Marco Polo's remark that Ahmad 'had so wrought upon the Kaan with his sorcery that the latter had the greatest faith and reliance on everything he said'.

Wives and daughters were sent home from his harem, stolen property was returned; his slaves were freed, his herds broken up, his remaining appointees – 581 of them – dismissed. That autumn his four sons were executed, Husain, Beijing's boss, being pickled as an additional disgrace, while the body of one of his brothers was flayed. Ahmad's crimes were publicly proclaimed. Other executions followed, including that of his assistant on the Secretariat, a Muslim protégé who had provided a daughter for Ahmad's harem in exchange for an appointment.

After his murder, Ahmad had been given an official burial. Five weeks later, Kublai ordered his tomb to be opened, his corpse to be beheaded in full public view and then his remains to be thrown outside Beijing's main north gate to be consumed by dogs. As the *Yuan History* laconically reports: 'Officials, gentry and commoners assembled to look on, and expressed approval.'

15

THE LIMITS TO GROWTH

I WONDER WHAT DROVE THE TWO OF THEM, GENGHIS AND HIS grandson Kublai. I think a psychoanalyst would say that both were driven by the same deep sense of insecurity. Genghis had been an outcast as a child, and seemed to have spent the rest of his life building security on a gargantuan scale. Kublai inherited what his grandfather had achieved, but because he was never fully accepted by traditionalist Mongols, his grandfather's people, at a deep level he never felt at ease. Luckily for their subjects, both had extraordinary leadership talents, which they used to push the bounds of empire as far as possible. Genghis did not live long enough to come up against any limits. But Kublai did, and the discovery of them was a shock. Behind all the trappings of greatness, I think there was a spoiled child stamping and refusing to take no for an answer.

Of course, it was all dressed up in ideology. To bring

China's millions into the empire was an astonishing achievement, but it was still just one more step towards the realization of that ultimate ambition: to have the world acknowledge his divinely ordained supremacy. It was this drive that lay behind Kublai's determination to expand. There was no threat to be countered, no strategic reason for conquest. It simply had to be done, period. Hence Japan; and hence four other adventures – Burma, Vietnam, Burma again and Java – which revealed how vain this ambition was. He might as well have aimed for the moon. Every adventure should have taught him that he had reached his limits; he refused to learn. Every setback made him more determined to repair the tattered mantle of invincibility, and every effort tore it more. He would go obstinate to the grave.

Hard as it seems to believe, he was even bent on attacking Japan again. In 1283 he ordered southern merchants to build 500 new ships, and two years later commissioned another 200 from the Jürchens in Manchuria. From the Koreans he demanded rice to feed the armies he proposed to send. Only in 1286 did his advisers manage to persuade him to drop the idea, because by then he was deeply embroiled elsewhere.

By the time of the second Japan débâcle, there were long-established links with most of the neighbouring peoples. Trade vessels had gone back and forth. An envoy had come from Annam (today's North Vietnam) in 1265. But trade and envoys were not enough. What Kublai wanted was recognition of his supremacy, the proof of which was tribute. And it was inevitable that he would want such recognition from Burma, because it abutted Yunnan, technically part of China since the Mongol invasion – headed, remember, by Kublai himself – in

1253. Yunnan had been left to its own devices with just a small garrison for 20 years, until in 1273 it acquired its first high-level administrator, Saiyid Ajall, the Turkmen from Bukhara whose grandfather had surrendered to Genghis in 1220. With Yunnan now brought fully into the empire, Kublai decided to send three envoys to demand Burma's submission.

Burma was not about to comply. The king, Narathihipate, was ruler of a considerable kingdom founded two centuries before by the Burmese, who had migrated into the Irrawaddy's tropical lowlands from the Yunnan highlands, absorbing the rich culture of the indigenous Mons. From their new nation, which they called Mranma (hence today's Myanmar), the Burmese reached out to Sri Lanka, India, Cambodia, Indonesia and China. With Pagan as its capital, it was prosperous, stable, the proud owner of myriad temples – 5,000 in Pagan alone – that glorified its Buddhist faith. To be told to offer tribute to China was an intolerable insult, especially as the message came from an area the Burmese believed had once been theirs. Added to pride, however, was insecurity. Burma had suffered uprisings and religious schism in the previous century, and the great age of temple-building was over.

Narathihipate was not the man to put things right. He was no true heir to the throne, having seized it by force. His people despised him, calling him 'King Dog's Dung'. Arbitrary and brutal, he kept a close eye on his 3,000 concubines. When he discovered that a favourite had plotted to assassinate him with poison, he had her put in a cage and burned. He wasted resources on an immense pagoda, the Mingalazedi, one of the last of Pagan's great temples – to which, being extremely nervous of assassins, he had a tunnel built from his palace. The pagoda's soft, pinkish bricks, much admired for the way they glowed at sunset, form a huge square-based pyramid on which an inscription records the king's boast that he was 'supreme commander of a vast army, the swallower of 300 dishes of curry daily' – though he wasn't referring to himself alone; he kept his sons and their families in the palace as well in case they turned against him. A Burmese proverb pretty much sums up his achievement: 'The Pagoda is finished, the great country ruined.'

When Kublai's envoys arrived, the king might have placated and negotiated; instead, he threw Kublai's demands back in his face, executing the envoys and then sending a force into the Thai buffer-state of Kaungai, thus virtually guaranteeing invasion.

For the next four years Kublai was otherwise engaged, conquering Song. In 1277 came action. To head the campaign, Kublai chose Saiyid's son Nasir al-Din, who had been helping his father set up Yunnan's administration. What followed was described by Marco Polo (who must have picked up the details later) with his usual admixture of fact and hyperbole.

The Burmese, with 200 war-elephants, had advanced against the invaders over the border along the high valleys, with their steep, forested sides, that lead to what is now the town of Baoshan. Blocking their path were Nasir al-Din's 12,000 men, their backs against a forest slope. Few of the Mongols had seen elephants. Certainly the horses hadn't. When spurred to advance, they refused. So Nasir al-Din ordered his men to dismount, approach on foot and use their bows. A single arrow won't have much effect on an elephant, but hundreds did, as Marco Polo noted:

Understand that when the elephants felt the smart of those arrows that pelted them like rain, they turned tail and fled, and nothing on earth would have induced them to turn and face the Tartars. So off they sped with such a noise and uproar that you would have trowed the world was coming to an end. And then too they plunged into the wood and rushed this way and that, dashing their castles against the trees, bursting their harness and smashing and destroying everything that was on them.

And destroying everything in their path, including the unfortunate Burmese infantry.

Now the cavalry came into its own, as Polo relates with the zest of a medieval epic poet, describing blows dealt and taken with sword and mace, arms and legs hewn off, and many a wounded man held down among the dead by the sheer weight of numbers. The Burmese fled, the Mongols pursued, using enemy mahouts taken prisoner to capture elephants. 'The elephant is an animal that hath more wit than any other; but in this way at last they were caught, more than 200 of them. And it was from this time forth that the Great Kaan began to keep numbers of elephants.'

Well, probably not 200, because Nasir al-Din, content with his victory, arrived back at Xanadu in July 1279 with just 12 elephants, having walked them over 2,000 kilometres cross-country. It was a victory, of a sort, for the king had fled down the Irrawaddy, earning himself another derogatory nickname: Tarokpliy Man, 'The King Who Ran Away from the Chinese'. But the climate was hellish, disease rampant and Nasir al-Din's troops far from home. All he did after the battle was tally up the households in the area (110,200 of them) and set up some postal stations. There was no conquest of Burma yet; this was unfinished business.

Then there was the matter of Vietnam – or rather, the matters, plural, for in the thirteenth century Vietnam was two kingdoms, Annam (in the north) and Champa. On the assumption that these realms, too, were already an un-acknowledged part of his empire, Kublai gave them both a chance to say so: in person, or by providing population registers that would prove useful for raising taxes and labour, or by delivering young relatives to act as proof of good intentions – that is, in effect, hostages. Annam sent some gifts, nothing more. In 1279 Champa sent an elephant, a rhinoceros and some jewellery. Next time, said Kublai, the king should come in person. In 1280 some more gifts arrived, but no king. It was time to insist.

Kublai placed matters in the hands of a certain Sodu, the governor in Guangzhou – Canton as it became to Europeans – the closest large port to Champa. His 5,000 troops and 100 vessels landed on the bulge of southern Vietnam, in the lagoon that led to the capital, Vijaya, now the city of Qui Nhon. They took the town, only to dis-cover that the king, Indravarman V, had headed for the hills inland. Sodu foolishly followed, convinced no doubt of quick victory in open combat. Instead, the Vietnamese became guerrillas, inflicting their own version of death by a thousand cuts. Sodu sent for reinforcements, and another 15,000 troops arrived, under Ataqai, a veteran of the Song campaign (he had been Bayan's number two in the final advance on the Song capital, Hangzhou). Yet neither he, nor further reinforcements under another veteran, Ariq-khaya, made any difference. The king remained uncaught, his troops undefeated, his guerrillas extremely effective in keeping the Mongols on edge in the forests of Champa's central highlands.

Some new strategy was called for. It was apparently Sodu's idea, which he proposed on a trip back to Xanadu: What if troops came overland, through Annam? Since Annam was supposedly a Chinese vassal, Kublai could surely send troops across his kingdom with impunity. Kublai liked the idea, and put his son, Toghan, in command, with Sodu as his number two.

But Annam had a new ruler, the third of the ruling Tran dynasty, Tran Nhan Tong; he saw the proposal as a ruse to invade, refused permission, and geared the country to defend itself, which, under Tran leadership, it could do very well. Under an elite of aristocratic officers, all males, except serfs, had to do national service, so a trained army could be called up in days. Accounts are not well sourced, but there is a ring of truth about the fervour they report. At first, the king hesitated. A protracted war would bring terrible destruction, he said to the supreme commander, Tran Hung Dao. Wouldn't it be better to lay down our arms to save the population? 'What would become of our ancestors' land, of our forefathers' temples?' the general is supposed to have replied politely. 'If you want to surrender, please have my head cut off first.' In early 1285, at a national assembly of village elders, Tran Hung Dao, already the embodiment of national resistance, put the matter to the vote: 'The enemy is strong; should we capitulate or fight?' Back came the cry: 'Fight!' But the top people were not setting a good example. The general chastised them in a proclamation much quoted as a classic of Vietnamese literature, a sort of Churchillian call to arms:

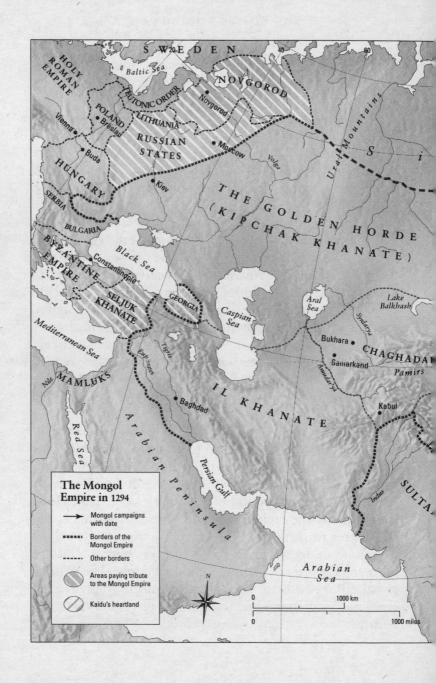

SWEDEN

Baltic Sea

NOVGOROD

HOLY
ROMAN
EMPIRE

TEUTONIC ORDER

Novgorod

LITHUANIA

POLAND

Vienna

Breslau

RUSSIAN
STATES

Moscow

Buda

Volga

Ural Mountains

S i

HUNGARY

Kiev

THE GOLDEN HORDE
(KIPCHAK KHANATE)

SERBIA

BULGARIA

Black Sea

BYZANTINE
EMPIRE

Constantinople

SELJUK
KHANATE

GEORGIA

Caspian
Sea

Aral
Sea

Lake
Balkhash

Mediterranean Sea

Syr Darya

Bukhara

CHAGHADA

Samarkand

Pamirs

Tigris

Euphrates

Amu Darya

IL KHANATE

MAMLUKS

Nile

Baghdad

Kabul

Red Sea

Arabian Peninsula

Persian Gulf

SULTA

Indus

N

Arabian
Sea

**The Mongol
Empire in 1294**

→   Mongol campaigns
     with date

▪▪▪▪ Borders of the
     Mongol Empire

---- Other borders

▨   Areas paying tribute
     to the Mongol Empire

▧   Kaidu's heartland

N

0   1000 km

0   1000 miles

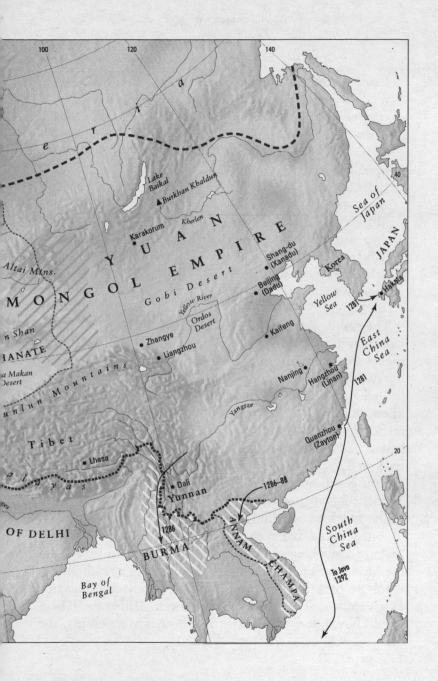

100 120 140

a

40

e r i a

Altai Mtns.

Lake
Baikal

▲ Burkhan Khaldun

Sea of
Japan

Karakorum

Kherlen

Y   U   A   N

Shang-du
(Xanadu)

Korea

JAPAN

n Shan

MONGOL EMPIRE

Gobi Desert

Beijing
(Dadu)

Yellow
Sea

Hakata

1281

HANATE

Yellow River

Ordos
Desert

Kaifeng

East
China
Sea

a Makan
Desert

unlun Mountains

Zhangye

Liangzhou

1281

Yangtze

Nanjing

Hangzhou
(Linan)

Tibet

Lhasa

a   l
y   a   s

Dali

Yunnan

Quanzhou
(Zaytoep)

20

1286–88

OF DELHI

1286

BURMA

ANNAM

South
China
Sea

CHAMPA

To Java
1292

Bay of
Bengal

I can neither eat nor sleep, my heart aches, and tears trickle from my eyes, I am enraged at being unable yet to tear the enemy to pieces, pluck out his liver and taste his blood. You who are officers and generals of our royal army ... you spend your time watching cock-fights, gambling, tending your gardens, looking after your wives and children. You are busy making money and forget about state affairs. But if the country were invaded by the Mongols, your cock's spurs would not be able to pierce their armour, your gambling tricks would not replace military strategy. You may possess immense gardens and fields but even a thousand *taels* of gold could not redeem your lives.

The people responded. Peasants called from their farms had their arms tattooed with 'Death to the Mongols!' and their banners emblazoned: 'Destroy the enemy's strength, repay the king's favour!'

Toghan, gathering an army in China's southern provinces, knew nothing of the opposition, either its spirit or its tactics. He really should have done, for the great Uriyang-kadai had taken the same route in his brief invasion back in 1257, before backing off in the face of Vietnam's intransigence and malarial heat. At first all went well. Toghan, advancing with an army reportedly of 300,000 (some speak of 500,000), a numerical superiority of two to one, forced back the Annamese troops, apparently making a mockery of their tattoos and flags. In June 1285 the Mongols reached Hanoi – Thang Long, as it then was – only to find that Annam's tactics were exactly the same as Champa's. The fall-back had been deliberate. There would be no decisive action. The houses were empty, the gardens stripped of food; the court and people had fled. The Mongols, now reinforced by ships sailing up the Red River, commanded the coast, the Red River delta – but not the interior, the forests and mountains, or the king's base at Thanh Hoa, 170 kilometres to the south. Guerrilla action, disease, lack of food and the fearsome summer heat began to eat away at Toghan's army.

After another month, Tran Hung Dao judged the moment right for a counter-attack. A battle at Chuong Duong, 20 kilometres downriver from Hanoi, carried the Vietnamese back into the capital, forcing the Mongols to retreat across the Red River. Another battle by a little river, the Tay Ket, which joins the Red River's ancient dyke a few kilometres south-east of Hanoi, sealed the Mongol defeat – 50,000 captured, Sodu himself killed and beheaded – leaving the remnants to be harried back to the border.

It took two years for Kublai to reform his shattered force and try again. Toghan clearly needed help, and he was sent it in the form of the veterans Ariq-khaya, Nasir al-Din and one of Kublai's many grandsons, Esen Temür. This time, the strategy would be different: a huge base was to be established just inland from Hai Phong, and a large-scale naval assault mounted as well as a land attack.

Tran Hung Dao's response, in early 1288, was sheer brilliance. On land, his strategy was the same – a scorched-earth withdrawal from inhabited areas, leaving the Mongols with nothing to conquer. Anticipating this, Toghan had prepared for a huge operation with some 500 vessels to bring in reinforcements and food up the Bach Dang river from Hai Phong. It was on the fleet that Tran Hung Dao focused his attention, planning to repeat a tactic first used 300 years before to defeat a Chinese fleet and ensure Vietnamese independence. The first step was to order troops to cut and sharpen hundreds of ironwood stakes. These were then ferried out 5 kilometres into Halong bay, to one of the thousand or more little islands that make the bay a famous beauty-spot (created, according to legend, when a dragon plunged into the sea, carving out crevices and valleys with his tail, and making countless caves in the craggy limestone). In the centre of the island, almost 200 metres up, was a particularly large yet well-hidden cave, into which 1,000 men would fit with ease. Here they settled with their stakes to watch as Toghan's ships slid past to make their way upriver.

Once the ships were out of sight, a small Vietnamese boat crossed from the mainland and picked up the troops and their sharpened stakes. A few kilometres upstream, in an area where the river broadened into mudflats at low tide, they waited for the outgoing waters to reach their lowest level. Then they planted their stakes, one to every square metre – some sticking up vertically, some pointing upstream – running in a zig-zag across the main channel, set just below the level of the water so that small boats would float clear of them. Tran Hung Dao himself came to check the work, so the story goes, thrusting his sword into the ground and twisting his hair into a chignon to get a clear view.

Assaults followed, of which we have no details. The result was that on 22 March (or thereabouts; some accounts mention 3 April or 8 April) the Mongol fleet, harried from the banks and shoreline, retreated downriver. Little Vietnamese boats acting as decoys slipped away above the stakes, a final attack slowed the Mongols, and then they were upon the stakes: many ships were impaled and torn open, fixed in place while others rammed into them, all helpless as Vietnamese fire-boats drifted in from upstream. Sloshing ashore through mud and water, the Mongols were easy prey for the forces ranged along the banks. Toghan was lucky to escape – to face Kublai's fury: the emperor banished his son to Yangzhou, 150 kilometres up the Yangtze from its mouth, and a very long way from court.

Over the years, the river at Bach Dang silted up, and the lines of stakes vanished beneath the river bottom. How do we know any of this is true? Partly because the spot where Tran Hung Dao stuck his sword in the ground to redo his hair was marked with a temple dedicated to him; but mainly because in 1953 the North Vietnamese dredged the river to improve navigation, and found the stakes. On 22 March 1988, the official 700th anniversary of the great victory, the Bach Dang Stake Yard was declared a historic site to commemorate the defeat of the 'northern feudalists'. The island where the stakes were hidden and its huge hidden cave – the Grotto of Wooden Stakes – are now tourist sites; and Tran Hung Dao is still remembered as the national hero who secured Annam's independence.

Kublai's involvement in Vietnam provides striking parallels with more recent events. A powerful ruler conceives the notion that the national interest will be served by sending troops to attack an extremely determined regime in the north. The foreign troops fail to achieve their ends. More troops are sent. Prestige is involved. A world-view must be sustained and it is inconceivable that a minor power can withstand an assault by the mightiest one on earth. For ten years the major power strives to achieve its end, struggling in quagmires and squinting for lights at the end of tunnels, only to be hounded into ignominious retreat.

Yes, there are interesting parallels with America and its war in Vietnam. But just as interesting are the differences. America in the 1960s was in the midst of the Cold War, in grim opposition to the USSR. There was at the time a logic behind the first step into Vietnam. Kublai, on the other hand, specialized in making enemies of people who posed no conceivable threat. It was all down to ideology.

There's a lesson in this on which the spirit of Kublai and the Americans would agree: never, ever, tangle with the North Vietnamese.

After that, there would be no thought of invading Champa. But there was still business to finish in Burma. In 1283 a force of 10,000 from Sichuan had tried to induce the king to submit, but he fled to the hills. Then, trying to avoid further trouble, he sent two monks to beg for peace. They knew they were on weak ground: 'Your majesty, art thou not the Bodhisattva [the future Buddha]? So vast are your domains. Pagan is a small country, but it has the Buddha doctrine which is flourishing. Don't send warriors into it. Come in only after the crops have grown.' Kublai promised, and was as good as his word.

In late 1286, with the defeat in Vietnam behind him, Kublai tried again, with more success that owed much to the internal state of affairs in Burma. King Narathihipate had just been assassinated by his son, Thihathu, who held a knife to his father's throat and forced him to drink poison. This was a kingdom in a state of collapse. The commander, Esen Temür, the grandson who had gained some experience in Vietnam, led his 7,000 troops down the Irrawaddy. When the Mongols reached Pagan, they stripped its monasteries of their gold and silver; then, unable to cope with the climate, they returned home, leaving Burma to more regicide, anarchy and Thai warlords. Dribs and drabs of tribute trickled out of northern Burma. But it was never enough to pay for the wars or satisfy a royal ego.

King Kertenagara of Java had done well for himself, having succeeded to one of South-East Asia's most successful kingdoms. Java, especially eastern Java, had a history of mini-empires. Three centuries earlier, one of them, Mataram, had grown rich on rice and spice. Rice grew well on the rich volcanic soil inland, and the island's ships monopolized the cloves, nutmeg and mace of the Spice Islands. Mataram had outperformed its great rival, Srivijaya, on the neighbouring Sumatra, until in 928 the great volcano Merapi, the source of the island's wonderful soil, erupted, spewing ash and rivers of hot mud down river valleys, burying towns and temples several metres deep. Mataram never recovered. But a surviving prince created a brilliant, if brief, successor state. Offered the throne at the age of 20, after four years spent in the refuge of a monastery, Airlangga rebuilt fast, establishing a new base near today's Surabaya, damming rivers, extending irrigation schemes. When he died in 1049, his empire collapsed into two rival kingdoms. One emerged supreme: Singhasari, founded by the orphan, thief and legendary hero Ken Arok in 1222 when he defeated the other, Kediri. It was this new empire of Singhasari that Kertenagara had inherited – a somewhat precarious inheritance, since its survival depended on both keeping control of the spice trade and keeping an eye on Kediri and its would-be rebels. Ambitious for more – indeed, some today see him as a forerunner of Indonesian nationhood – he had allied himself with Champa by marrying a Champa princess, and in 1284 tried and failed to take Bali and, in the other direction, a bit of Sumatra.

Kertenagara was not best pleased, therefore, when an envoy called Meng Chi arrived from Kublai in 1289, bearing a rude demand for submission. Kertenagara punished Kublai for his impertinence by having the envoy's face tattooed, so that when he reported back to court the insult was plain and public. It demanded revenge. Kublai ordered a battle fleet to be made ready in the south commanded by Shi-pi, a veteran of the Song campaign. Under his overall command, ground forces would be led by Kao Xing and naval forces by a Uighur named something like Ikh-Musu. Kublai told them it would be a walkover: 'If you occupy that country, the other smaller states will submit of themselves; you have only to send envoys to receive their allegiance.' For three years they mustered their forces in Quanzhou (Zayton): 1,000 ships, 20,000 troops, a year's supply of grain, 1,000 kilos of silver for new supplies.

So Kertenagara had plenty of time to prepare for the assault; but he misread Shi-pi's strategy. Assuming the commander would work his way southward along the coast, calling in on both Champa and Malaya, he despatched forces there to ambush the Mongol fleet. This was a fatal mistake. Shi-pi covered the 4,000 kilometres to Java non-stop. It was a high-risk strategy – 'The wind was strong and the sea very rough, so that the ships rolled heavily and the soldiers could not eat for many days' – but it paid off. Shi-pi landed his troops in 1293, unopposed because meanwhile Kertenagara had become involved in a war with his neighbouring state, Kediri, and been killed. All the native troops were off fighting in the south.

Shi-pi should have had the walkover Kublai had promised. In fact, he was instantly caught up in local politics. Kertenagara's son-in-law, Vijaya, an equally ambitious and far more devious character, sent him a message offering submission in exchange for help against Kediri, backing his offer with gifts of incense, perfume, rhinoceros horn and ivory. Shi-pi agreed. Vijaya sent details of the territory – on the Brantas river, at the foot of Mount Wilis, 105 kilometres south-west of Surabaya, rich in rice, a harbour on the coast, all explained on a helpful map – and the Mongols went in. A week later, 5,000 of Kediri's troops were dead, their leader had been executed and the place was in Shi-pi's hands.

All that remained was the ceremony to celebrate victory and, of course, accept Vijaya's promised submission. Vijaya requested 200 unarmed men under two officers as an escort back to his capital, Majapahit, supposedly to fetch gifts. On the way, Vijaya's men killed the unarmed escort, and then turned on the Mongol force. Shi-pi fled, leading his troops in a 150-kilometre fighting retreat to the coast, back into the ships, and away for home – where Kublai rewarded him for his failure and the loss of 3,000 men with 17 lashes and the confiscation of one-third of his property.

Two years later Kublai's successor restored Shi-pi to favour. After all, as an adviser pointed out, he had travelled 12,000 kilometres, reached countries never reached before and made a terrific impression on the natives. So ended another disaster, with honour satisfied by self-deception.

For Kublai, this adventure was a fine example of the Law of Unintended Consequences. Setting out to punish one king, Kublai had managed to help his legitimate successor secure the throne and establish a new dynasty and a nation-state. Over the next 50 years Vijaya's new creation, Majapahit, grew into a rich and powerful empire that included a good deal (some say all) of Indonesia – exactly the opposite of what Kublai had intended.

16

HOW THE EAST WENT WEST

FOR MOST OF KUBLAI'S REIGN, THE IMPACT OF CHINA ON THE West was, frankly, fairly negligible. It was only after his death that he became famous, and that was almost entirely thanks to one man who has been much quoted in earlier chapters: Marco Polo.

To understand the difference Marco made, look at what was known of China and Central Asia before Kublai. In the twelfth century, Europeans and Middle Easterners had only the vaguest ideas about China. In Christian Europe, maps were not really maps at all, but diagrams of beliefs in which the Last Judgement and the Garden of Eden were as prominent as land masses and oceans. Monsters had leading roles: men who fed on the smell of apples; the Sciopod, who used his giant foot as a sun-shade. The only continents were Europe, Asia and Africa, which appeared as neat segments of a circle or unshaped blobs. Asia and India were identical; China, simply absent. Arabic geography, of which Europe knew little, was better, but not much. A Spanish Jew, Benjamin of Tudela, travelled from Ceylon to China in the late twelfth century, but recorded few details, and his Hebrew *Itinerary* was unknown to Christian Europe until the sixteenth century. None of the Nestorian Christians who undertook missionary work in Central Asia wrote accounts, or at least none that were copied. Other Christians knew that they were there, and dreamed up another legend, about a non-existent Christian king, Prester John.

So when Genghis's Mongols burst upon Europe, they sprang out of the dark. With Genghis's devastating sweep across Central Asia and into Persia (1219–23), the initial burst of optimism that these were Christians coming to rescue the Crusaders rapidly gave way to fear and trembling. Europeans seized on the name of one group of Mongol subjects, the Tatars, and called all Mongols Tartars – people from Tartarus, the hellish nether regions of antiquity. Minor shocks were like omens of doom. In 1238, the fish-traders of Novgorod forfeited their usual trip to Norfolk for North Sea herring and stayed home to fight the invaders, causing a glut of fish in Yarmouth. The Hungarian king received a threatening letter from Batu, khan of the Golden Horde, Genghis's grandson and Kublai's cousin: 'As for you who dwell in houses and have fortresses and cities – how will you escape my grasp?' Then in 1241, the storm broke. Russia, Poland and Hungary fell. European leaders almost united to fight back. Crusades were proposed, pleas for help and co-operation exchanged between rival leaders. In fact, there was no time to organize anything, because suddenly the Mongols were gone, drawn back home by the death of Ogedei.

After illusion and stark terror came a reality check, in the form of two papal envoys to Karakorum: Giovanni (John), a cleric from what was then Plano (or Piano) Carpini or Carpine, and is now the town of Magione in Umbria, who was at Güyük's election in Karakorum in 1246; and Friar William, from Rubrouck in north-eastern France, who met Mönkhe in 1253–5. Both brought back uncompromising demands from the Mongol khans. 'By the power of God, all lands, from the rising of the sun to its setting, have been made subject to us': that statement in a letter to the pope from Güyük captures their view succinctly. Other envoys were sent to meet the Mongols in the Middle East. As a result, the West acquired detailed, realistic information about Genghis's successors and their people, mainly as a result of Carpini's account, which was leaked before he arrived home. Copies circulated widely (whereas Rubrouck's brilliant report lay uncopied for three centuries). What people read – and heard from Carpini himself, as he toured Europe on his return from the Mongol court – did nothing to calm their nerves. In the event, the direct threat turned out to be over: the Mongols over-reached themselves, then settled back into their new mini-empires in southern Russia and Persia, where they began to engage in the normal activities of states – establishing relations with outside powers, forming alliances and squabbling with each other. Of these states, Europe knew a good deal.

Meanwhile, a new world had emerged in the Far East – Kublai's – of which the West knew nothing. No missionaries were despatched from Rome, nor envoys from any other ruler, until the 1290s – and even then communication was limited, mainly because of linguistic problems. Interpreters were few and bad, no-one stayed long enough to become fluent in either Chinese or Mongol, and any-way the Mongols showed no interest in becoming Christian. True, there were Nestorians among them – notably Kublai's mother, Sorkaktani – but they were so embedded in Mongol and Chinese society as to be no help at all to mainstream Catholics. As the Persian khan Arghun said to the pope in a polite refusal to accept baptism: 'If one prays to Eternal Heaven alone and thinks in the appropriate manner, is it not as if one had accepted baptism?' In brief, they were unconvertible.

The major conduits for information should have been the trade routes. Unfortunately for historians, traders were mainly interested in trade, not travel and social comment. Although several routes were open, thanks to Mongol rule, few made the demanding journey overland themselves. A fourteenth-century anonymous Florentine noted the time taken to travel all the way from Ukraine to Beijing: 250 days, give or take. In addition, scholars now believe that the idea of a peaceful high road across the Pax Mongolica is overstated, because the Mongols were in an almost constant state of bickering or open warfare for most of Kublai's reign. When Hulegu and Berke were fighting each other in the 1260s, both slaughtered each other's traders. Who would risk life and spend 18 months struggling back and forth across Asia to fetch goods you could pick up from middlemen closer to home?

There was always the sea route, of course; but this, for westerners, was even worse. It started in the Persian Gulf, because no-one would be sailing around southern Africa for another two centuries. From there, it took up to two years for Arab ships to reach the East, with the risks along the way of nasty death from pirates, storms and structural collapse of hulls held together by rope (a hazard mentioned by Marco Polo). Again, no-one wrote up the experience.

Some did make the land trek later, after Kublai's death, because there were profits to be made along the way for the lucky and the knowledgeable. But the only ones to have done this in Kublai's time were the Polos, who financed their first journey by selling merchandise in Constantinople, where they bought jewellery which Berke, khan of the Golden Horde in Sarai, took in exchange for unspecified goods that they sold later as they journeyed eastward.

As Venetians and merchants, the Polo family firm of three brothers was uniquely placed for travel eastward. Venice owned bits of Constantinople – recently seized by Latinized Christians from Greek Orthodoxy – and Acre in Syria, and Soldaia in the Crimea. Venice dominated the trade routes that linked Russia to Egypt, the Middle East to Italy. Fortunes were to be made from Baltic amber, honey, wax, Russian furs and slaves. Around 1260, two brothers, Nicolò and Maffeo, set out to trade in jewels with the Mongols of southern Russia, the Golden Horde. When they arrived, two catastrophes upset their plans. The Greeks retook Constantinople and blinded or killed 50 Venetian merchants; and the two Mongol sub-empires, the Golden Horde and Persia, went to war. There was only one safe direction: due east.

In Bukhara, three years later, a Mongol mission to their overlord's overlord, Kublai, offered to take them to the emperor's court. A year later, they were with Kublai. He questioned them about the papacy and the Roman version of Christianity, and then helped them on their way home, giving them one of the gold or silver tablets (*paiza*) that acted as a combined passport and requisition order, allowing them to make use of official Mongol way-stations on their return journey. He sent them off with a request to bring him 100 men who could act as missionaries, and also some oil from a lamp in Christ's Sepulchre in Jerusalem. This was not just tolerance, but good politics. Kublai was beset by many disputatious clerics of several religions, one of which was Nestorian Christianity. His mother had been a Nestorian. A hundred Christians from a different sect would allow him to create another special interest group, and prevent any one sect becoming dominant.

Back home in 1269, Nicolò was reunited with his son Marco, now 15. Unfortunately for Kublai's request, the pope had died, and a new appointment was much delayed. Two years later, drawn by the wealth and opportunities they had seen in Kublai's China, the brothers set out again, taking Marco with them.

In Acre they consulted an old friend, the archdeacon Teobaldo Visconti, which turned out to be a fortunate decision, because, by an extraordinary coincidence, he was appointed pope and was able to give them official credentials. Three and a half years later – in the summer of 1275 – they were back with Kublai in Xanadu.

Scholars have long debated how much of Marco's account is authentic. Opinions range from very little to almost all. On the minus side, Marco worked with a co-author, Rustichello: a ghost-writer who, since he was a professional author keen to make the book appealing, gave Marco's words a literary spin. There are blatant intimacies and much use of the first person, as if the author is button-holing the reader, and faux-casual asides, like 'Oh, I forgot to mention such-and-such.' Actually, he *was* button-holing, not the reader exactly, but the listener, because this was a time when texts were designed to be read aloud. Later, Marco himself and various editors added, subtracted and rewrote, creating several different versions; there is no original text.

The chattiness, combined with a tabloid habit of being economical with the truth, should often give us pause. Some have even wondered whether he could have plagiarized the lot from other books. To this the short answer is no, he couldn't. The book is crammed with details that no westerner could possibly have known (like the marble of Xanadu). Even his distortions, like the help with making the catapults of Xiangyang, can be put down to exaggeration rather than fantasy. When he and Rustichello were at work in the last years of the century, no-one else in the West had a clue what had been happening in China, so lies could have sold as well as truth. Now, of course, scholars are adept at using other sources to tell truth from falsehood; and on the whole, with a few notable lapses, Marco stands the test.

It is Marco Polo's account of his 17 years in China that told Europe almost all it knew of Kublai. For later historians he was an invaluable eye-witness, because he arrived overland, before the conquest of the south was complete, and plunged right into the heart of China. Others coming later arrived by sea, and saw mainly southern ports. The Polos were there at the heart of things, at Kublai's court, insiders as far as it was possible for foreigners with only a smattering of the language to be: Marco may have picked up some spoken Mongol and Chinese, but he couldn't write either. Kublai used Marco as an envoy, a post which Marco magnifies in importance;

in fact he was probably more of a freelance reporter, able to provide an independent view of places, people and events.

So popular were the Polos that Kublai several times refused them permission to leave, finally allowing them to go in order to escort a Mongol princess as a bride to the Mongol ruler of Persia, Arghun. Again he gave them two of his gold passports, so that they should be well taken care of, and told them to deliver messages to all the Christian kings of Europe. In a convoy of 13 four-masted ships, they reached Persia in 1293 or 1294, after two years and many disasters. By then Arghun was dead. The princess was married off to his son, and the Polos arrived back in Venice in 1295.

Somehow, in some scrap between Venice and Genoa, Marco found himself in a Genoese gaol – confined in some comfort, apparently, because it was here that Rustichello ghosted the *Travels*, which was finished before their release, probably in 1300. Marco, now in his mid-forties, married, had three daughters, lived comfortably, and died aged 69 in 1324.

It is hard to know whether people at the time believed his book or not. It was all very far away and extraordinary, and there was nothing else to substantiate it. Some say it was seen as no more than a collection of fables. But Marco makes a whiter-than-white claim right at the beginning, addressing the reader:

> Ye shall find therein all kinds of wonderful things . . . according to the description of Messer Marco Polo, a wise and noble citizen of Venice, as he saw them with his own

eyes. Some things indeed there be therein which he beheld not; but these he heard from men of credit and veracity. And we shall set down things seen as seen, and things heard as heard only, so that no jot of falsehood may mar the truth of our book.

But then, if he was lying, he would say that, wouldn't he? Nevertheless, two things carry conviction: the amount of detail and the lack of unsubstantiated legends. It has the ring of truth, and that's what appealed.

The *Travels* must have been immensely popular among the small number of people able to obtain or borrow a copy, for within 25 years it had been translated from its original language, probably a hybrid Franco-Italian, into French, Tuscan, Venetian, German and Latin, each version being re-edited to make it conform to the prejudices of its readers. But what exactly is meant by popularity is anyone's guess. No-one knows how many copies were made, who read them, or how many heard the book being read out loud as if it were an epic being recited by a bard. As one historian of printing, Elizabeth Eisenstein, has written: 'Just what publication meant before the age of printing or just how messages got transmitted in the age of scribes are questions that cannot be answered in general.' All that can be said is that for two centuries the demand for books had been growing steadily, though from a very low base. Most books were religious, and great cathedrals had *scriptoria* of copyists who continued, very slowly, to build libraries that were meagre by later standards, intellectual treasures by their own. Cathedral libraries seldom contained more than 200 300 books. The few great universities boasted not many more. In 1338 the Sorbonne had 338 reference books, carefully chained, and 1,728 books for loan, all of Latin authors, except for one in French, a copy of the epic *Roman de la Rose*. For an individual other than an aristocrat to own a single book was rare, to own one in an everyday language even rarer.

Still the copies multiplied – 85 have survived – many with glorious and utterly spurious illustrations, turning the book into a work of art as much as reportage. Those who took Marco most seriously were his Latin trans- lators, for they were trying to assess China for possible conversion. To one, Francesco Pipino of Bologna, Marco was 'respectable, veracious and devout', as were his father and uncle; a judgement which is then artificially fulfilled by additions describing non-Christian religions as abominations. For Latin clerics at least, Marco was reliable. Some time in the 1330s a Dominican friar, Jacopo d'Acqui, told a story about the dying Marco: 'Because there are many and great things in that book, which are beyond all credence, he was asked by his friends on his death-bed to correct the book by removing everything that went beyond the facts. To which his reply was that he had not told one-half of what he had really seen.'

Slowly, therefore, merchants began to explore the possi- bilities suggested by Marco. There were enough Genoese making the overland journey by 1330 for Francesco Pegolotti to offer some advice, with rather off-putting casualness: the road to China was 'quite safe by day and by night', he said, unless you happened to die en route, in which case the local warlord would take everything you owned.

Missionaries, too, had taken up the challenge. A Franciscan, John of Montecorvino, set up the first Christian church in Beijing in 1294, the year of Kublai's death. Another Franciscan, Odoric of Pordenone, who arrived in 1322, wrote an account that became almost as famous as Marco's.

Of those early Christians, traces survived that very nearly support one of Marco's more outrageous claims, that for three years he governed the city of Yangzhou. In the autumn of 1951, just after Mao's Communists had taken power, a workforce was knocking down the walls of Yangzhou and using the rubble to build a new road. Workers had spotted a slab of marble with some strange markings on it. They handed it to a local antiquarian, who recognized what looked like scenes from the life of a Christian saint. Puzzled, he crated it up and sent it to a friend near Shanghai, a young Jesuit, Francis Rouleau, who was packing to leave, having been thrown out of the country by the new regime. Rouleau, well aware of the delicacy of researching religious imagery with the Communists looking over his shoulder, took rubbings and photographs. The slab vanished after he left, but from his records he made a report on what he had seen and examined.[1] It was a tombstone, decorated with scenes from the life of St Catherine – suitably so, given the name of the deceased: Katerina Yllionis, who died in July 1342. A few years later another tombstone turned up in Yangzhou, that of Katerina's brother Antonio, who had died in November 1344. Both were the children of Antonio 'Ilioni', as records in his hometown of Genoa spelled him. He had been executor of the estate of a friend who had come to China, done well there and, it seems, founded a little community. Indeed, Odoric mentions

[1] Father Francis Rouleau, SJ, 'The Yangchow Latin Tombstone as a Landmark of Medieval Christianity in China'.

staying with Franciscans in Yangzhou in 1322, and also records three Nestorian churches. A Christian community had apparently been there for some time. Long enough, perhaps, for Marco to have been sent by Kublai to take it under his wing? To have been the governor not of the city, but of its Christians, a position that Rustichello either misunderstood or nudged him into upgrading?

In any event, from Marco, merchants and missionaries, news of Kublai filtered into public consciousness.

There's an item of information that Mongolists from time to time toss out that intrigued me. Did you know, they say, that Phags-pa's script is portrayed by the thirteenth- and fourteenth-century master, Giotto? It's one of those insignificant-but-interesting, coffee-time, drinks-party things: *I was talking to this Japanese academic the other day, and he told me . . . Good heavens, that's amazing . . . Giotto? Really? Where? . . . Oh, I think it was something to do with the robe of Christ*. I had heard and read this a few times, and decided to check it out.

Yes, there could be a link between Kublai Khan and Giotto. His name was Rabban (Master) Sauma, a monk who journeyed west from Kublai's realm and was the first known traveller ever to arrive in Europe from China. Sauma was a mirror-image of Marco Polo, with differences: his stay in Europe lasted less than a year, and he was an official envoy who rated top-level meetings. His is a wonderful tale, which vanished in its original Persian form, surviving only in an adulterated Syriac translation undiscovered until the late nineteenth century. The man and his adventures have been superbly resurrected by Morris Rossabi in *Voyager from Xanadu*. 'In these days when multiculturalism is in the air,' he says, 'it seemed fitting to write about a man who flourished in a variety of cultures and who worked to build bridges between them.' But there's more to the story than that: it is one of history's what-ifs, for Sauma very nearly succeeded in forging an alliance between the Mongols and Christian Europe, an alliance that could have changed the course of history. So, for the next few pages, put Giotto out of mind and focus on Sauma.

Sauma was an Önggüd, one of a Turkish tribe that lived on the Yellow River in today's mid-China and had early on thrown in their lot with Genghis. Living on a major trade route westward, they had converted to Nestorian Christianity, the sect which claimed Christ had two natures, divine and human, and that Mary was the mother of the human, not the god. Declared heretical by Rome, the Nestorians had gone their own way very successfully in Central Asia and China, winning a reputation as good doctors and good businessmen who were remarkably tolerant of local practices. Members included Kublai's mother Sorkaktani and Hulegu's wife. The Önggüd appealed to Genghis because they made good officials. Later, they proved good allies to Kublai in his fight against his cousin Kaidu.

Sauma, born around 1240, joined the priesthood at 25 and became a hermit in mountains 50 kilometres south-west of Beijing. Famous for his asceticism and learning, he would have remained in scholarly seclusion had he not been joined after some years by an eager 15-year-old student named Markos. For a decade master and pupil remained isolated from the world, untouched by the momentous changes going on around them, until Markos became convinced that they should go to Jerusalem to receive the highest level of absolution he could think of. Since the two priests feared neither hardship nor death, Nestorians in Beijing backed them, and so did Kublai. The two priests were good publicity in his efforts to keep the sympathy of the sect to which his mother had belonged. In addition, by chance, this was about the time the Polos returned to Beijing with young Marco, so Kublai could well have been hoping for a boom in East–West contacts overland. Sauma and Markos might be able to bring back western experts who would be useful in his new Beijing. He gave them one of the official golden passes, *paiza*, which allowed them to make use of the postal relay system and to claim care en route. They gathered a caravan of camels, grooms, cooks and guards, and set off, probably in 1275.

It took a long time. The first leg took them back to their homeland on the Yellow River and on through Xinjiang via the Gansu Corridor, skirting the Takla Makan desert to Hotan, the multinational oasis at the base of the Kunlun Mountains. Now they were out of Kublai's protection, into Kaidu's territory. The place had become notorious for brigands. Wisely they headed for Kaidu's camp in Talas, carefully not mentioning either Kublai or Persia, both Kaidu's current enemies. Then on across mountain and desert, enduring heat, bitter winds, avalanches, hunger, thirst and several robberies, and so at last via Tus (today's Mashhad, in north-east Iran) to Kublai's nephew, the Il-khan Abaqa, in his former capital Maragheh; because here, by chance, the Nestorian leader, the Catholicos, Patriarch Mar Denha, was staying. After an emotional meeting and a tour of the local Nestorian sites, they town-hopped westward to Arbil in northern Iraq. Then came a sudden change of plan. The

Catholicos summoned them to Baghdad and gave them a new mission: to win the ear of Abaqa for Nestorians. Off then to Tabriz, the Il-khan's new capital, undamaged during the Mongol invasions because, unlike Baghdad, it had surrendered. In this cosmopolitan centre, with its rich markets, many Christian sects and Italian merchants, they showed Abaqa the *paiza* from Uncle Kublai, and received all the recognition the Nestorians wanted, and all the help they needed.

As it happened, there was war further west, so they were stuck; but in great comfort, because the Catholicos promoted them both, Markos to be a metropolitan, equivalent to a bishop, and Sauma to 'visitor general' in China, a sort of roving ambassador (not that he would ever have a chance to perform this role). No, no, they demurred, they wanted a simple life, they wanted to go on with their pilgrimage. But they had no choice. They accepted, and put their travels on hold.

Events now took a most surprising turn. A year later, the Catholicos was dead, and the 36-year-old Markos was appointed to succeed him. For the next five years, he and his middle-aged master were absorbed by local and church politics – the death of Abaqa, a vicious round of in-fighting and final confirmation of their offices.

In 1286 the new Il-khan Arghun found himself needing support against Egyptians and other Muslims, and came up with an extraordinary idea. He wanted to approach Europe to suggest another crusade, Christians and Mongols together against Islam. Considering the horror caused in Europe by the Mongol advance only 40 years before, this sounds totally bizarre; but rather less so, taking into account that there had been some co-operation between Mongols and Christian crusaders 20 years after that. The deal was this: in exchange for Europe's help, Arghun would deliver Jerusalem to them. To set the scheme in motion, he needed a sophisticated, well-travelled, multi-lingual envoy, and Sauma was just the man. He knew Turkish, Chinese and probably Mongol from childhood. Now he knew Persian as well. There were many Italians in the Il-khanate, so interpretation was no problem.

Arghun gave Sauma letters to the pope, the Byzantine Emperor, and the French and English kings. In 1287, the ambassador and three companions left for the Black Sea, where they took a ship to Constantinople. Here he met the Emperor Andronicus, saw the sites, admired relics – and achieved nothing much, for an anti-Muslim coalition meant eastern and western churches working together, which was not about to happen.

And so, in June 1287, he and his small entourage, minus Markos (who as Catholicos had duties closer to home), sailed past Sicily and an erupting Mount Etna, to Naples, and then overland to Rome, only to discover that the pope was dead, and a new one not yet chosen. Sauma was greeted instead, with due respect, by the cardinals. They asked him first about his native land, and his unrecorded reply must have been the first detailed report of Kublai ever heard in Europe. Then they moved rapidly on to his faith, with questions he answered so carefully, emphasizing early church fathers rather than the contentious matters of Christ's nature and the exact status of the Holy Spirit, that the cardinals did not entirely grasp that they were dealing with a supposed heretic. They were hugely impressed with his erudition. 'It is a marvellous thing,' they said, 'that thou who art a Christian, and a deacon of the Throne of the Patriarch of the east, hast come upon an embassy from the King of the Mongols.'

But on the matter of a crusade, they could not commit in the absence of a new pope.

He was told all the stories and shown all the sights – the place of Paul's martyrdom (where Paul's severed head had leaped in the air three times, crying 'Christ! Christ! Christ!'), one of Jesus's seamless robes, some wood from Jesus's cradle, the original Crown of Thorns – and appreciatively took all these relics and tales at face value.

But he was anxious to move on. His mission was still only half done. There were the kings of France and England still to see.

Leaving the heat of Italy behind, it took Sauma a month to work his way from inn to inn along France's dusty dirt roads. Now about 60, he must have been near breaking point. But in Paris, France's ambitious teenage king, Philip the Fair, gave him a great reception and a comfortable house. Once recovered, Sauma put his case. Philip seemed to be impressed. If Mongols were ready to help retake Jerusalem, what could Christians do but respond? In fact, he was eager to make a display of strength for reasons of his own – to gain control over English domains in France, to assert French claims to Flanders, to keep the Vatican from siphoning off funds from French church properties.

Assuming that Philip was now a fully paid-up member of the Mongol–European Alliance, Sauma moved on to Edward I of England, who fortunately was in his French colony, Aquitaine. Sauma reached Bordeaux after a three-week journey in October 1287, identified himself, and was at once invited to see the king. After presenting Arghun's gifts of jewels and silk, Sauma put forward the idea of a crusade. Edward loved it. He himself had vowed to take up the cross that spring. It fitted his plans precisely. Sauma surely believed he had two-thirds of his task done; the final third would fall into place when he returned to Rome.

As if to seal the pact, Edward invited his new ally to give him and his court communion according to his own rite, which differed only in minor respects from the Roman one. This was followed by a feast, which would have been lavish – one of Edward's other banquets fed hundreds of guests with 10 oxen and 59 lambs – though it might have crossed Sauma's mind, as the only person in the world able to make such a comparison, that a few hundred was no match for the 6,000 who dined in Kublai's great hall in Beijing.

Everything now depended on Rome, for without the pope there could be no crusade. Still, however, there was no pope. Winter was closing in. Sauma headed south, to the mildness of Genoa – a garden paradise, as he called it, where he could eat grapes year-round. After three months of growing frustration came the news: *habemus papem*, Jerome of Ascoli, enthroned as Nicholas IV on 1 March 1288.

An invitation followed, and an audience, with a fine speech from Sauma, the delivery of Arghun's gifts and a generous response from Nicholas. Sauma was an honoured guest, he said, and would of course stay for Easter. Sauma was delighted, and asked to celebrate mass. His request was granted and the mass was held, with hundreds watching. No-one understood a thing, but all approved the actions. Sauma countered by asking to receive communion from the pope himself. So it happened, before a huge crowd, on Palm Sunday, with further celebrations on Passover (Maundy Thursday), Good Friday, Holy Saturday and Easter Day.

Now Sauma requested permission to leave for home.

Nicholas demurred, Sauma insisted: he needed to tell his own people of his generous reception. Sauma also took the liberty of asking for some relics. The pope was momentarily fazed: if we gave relics to all who asked, he said, there wouldn't be any left; but, he added, in this case he would provide some – a piece of Jesus's clothing, something of the Virgin's scarf, a few assorted saintly relics; and for Markos, the Catholicos, a bejewelled crown of gold, a purple robe lined with gold thread, socks decorated with pearls and a papal ring . . .

. . . and several letters, confirming the position of Markos and Sauma, and another for Arghun, which at last came to the point. Jesus had given authority to Peter, and thus to all succeeding popes. Arghun should recognize the true faith. As for a crusade, it was up to the pope to proclaim, not others to suggest, because he would bear responsibility for its success or failure. Let Arghun convert, accept papal authority, and God would give him the strength to seize Jerusalem and become a champion of Christianity. In brief: no practical aid, no crusade.

Still, when Sauma reached Persia in September, Arghun was pleased. There was, it seemed, a foundation for peace and diplomacy (and this, remember, was only some 60 years after Genghis's death, and a mere 30 since the destruction of Baghdad and Kublai's succession). There was a three-day banquet for Sauma and the Catholicos.

Of course, the crusade idea was dead in the water. Arghun tried to summon interest in France and England, but got only evasive answers. He himself was sidetracked by challenges from the Golden Horde and rebellious Muslims. He died in 1291, along with his dreams of further conquests. By then, it was too late anyway. The same year the Egyptian Mamluks took Acre, the last

Christian outpost in the Middle East, and the crusading era came to an end.

And Sauma ended his days with a fine, new, well-endowed church, spending as much time as possible with his old friend Markos, both no doubt hardly able to believe their transformation from hermit and avid pupil. In late 1293 he fell ill in Baghdad, harboured his strength until Markos arrived to say farewell, and died in January 1294, coincidentally within a month of Kublai himself. With Markos grief-stricken at his graveside, he was buried in Baghdad's main Nestorian church.

What if Nicholas had backed the alliance? The papacy, France, England and the Mongols would have joined the crusaders in defending their castles in Syria, possibly with some strange consequences: Islam pushed out of the Middle East; Jerusalem delivered to the pope, under an English– French–Italian–Mongol administration; Arghun a Christian convert; Christianity taking a leap into Central Asia . . . and all because Kublai had decided that Sauma and Markos had a role to play in his plans.

And now, to echo Marco, I must mention another thing that I had forgotten: Sauma's possible link with Giotto, in the form of strange writing on Christ's robe in one of Giotto's paintings.

Rabban Sauma would surely have had his *paiza* with him in Rome. It would have been seen and admired, its script copied. Twelve years later, Giotto was in Rome, in time for the huge centennial celebrations of 1300 held by Pope Boniface VIII, no doubt gathering ideas to inject into future paintings. In 1305 he was in Padua, about to begin work on his greatest masterpiece, the Arena Chapel frescoes: 67 paintings that cover the whole interior with scenes from the life of Christ. One of the aspects of his originality was his readiness to paint elements of contemporary life into his creations. Famously, he included in his *Adoration of the Magi* a Star of David that was in fact Halley's Comet, which had made a particularly spectacular appearance in October–November 1301.

I searched every robe of Christ in the Arena Chapel: no strange writing there. But two pictures made me look closer. In the Nativity, the Virgin lies in the stable, rather well dressed given the circumstances. On her dress, just visible beneath her cloak, is a hem displaying some rather oddly familiar designs: squiggles and lines making squares. In the Resurrection fresco, *The Angel at the Tomb*, the same patterns decorate the hems of garments on Roman soldiers who are asleep, unaware of the miracle taking place right beside them; and they are there again on the hem of Mary Magdalene's dress.

I'm sorry to spoil a good story, but these patterns are not Phags-pa's letters. They might, however, just possibly be pastiches of them, the sort of thing that Giotto might have added to provide a touch of exoticism – brought from the mysterious East, moreover, by a Christian. It's a detail; and a bit of a stretch (17 years between Rabban Sauma's visit and Giotto's painting); and perhaps it's mere coincidence. But it's odd, nevertheless. Perhaps there really is a chain of causes and effects linking Xanadu and Padua: a Chinese emperor worried about communicating with his subjects, a brilliant Tibetan monk, a long-distance Turkish Christian traveller, a pope eager for knowledge of the Mongol empire – and an artist injecting a hint of chinoiserie into his masterpiece.

* * *

Thinking about the possible transmission of a new script raised a question in my mind. Much of this book has been about Kublai's extraordinary achievements, but the flip side of his life and times is equally intriguing: his failures, his limitations. Given his skills in leadership and his intellectual range, what more might he have done? There is a particular link that might have been made between East and West that would have transformed our world in astonishing ways.

The question is this: why didn't Kublai invent printing with movable type? He had it right there in his hands.

Consider:

Kublai, uniquely placed astride several cultures, knew that no existing script was good enough for his purposes: all were either too hard or too obscure or unacceptable to other members of his imperial family. In theory, Phags-pa's script solved the problem pretty well, even if in practice it did not take root.

Kublai was immersed in books – by the thousand in his own government, by the million in society at large. But the books were not produced by the method invented in the West by Johannes Gutenberg in about 1450: using movable metal type to make up many pages at a time and run them off printing presses. The eastern method of printing, which had been in existence since the fifth century, was to cut text or a picture in reverse into wood, cover this block with ink and print from it onto paper. At first, the technique had been used to make seals, stamps and religious pictures; then, in the late eighth century, the first books appeared. The technology was basic, effective and technically easy, but hampered by fundamental inefficiencies. It took days to make a block, pages could only be printed one at a time, and the information could only be used in that form: the block. Every new page demanded a new block; every new book, many new blocks. Discarded blocks of out-of-print books clogged the yards of printing works. Often, they simply became firewood.

The solution was obvious. If each character had its own block, as in stamps, you could make up any text you liked, and reuse the characters after printing. No need to carve every page; no need for the millions of discarded blocks. Remember Pi Sheng, who supposedly invented printing with movable type in the eleventh century? His idea was to cut his characters in wet clay, in reverse, and bake them. To print, he selected his characters, put them in a frame, inked them, and took a rubbing with cloth or paper. The technique worked; the technology improved and was adopted by the Koreans, whose first book printed with movable metal type appeared in 1234. The Mongols had first invaded Korea in 1216, with much back-and-forth over the next 50 years. It was Kublai who finally made Korea part of the Mongol empire in 1271. So possibly Kublai himself, and certainly his scientific advisers, knew about printing with movable metal type.

They also knew the problems. It was even more trouble than block-printing. The business of choosing the correct character from at least 8,000, maybe 40,000 or more depending on design requirements, offered no advantage in design and not much in speed. Besides, it was an implied threat to two ancient skills, calligraphy and block-carving. True, there were those who remained intrigued by the idea. In 1297 Wang Zhen, a magistrate from Dongping in Shandong province, made 30,000 wooden characters set out in two revolving round tables, which gave easier access to the type. Later, governments produced some astonishing publications with movable type – such as a 1726 encyclopedia of 5,000 volumes that used 250,000 characters – but for day-to-day use this method of printing remained too cumbersome to be more than a technological oddity.

Kublai was thus in a position to see the *real* problem behind both block-printing and movable-type printing: namely, China's writing system. China's script records syllables.[2] It is this that held back Chinese printing until modern techniques and modern demands – mass-market books, newspapers – made it worthwhile to develop the industry in the twentieth century.

But Kublai had the answer, right there, in front of his face. It existed in the form of the alphabetical script adopted from the Uighurs on his grandfather's instigation. It existed again in the alphabetical script devised by Phags-pa. He thus formed another link in the chain that led back 3,400 years to the point when a Middle Eastern immigrant community in ancient Egypt started to adapt hieroglyphs and stumbled upon that revolutionary invention, the alphabet.

Like Chinese, other early writing systems – Egyptian hieroglyphic, Mesopotamian cuneiform – were based on syllables, which seem the natural basic components of language. But language has a much more fundamental level, namely the meaningless bits and pieces of noise that make up syllables. The genius of the alphabet – any alphabet – is that it uses a few symbols, no more than a

---

[2] With two exceptions, as I discovered with relief in my first struggles to memorize written characters – the free-floating *r* and *dz* sounds, e.g. in *nar* (where) and *beizi* (cup). These sounds are meaningless on their own, and could thus qualify as 'letters'.

few dozen, to represent the whole range of linguistic sounds, even non-sounds (like the silent gathering of energy before the little explosion that begins the letter *p*). It is not a one-to-one match between sound and symbol, as is often claimed. Its great strength is its fuzziness, which confers flexibility. It's this quality that allows it to represent any sound in any language, once you have mastered the conventions of that particular system of transliteration: a Chinese *r* is a sort of buzz (like the *s* in treasure), a French *r* is a Scottish *ch*, a German *r* is a throat-rattle, a child's *r* in English is often a *w* (*w*ound the *w*agged *w*ocks the *w*agged *w*ascal *w*an). This combination of fuzziness and simplicity gives it a massive advantage over scripts based on syllables.

So Kublai had at his disposal several of the major elements that in Gutenberg's hands almost two centuries later helped the Renaissance on its way. Out went scribes and their beautiful, slow ways; in came the printing-press, and a slew of advances, all feeding on each other: mass markets and universal literacy and cheap books and scholars exchanging information and standing on each other's shoulders. Copernicus's ideas were unreadably obscure, but once printed they remained in libraries, waiting for Galileo to confirm them. A scribe took a week to copy a couple of high-quality pages, years to copy a single bible. Gutenberg and his team perfected a whole new technology and printed 180 copies of his famous bible in two years. By 1500, 250 printing operations across Europe were producing 2,000 titles – over 200,000 books – per year. In 1518–25, Germany alone printed a million books each year; and one-third of them were by Martin Luther, whose anti-papal *Ninety-Five Theses* kick-started the Reformation and who has therefore, with some justification, been blamed and praised alike for causing the greatest split in the Christian church. And from the Renaissance and the Reformation sprang a new Europe, a Europe that seized the world, dominated trade, founded nations, discovered new lands – precisely what Genghis and Kublai intended for their empire.

A revolution of this nature might have been initiated under Kublai's aegis. Kublai's China had the technology, the ships, and the intercontinental links by sea and land to back his imperial ambitions. He or his extremely bright advisers might have taken the next steps, which was to turn Phags-pa's script into metal type, set it in frames and start printing. There was even a good financial reason to do this. In Europe, the push came from religion: the need to ensure that all Christian institutions were reading the same approved and error-free Bible. In Kublai's China, the push might well have come from the need to print vast amounts of paper money, with complex designs and several colours to prevent counterfeiting.

Why didn't it happen?

There were several vital technical steps that were missing. One was the right sort of paper. In China, paper was soft and absorbent as toilet-paper, ideal for scribes working with brushes and for block-printing. In Europe, scribes working with quills needed a much firmer, non-absorbent surface, which was the sort of paper Gutenberg needed to produce crisp, tiny lettering. Second, China did not have olives or grapes that needed to be squashed with heavy-duty presses, the devices that Gutenberg adapted to make the printing press. And third, someone would have needed to come up with Gutenberg's astonishing invention of the hand-mould, which could produce several hundred new lead types per day. This device, which now exists only in museums, was fundamental in printing for 500 years.

There is a final, and perhaps fundamentally crucial reason why there was no Yuan printing revolution. The purpose of printing is the transmission of information, and I believe – I am sorry to say this – that the Mongols had no information they wished to transmit. Deep down, what Kublai had created was Mongolia Inc., a vast corporate entity dedicated to creating wealth and power for itself, with nothing at the end save its own eternal survival. This had always been a problem. One of Genghis's main characteristics was his toleration. It was to him clearly true that Heaven had chosen him and his heirs for universal rule. But why this should be so was a mystery. All his life he wondered about it, hoping that perhaps other religions had the answer. His restlessness and tolerance were inherited by his successors, Kublai included – and he had no answers either. There was no great new truth to be promulgated. Nor, of course, did the Mongols have a tradition of great literature or great art. All they could do was to encourage the transmission of the art and literature of their subjects, the Chinese.

There is, therefore, an intellectual and artistic hollowness to the Mongol imperial enterprise. Its aim was purely to conquer and govern and finance itself. And I am not sure that this is enough of a message for any government, let alone one controlling an empire the size of Kublai's. In the end, the Mongols had nothing much to say.

As it was, Gutenberg gets the credit, and Marco Polo's *Travels* moved from script to print, with ever-increasing exposure. Long before the first printed editions – German, in 1477 – came off the press, the route taken by Marco had been closed off by the collapse of the Mongol empire and the Muslim resurgence spearheaded by the Turkish seizure of Constantinople in 1453.

Not wishing to be beholden to Muslim middlemen, Europe's merchants turned again to the sea route to the East. Traditionally, the goods they sought – silks, precious stones and, in particular, spices – were brought by Chinese junks to Malaysia, by Arab ships to India, Persia, Africa and Arabia, and thence via the Red Sea to the Mediterranean. But this was a galling arrangement. Eastern pepper underwent a 50-fold increase in price on its journey to European kitchens. Clearly the thing to do, from the European perspective, was to fetch it yourself. Hence the race to discover and sail around the Cape of Good Hope; and hence Columbus's big idea – to reach the East by sailing round the world the other way, westward.

Let me repeat: his aim was to get to China and the land of the Great Khan. But wait a minute. We are now in the 1490s. Marco's book appeared around 1300. Two centuries have elapsed, *and the Great Khan is still alive?* Of course he can't be. But when the Muslims slammed the door on the overland route in the mid-fourteenth century, it was as if China entered a time-warp for Europeans. No-one had a clue what was happening out there. As far as they were concerned, Kublai Khan was immortal, and no-one seemed to question this extraordinary assumption. As John Larner puts it in *Marco Polo and the Discovery of the World*, 'For Europe, the Great Khan [i.e. the last Yuan emperor] still lived and reigned 130 years after his expulsion from China.'

Columbus – Cristoforo Colombo – was a rough-and-ready Genoese driven by his obsession, his dream. Having tried for years to get backing from Portugal, he eventually won it from Spain, which turned out rather well for everyone, except America's indigenous peoples. It has become a commonplace of historical writing to say that Columbus was heading for Kublai's China as his first stop because he had read Marco Polo's descriptions of it. Supposedly, he carried the *Travels* with him on his first voyage in 1492 to make sure he could find his way when he got there. Whether this is true or not has been a matter of intense and highly technical controversy among scholars, but there is now a reluctant majority verdict that he didn't. The arguments are well summarized by John Larner. In brief: Columbus *did* own a copy of Marco's book (in Latin, printed in 1490), but, not being a great reader, he seems to have acquired it only *after* his return from the New World, to check what it was he had discovered.

His inspiration for the journey could have come from several sources, for by the fifteenth century Marco had become fully accepted as a reporter rather than a fantasist, and his information was being incorporated into 'maps', if such fanciful creations can be called maps. And Columbus may have had direct access to his ideas as the result of a letter written by a Florentine astrologer and scholar called Pozzo Toscanelli, who was a member of a sort of unofficial pan-European society of scholars. This same group included a Portuguese cleric, Fernão Martins, who became canon of Lisbon and adviser to Alfonso V of Portugal. To him in 1474 Toscanelli sent a map, with a letter: 'I have spoken with you elsewhere about a shorter way, travelling by sea, to the lands of spices than that which you are taking by Guinea . . . It is said that in a most noble port called Zaiton' – which he then describes in Polo-like terms. '[It] is under a prince who is called the Great Khan,' who rules many cities including the 'noble and very great city of Qinsay', which lies in the province of Mangi (southern China) near the province of Cathay (northern China). It happens that Columbus was in Lisbon at the time. As Larner suggests, it is possible that he saw or copied Toscanelli's letter, and thus acquired Marco's information at second hand.

That he had it is certain. When he left in search of Cathay in 1492, he recorded in his journal that his royal backers, Ferdinand and Isabella, had given him letters for 'the Great Khan and for all the kings and lords of India'. When he reaches Cuba, he learns of a river ahead and 'says he will endeavour to go to the Great Khan who he thought was in that region or to the city of Cathay which is in the Great Khan's possession, which he says is very large according to what he was told before he left'. (The reference to Cathay as a city and the words 'what he was told' both suggest an oral source of information rather than a reading of Polo.)

It is an extraordinary chain of causes and effects. Kublai welcomed Marco, who wrote his *Travels*, which indirectly inspired Columbus in his epoch-making voyage. Perhaps this was Kublai's greatest contribution to world history: that he was the magnet that drew Columbus westward, and put the Old World in touch with the New.

By 1492, then, Kublai had become rooted in the western consciousness, no longer as the nightmare his grandfather had been, but as an end-of-rainbow monarch of infinite wealth and glory. It is in this form that he comes through to English-speakers today, thanks to distorted versions of Polo, an opium-induced vision and a famous interruption.

Polo's *Travels* came via an Italian translation (by Ramusio) to the English compiler of voyages of discovery, Richard Hakluyt, whose massive three-volume work appeared in 1598–1600. This, plus Hakluyt's unpublished work, plus additional material, was then edited by his colleague Samuel Purchas into an even larger work published in various editions, concluding with *Hakluytus Post-humus, or Purchas His Pilgrimes* in 1625. In this compendium we read: 'In Xamdu did Cublai Can build a stately Palace, encompassing sixteen miles of plaine ground with a wall, wherein are fertile Meddowes, pleasant Springs, delightful Streames, and all sorts of beasts of chase and game, and in the middest thereof a sumptuous house of pleasures.'

For the famous story of the vision and interruption, we go forward 170 years, to an evening in June 1797. The scene is an isolated hillside farm on Exmoor near the coast between Porlock and Lynton. Enter the poet Samuel Taylor Coleridge, who is staying here. He has been out on a long walk communing with nature and has been suddenly taken short with a terrible stomach upset – dysentery, he calls it. He takes some opium, reads the passage in Purchas, falls asleep and dreams a wilder version of what he has just read. He is dragged from sleep by 'a person on business from Porlock' – one of the most famous incognitos in literary history, kept anonymous because Coleridge was developing a habit, and this (so some have suggested) was probably his dealer. He is aware that he has on the tip of his tongue a poem some 300 lines long. The deal takes an hour, by which time he has forgotten most of the poem. He recalls a few lines, and wrestles together enough a few weeks later to make the 'fragment' that has become one of the most famous poems in the English language:

In Xanadu did Kubla Khan
A stately pleasure-dome decree:
Where Alph, the sacred river, ran
Through caverns measureless to man
Down to a sunless sea.
So twice five miles of fertile ground
With walls and towers were girdled round:
And there were gardens bright with sinuous rills,
Where blossomed many an incense-bearing tree;
And here were forests ancient as the hills,
Enfolding sunny spots of greenery.
But oh! that deep romantic chasm which slanted
Down the green hill athwart a cedarn cover!
A savage place! as holy and enchanted
As e'er beneath a waning moon was haunted
By woman wailing for her demon-lover!
And from this chasm, with ceaseless turmoil seething,
As if this earth in fast thick pants were breathing,
A mighty fountain momently was forced:
Amid whose swift half-intermitted burst
Huge fragments vaulted like rebounding hail,
Or chaffy grain beneath the thresher's flail:
And 'mid these dancing rocks at once and ever
It flung up momently the sacred river.
Five miles meandering with a mazy motion
Through wood and dale the sacred river ran,
Then reached the caverns measureless to man,
And sank in tumult to a lifeless ocean:
And 'mid this tumult Kubla heard from far
Ancestral voices prophesying war!
The shadow of the dome of pleasure
Floated midway on the waves;
Where was heard the mingled measure

From the fountain and the caves.
It was a miracle of rare device,
A sunny pleasure-dome with caves of ice!
A damsel with a dulcimer
In a vision once I saw:
It was an Abyssinian maid,
And on her dulcimer she played,
Singing of Mount Abora.
Could I revive within me
Her symphony and song,
To such a deep delight 'twould win me,
That with music loud and long,
I would build that dome in air,
That sunny dome! those caves of ice!
And all who heard should see them there,
And all should cry, Beware! Beware!
His flashing eyes, his floating hair!
Weave a circle round him thrice,
And close your eyes with holy dread,
For he on honey-dew hath fed,
And drunk the milk of Paradise.

This has, of course, absolutely nothing to do with Kublai, for Xanadu never had any chasms, caves or forests, and certainly boasted no incense-trees, only a slowly flowing river and rolling treeless hills; the sea, which is no less sunny than any other, is two days' hard ride away. It has everything to do with the Quantock hills, the wild Somerset coast, the glorious wooded slopes, a host of literary references, Coleridge's love of nature and a growing addiction to opium. I'm not sure the poetry works all that well today. 'Momently' is an odd word to use twice in six lines. But that's a quibble. It is the surreal mix of images that makes the magic, which is why the name of Kublai Khan echoes in the minds of English-speakers who have never heard of Coleridge.

And why the name of Xanadu does too. Film buffs are surprised to learn that it's a real place, because they know it as Charles Foster Kane's spooky estate in Orson Welles's 1941 film, *Citizen Kane*. Pop enthusiasts of a certain age recall it as a song by Olivia Newton John. IT experts know it as the name given by the visionary Ted Nelson to the idea that all the world's information could be published as hypertext: Project Xanadu, 'the explicit inspiration for the World Wide Web', as the website puts it, continuing:

> About the name: No, we did not get it from Olivia Newton-John. It is an actual place in Mongolia [China, actually, Ted] which is described in a poem considered by many the most romantic poem in the English language . . . This poem's tradition also associates the name 'Xanadu' with memory and lost work, because Coleridge said he lost part of the poem due to a mundane interruption. We chose the name 'Xanadu', with all these connotations, to represent a magic place of literary memory and freedom, where nothing would be forgotten.

Listening to these echoes down the distorting corridors of time, we're a long way from Kublai's Shang-du. But it was he who gave the yell that started it all, and I think he would have been gratified.

17

A HOLY MOUNTAIN,
A SECRET GRAVE

THE TURNING POINT WAS 1281, WHEN KUBLAI WAS 66. HIS empire had reached its limits, and there is, by hindsight, a sense of desperation to his efforts to extend it further. From a modern perspective, a psychologist might suggest that he, the world's most powerful man, was fighting off any recognition that dreams must die, ambitions fade, the body age, and that the best he could hope for was an empire that endured within the borders he had set for it.

What was his demon? Depression, for a start. In 1281 his favourite wife, Chabi, his chief companion and adviser for 41 years, died. In the first 20 years of their marriage, before he became emperor, she bore and raised four sons, including his heir Jingim, and five daughters, making sure the children were educated in all the cultures that surrounded them, Mongol and Chinese, Buddhist and Confucian. She was famous for her frugality and good sense. She used to tell the court ladies to collect old bowstrings, because they could be used as thread and woven into cloths. She redesigned Mongol hats, giving them a peak as protection from the sun. She was not blinded by her husband's successes. After the victory over the Song capital in 1276, she is supposed to have warned him against overweening ambition: 'Your handmaiden has heard that from ancient times there has never been a kingdom that lasted a thousand years.' It was she who made sure the captured Song empress was treated with due respect.

Then there came scandal with the murder of the grasping and unpopular Muslim minister, Ahmad, bringing with it the sudden proof of Kublai's poor judgement. Still, at least the succession was secured, in the form of Jingim, Pure Gold, second son of Kublai and Chabi, now in the prime of life at 38. He had always been the intended heir since the death of an elder brother in childhood. After Ahmad's murder he came into his own, and Kublai rallied enough to take another wife, Nambui, a distant cousin of Chabi's and possibly selected by her before her death in order to give her husband the support he needed. It seemed to work. He was clearly still fit enough to face life because, at the age of almost 70, he managed to make Nambui pregnant. Having borne a son, she began to act as his go-between, protecting him from overwork.

Jingim was increasingly the man in charge, so much so that in 1285 a senior official floated the idea that Kublai abdicate in favour of his son. Somehow, despite Nambui's protection, Kublai heard this, and flew into a rage. In the ensuing crisis, with Kublai no doubt suspecting his son of disloyalty, tragedy struck again. Jingim fell ill from some unspecified disease and died.

* * *

There was still a remnant of the old Kublai left; enough for one last effort. He would need it. All this while Kublai's troublesome and ambitious cousin Kaidu had been active in Central Asia, often almost forgotten in China amid the business of administration and foreign adventuring. But he had been busy building support all around the fringes of the empire, reaching out southward into Tibet and at the same time eastward to Manchuria. If Kublai was not careful he would find himself cut off from his own hinterland.

In Tibet, Phags-pa's successor on his death in 1280 had been a 13-year-old boy plucked from the Mongol court, causing much resentment locally. In 1285 one Buddhist sect, the Brigung, turned to violence, attacking the monasteries of Phags-pa's sect, the Saskya. Perhaps this was spontaneous; but Kaidu saw his chance. His protégé Duwa came in to aid the rebels, while at the same time slicing away at Kublai's garrisons and postal relay stations in Uighur lands – today's Xinjiang. Duwa laid siege to the town of Khara-Khocho (now ruins 45 kilometres east of Turpan) for six months, attacking the earthwork walls with a dozen catapults and 100 naphtha-throwers – all to no avail. He gave up only when the town's desperate commander lowered his daughter over the walls as a gift. The following year, Kaidu took Ürümqi (Beshbaligh as it then was), the Uighur capital. In 1288, 1,050 craftsmen abandoned Khotan (Hotan) and Kashgar for safer bases back east. It was all proving too much. The following year Kublai ordered a total retreat from Xinjiang, leaving Kaidu with double his original territory. But only briefly. Kublai despatched a junior grandson at the head of an army. The rebel HQ was destroyed, 10,000 died (so sources claim: it sounds high), the postal relay stations were made good and Mongol authority was restored, turning Tibet into a backwater for the next century.

Meanwhile, Kaidu had been active elsewhere. In 1287 he threatened to link up with a new challenger, a feisty 30-year-old prince named Nayan, a descendant of Genghis's half-brother Belgutei, in Manchuria. Kublai was faced with the grim prospect that all the northern reaches of his empire, a great arc of steppeland from Xinjiang, across his original Mongolian homeland and into Manchuria, would fall away to become the pastoral–nomadic empire to which the rebels aspired. So, to investigate, Kublai picked a hero: Bayan, general, Grand Councillor, conqueror of the Song campaign. (I know Bayan vs Nayan is confusing, but that's the way it was.) According to one source, Bayan was about to accept Nayan's invitation to a banquet when he learned it was a trap, and managed to escape in time. Kublai decided on firm action. Though the details are obscure, he sent Bayan to keep the two rebels apart by occupying Karakorum, while he himself led another army against Nayan.

Marco tells the story in his usual overblown way. In 12 days Kublai gathers his troops, 360,000 cavalry and 100,000 infantry – impossible numbers that we should at once cut by 90 per cent. Even so, 46,000 is a significant force. Astrologers are consulted, and predict victory. Scouts are sent out ahead to arrest anyone they see, thus preventing word of the advance leaking out. Kublai is lifted into his mobile battle-station, a miniature fortress borne by four elephants harnessed together abreast. A 20-day march brings them to a plain, probably somewhere in the vast open spaces of Mongolia's south-eastern steppes.

The rebels are surprised, but form up, both sides singing to the accompaniment of 'certain two-stringed instruments'. Then kettle-drums – cauldrons a couple of metres across, covered in buffalo-skin – boom out the order to attack. Arrows fall like rain, men clash with mace, lance and sword, the wounded cry, the battle sounds like thunder, as battles commonly did in the clichés of medieval romances. Kublai wins; Nayan is captured, and executed in the traditional way for princes, without the shedding of blood. 'He was wrapt in a carpet, and tossed to and fro so mercilessly that he died.'

Kaidu, ever the strategist, pulled back westward to avoid a battle, preferring to keep his forces intact for hit-and-run assaults (and also, surely, distracted by conflict that had broken out with Persia, with which he remained in constant enmity for the rest of his life; but that's another story). So there was no showdown; but at least his retreat prevented a possible link-up between the rebels in Central Asia and Manchuria.

With Bayan in control in Karakorum and re-establishing control over surrounding areas, Kaidu, de facto khan of Inner Asia, did not attempt anything large scale for the next three years. Bayan was blamed for allowing him to escape – some even accused him of collusion with Kaidu, forcing Kublai to relieve him of his command and banish him to Datong in northern Shanxi province to await further orders. Before Bayan went, however, Kaidu was rash enough to return, and this time received a sharp lesson, with the loss of 3,000 men into captivity. That was enough to pen him up in his own territory, behind frontiers garrisoned by Yuan troops. But nor was there any further attempt by Kublai to regain control of Central Asia. The two had reached stalemate.

That stalemate lasted until Kublai's death in 1294, and beyond. His heir, Temür, having abandoned his grandfather's grandiose schemes for overseas expansion, thought he could finally tackle the task of crushing rebellion at home. He was wrong. In September 1301 he sent a massive force, vastly outnumbering Kaidu's, and the two met in a series of four battles in south-west Mongolia, where the Altai mountains begin to fall away into the Gobi's gravel plains. Sources disagree on who won. It seems fair to say it was a draw. So there was no final solution; nor would there be with Kaidu, because, despite the efforts of his Chinese doctors, he died shortly after the battle – of wounds, according to Rashid, or perhaps of sheer exhaustion after 45 years of campaigning. He was, after all, almost 70.

Duwa, now king-maker, crowned Kaidu's first-born, Chapar – not a popular choice: an 'extremely lean and ill-favoured' youth, according to Rashid – but remained dominant himself, eliminating all those heirs of Kaidu who had opposed him, until his death. Thereafter Chapar regained control, saw the struggle was in vain and surrendered to the Yuan in 1310, finally making the journey to court that his father had refused to make in 1264, and bringing to an end the challenge to imperial authority from Central Asia.

Personal losses, rebellion, defeat abroad: it was all too much. Kublai turned to food and drink. At court banquets he gorged on boiled mutton, breast of lamb, eggs, saffron-seasoned vegetables in pancakes, sugary tea and, of course, the Mongolian drink of choice: *airag* (fermented mare's milk, otherwise known by its Turkish name, *kumiss*). It was the drink in particular that undermined him. *Airag* and wine – he consumed both in prodigious amounts. As he became less active, as his powers waned, he put on weight, ballooning year by year into extreme obesity. He must have known it would kill him, but he didn't care. Knowing he had not much longer to live, he made peace with the spirit of his lost heir by nominating Jingim's third son, Temür, as his successor.

He also knew where he wanted to be buried: back in the land of his birth, in the heartland of the Mongol people, where the last of the Siberian mountain ranges, the Khenti, begin to give way to grasslands. This was where his grandfather, who had started it all, had been born, and this is where he was buried. Genghis, too, had died far from home, in the Liupan mountains of Ningxia province, just on the verge of the conquest of Xi Xia. For three weeks, his funeral cortège had carried his body northward, back across the Yellow River, along the Helan mountains, into the high grasslands of today's Inner Mongolia, across the Gobi's gravel plains and the grasslands of Mongolia itself, across the Kherlen river to the mountain that had been considered sacred by the Mongols from when they first arrived there some time around AD 800. Its name was Burkhan Khaldun – Holy Khaldun, as it is usually translated (though there are those who say that *burkhan* was nothing but an old word for 'willow'). Genghis knew this area – the two rivers of Kherlen and Onon, the Khenti mountains that give birth to them, the open grasslands they run through – like his own saddle. Burkhan Khaldun was the mountain on which Genghis had often eluded his enemies, on which it had come to him in a revelation (or so his people believed, because he told them so) that he had the backing of the

Eternal Sky, Heaven above, to create a nation and an empire. He had promised to give thanks to Burkhan Khaldun every day. The place and the occasion had been captured in oral traditions, and then set down in the Mongols' foundation epic, *The Secret History of the Mongols*, by Shigi, adopted into Genghis's family as a boy. It was inconceivable that Genghis would be buried anywhere else, and equally inconceivable that his people would allow it ever to be desecrated. People often say that no-one knows where Genghis is buried. Don't believe them. Everyone in Mongolia knows within a few square miles where Genghis is buried. It is the exact spot on Burkhan Khaldun's vast, rounded, rocky, forested, scree-covered flanks that is the mystery. Horses were allowed to roam over the site, guards were placed at a suitable distance, trees grew, and to this day the site of the grave is unknown. Today treasure hunters eye Burkhan Khaldun as the place where one day a great find will be made, revealing infinite riches. Mongols say it should never be found, as Holy Genghis intended.

It was surely with a proprietary eye on this spot that in 1292 Kublai put one of his grandsons, Kamala, in charge of Genghis's *ordos*, his tent-palaces and estates. As the Persian historian Rashid ad-Din wrote only a few years after Kublai's death, the estates included

> the Great Khorig [Forbidden Precinct] of Genghis Khan, which they call Burkhan Khaldun, and where the great *ordos* of Genghis Khan are still situated. These latter are guarded by Kamala. There are four great *ordos* and five others, nine in all, and no one is admitted to them. They have made portraits of them [the family] there and constantly burn perfumes and incense.

My guess is that Kublai wanted to make sure that he, Kublai, and not Kaidu or any other rebellious upstart, laid claim to this sacred site. The tent-shrines must already have been in existence when Kamala arrived, guarding a grave site dug 70 years before, and long since overgrown. But tents are temporary things. In due course, nine would later become eight, the Eight White Tents which acted as a travelling shrine, drifting back and forth across Mongol lands until finally settling south of Dongsheng in Inner Mongolia, where they were transformed into today's Genghis Khan Mausoleum. Kamala needed something permanent in which to perform rites honouring Genghis and, in due course, Kublai. As Rashid adds, 'Kamala too has built himself a temple there.'

Burkhan Khaldun appears as Khan Khenti – the King of the Khenti – on maps. There are those who say they are not identical, but I don't believe them, and nor does the government, because every three or four years ministers and MPs by the dozen go there to do honour to the mountain, to Genghis, and also, if they think about it, to Kublai. They travel in many 4×4s, well equipped with winches, because it is quite a trip, as I discovered when I made it in 2002.

From Ulaanbaatar, you take the road east for 100 kilometres to the coal-mining town of Baganuur, an unappealing stack of Communist-era apartment blocks. That's where the paved road runs out. Then you head north over grassy hills, following a loose network of tracks – this is what Mongolians normally mean by a 'road' – which lead you to Möngönmört (meaning At the Silver Horse). You head on, with the Kherlen on your right, into the uninhabited region that is now the Khan Khenti National Park. The tracks converge on a surprisingly solid wooden bridge (after all, the government comes this way sometimes). Beyond, you're on a single track, often muddy, sometimes impassable after a storm, bouncing through low willow bushes and scattered firs. After 25 kilometres you come to a peat bog and a ridge, the Threshold. If the car can climb the ridge, you are greeted with a stupendous view across the upper Kherlen, and a shocking descent over rutted peat that is either a morass (in wet weather) or as rough as tank-traps. Descending, if you dare, you cross the Kherlen (very shallow, with a stony bottom). At this point Burkhan Khaldun comes into view: 2,452 metres, not very high, but a Schwarzenegger shoulder-muscle of a mountain, a sort of Mongolian Ayers Rock, but seven times the size. Proceed for another 18 kilometres straight ahead, along a valley that closes in on you steadily until you reach a sign and a collection of tree-trunks all leaning together and covered in bits of blue silk and Tibetan prayer-sheets. This is an *ovoo*, a shrine, such as would normally be made of stones, if there were any stones in soil made soft by pine-needles. You are at the base of Burkhan Khaldun, and now you must climb. It will only take you a couple of hours to reach the top.

Very soon you reach a place that was once quite clearly artificially flattened. This area too is considered holy. Here is another silk-draped *ovoo*, with little offerings at its base: vodka bottles, saucers for incense-sticks. This was where Kamala's temple once stood, no doubt about it. In 1961 Johannes Schubert from Leipzig, the first westerner to climb the mountain, found many semi-circular roof tiles and bits of pottery here. Now you have to hunt around for such things. I found two bits of tile, which ignite an imaginary scene whenever I pick them up: the 29-year-old Kamala watching 50 Chinese builders at work on the wooden walls and pillars, while nearby tilers shape local clay into curved roof-tiles which they lay to dry on a tree-trunk covered with sacking. Later they will be baked in an oven that stands ready nearby.

Kamala would have been keen to get the job done. He knew his grandfather did not have long to live.

And indeed, a year after Kamala returned, Kublai, now well into his 80th year, was hardly able to function except through his wife Nambui.

On 28 January 1294, New Year's Day by the lunar calendar, Kublai was too ill to attend the usual ceremonies in Beijing. No dressing in white, no great reception to receive tributes and praise from visiting vassals, no reviewing the parade of richly caparisoned elephants and white horses, no presiding over the banquet in the Great Hall. Everyone must have known the end was near. A messenger was sent galloping off to the only man who might be able to lift the emperor's spirits: Bayan, still awaiting his next assignment in Datong, 300 kilometres away. Three days later – no more, surely, in these circumstances – Bayan was with the emperor. But there was nothing to be done, except promise eternal loyalty. Kublai knew his end was near, and asked that Bayan be one of the three executors of his will (the others were the chief censor and the director of political affairs on the Secretariat). He weakened steadily, and on 18 February he died.

Two days later, the funeral cortège was ready. Considering Kublai's wealth and the money he had been spending on his campaigns, it would have seemed quite austere. Still, the entourage would have run into the hundreds: members of the family and government who were fit enough for the journey, plus guards, drovers, grooms, cooks, household servants, accompanied by spare horses, carts for the women, carts for the tents, and camels carrying all the paraphernalia suitable for a royal procession that would be on the road for three weeks and 1,000 kilometres. Somewhere quite near the front, behind a guard, would have come Kublai's hearse: a wagon bearing a tent, concealing a large coffin, well-sealed and packed with spices and other preservatives. Covering perhaps 50 kilometres a day – good going for such a crowd – the line would have wound through Beijing's guardian mountains where the Great Wall now runs, over ridges and valleys to the old Mongol–Chinese frontier at Kalgan (today's Zhangjiakou) and up on to the Mongolian plateau; avoiding the right turn to Xanadu – it would mean at least a two-day delay – it would have set out over the Gobi's dusty wastes, until at last the gravel gave way to grassy hills, and the shallow Kherlen, and finally the foothills of the Khenti.

Where he lies I doubt we shall ever know. There is a place, a half-hour's climb above Kamala's temple, where you leave the trees, now stunted and thinned by the height, and step out on to level ground. The summit is still a way ahead, sometimes a breaking wave of rock, sometimes invisible in cloud. The area on which you stand looks like a cemetery. I thought it was when I first saw it, because others think so too. The 'graves' you see are irregular puddles of stone, anything from a metre to three metres across. There are, I would guess, several hundred of them. It is easy to imagine them as graves, the piles of stone as flattened burial mounds. But there was something that didn't fit. The stone-puddles are irregular blobs, and they are all flat. Yet round about were several *ovoos*, stone ones, standing a metre or so high. Enough people come up here today to make and preserve *ovoos*. So why not preserve the 'graves'? And this was on the main path to the summit – not the best place for a secret burial, surely?

I now believe the features to be geological, the result of centuries of frost working magic on loose stones. These cold-weather and permafrost processes are the subject of much study by a rare breed of scientists called cryogeologists. If you glance at a cryogeological textbook, you see patterns – polygons, circles, rings and mounds – that look disturbingly artificial, like fairy rings in stone. Indeed, some early explorers who first saw them in the Arctic landscapes thought they were artificial. But they are all the result of temperature changes that cause minute expansions and contractions in stones, causing them to sort themselves into different sizes and shapes. No-one knows how long it takes, because it happens on geological timescales. They are no more artificial than snowflakes or the polygons of mud in dried-up lakes.

These stony circles suggest a perverse thought. Would not these natural 'graves' offer perfect camouflage for real ones? Who would ever know which among the hundreds was real? Even today, with modern archaeological techniques, it would take millions of dollars and years of work to research them all. Frankly, it's not going to happen.

Of one thing I am certain: Kamala would not have got the wrong place.

A scene replays in my mind whenever I recall my climb. A line of men is winding up through the slender firs, emerging onto this open ground. They are dressed in furs against the bitter cold, and their ornate leather boots with turned-up toes scrape through a thin covering of snow to the hard earth beneath. Six men – no, eight, for their burden is heavy – shoulder two poles that carry a simple coffin draped in blue and yellow silk. There are no lamas in attendance, no Buddhist trappings: this is a return to the austere, nomadic tradition that Genghis loved. Led by a masked shaman with a drum and rattle, the men proceed to the edge of the plateau, where there opens up a stupendous view: a snow-filled valley, a frozen river winding away to distant mountains. It is the land their khan never saw and yet called home.

A small group has been up here for some time, and with gloved hands they have removed stones from one of the hundreds of stony circles. A fire was lit in the shallow depression to melt the iron-hard earth. Slow digging with iron spades has made a grave. Now there is a reverent deposition, followed by prayers and an invocation by the shaman, accompanied by a steady beat on his drum; then the stones are replaced one by one until nothing separates this circle from any other. Kublai is beside his grandfather Genghis, and both are part of the landscape from which they and their empire sprang.

EPILOGUE: THE LEGACY OF THE GREAT KHAN

SHORTLY AFTER KUBLAI'S BURIAL ON BURKHAN KHALDUN, AN assembly was called to decide which of two of his grand-sons would succeed him, Kamala or Temür (Temür, Kublai's provisional choice, had never been confirmed as heir). There was a dispute. A matriarch suggested a solution: Kublai had said that whoever knew the sayings of Genghis best was best suited to rule. It was agreed that the two claimants would compete. Temür, the younger, being eloquent and a good reciter, declaimed well, while Kamala, who stammered, could not match him. All cried out: 'Temür knows them better! . . . It is he that is worthy of crown and throne!'

Temür's inheritance was, in theory, astounding. His family ruled China, Korea, Tibet, Pakistan, Iran, most of Turkey, the Caucasus (Georgia, Armenia, Azerbaijan), most of habitable Russia, Ukraine and half of Poland – one-fifth of the world's land area. In fact, as with Kublai's,

Temür's hold over the further reaches of this pan-Eurasian empire was nominal. Its nomad roots were a romance in the minds of the soft Mongol aristocracy, who seldom if ever visited Mongolia and who had as much connection with their 'homeland' as New York Irish marching down Fifth Avenue on St Patrick's Day. The empire became a crumbling edifice, its cracks papered over by memories of its founder.

The Golden Horde in southern Russia had begun two centuries of rule still known to Russians as the 'Tartar (or Tatar) Yoke'. Its Mongol rulers – ex-Mongols, as they soon were – turned to Islam, working closely with the rulers of Egypt, with whom they exchanged diplomatic correspondence complete with gold lettering and elaborate salutations, all in Turkish. Supposedly every khan had to be one of the Golden Kin, a descendant of Genghis, but as time went on almost any would-be ruler could make that claim. When a resurgent Russia under Catherine the Great annexed the Crimea in 1783, its khan was still proclaiming his Genghisid ancestry.

In Persia, the Il-khans (subordinate khans), as they called themselves, enslaved, plundered and taxed to the limit, entrenching ordinary people in bitter hostility to their rule. Trade favoured cities, which generated enough wealth to enable the Mongols to keep a precarious hold, even as they lost contact with their roots. Hulegu's great-grandson turned Muslim, and fought other Muslims, all with no gain. In 1307, a Mongol embassy to Edward II in England was the final, useless attempt at self-promotion. Thirty years later, the last of the Mongols died with no heir, and Mongol rule vanished.

In Central Asia, Chaghadai's heirs ruled over a vague expanse constantly riven by religious dissension, wars and internecine strife. Here nomadic traditions remained strong, as did the urge to conquer. Constrained by Mongol rivals east and west, Chaghadai's heirs looked south to Afghanistan and India, invading several times, and inspiring a tradition that endured when Mongol rule fell into the bloody hands of Tamerlane. Though not in a direct line from Genghis, he justified himself as a re-incarnation of Genghis – modest roots, heavenly favours, brutal conquest and all. It is this claim that explains why Tamerlane's descendant Babur called himself 'Mughal' when he seized power in India in the early sixteenth century, establishing a dynasty that ended when the British shuffled the last Mughal off the throne in 1857. His name, by the way, was Bahadur, a distant echo of the Mongol *baatar*, hero, the second element in the name of Mongolia's capital, Ulaanbaatar (Red Hero). Modern English contains a fossil remnant of the same word: a 'mogul', originally a wealthy Indian, then a wealthy Anglo-Indian, is now a media tycoon.

For another 73 years after Kublai's death, his descen-dants in China linked east and west, sharing with distant relatives the free flow of trade, diplomats and experts. But the Mongols were on shaky ground. Nomads no longer, they never became truly Chinese. Though some of Kublai's ten successors could speak Chinese, not one of them learned to write it well. Rulers and ruled despised each other. True, there was a peace dividend: the popu-lation rose back towards its former levels; trade flourished. But Mongol authority depended on power, and power seeped away.

Successions were disputed, conspiracy and assassin-ation thrived. In 1328, a two-month civil war ended in executions. In 1331, plague ravaged parts of China, perhaps the beginning of the Black Death that would soon spread to Europe. In Henan province, 90 per cent of the population died. Then the Yellow River broke its banks, drowned uncounted thousands and set itself a new course to the sea. Rebels, sensing that the Mandate of Heaven was being withdrawn, seized the Huai and Yangtze basins. Pirates raided coastal shipping. In plague-ravaged Henan, rebels known as Red Turbans even briefly restored the Song dynasty (1355–60). When the emperor, Toqtoa, tried to restore order and repair the damage, he did so by printing paper money, which led to hyperinflation and forced a return to silver and copper coins.

At last, hatred, corruption, plague, inflation, disaster and disorder, heaped one on another, reached tipping point. In 1368, a former monk drove the last Mongol emperor, Toghon Temür, back to the steppes of Mongolia, leaving some 300,000–400,000 Mongols to fall into the vengeful arms of the Ming. With him went 60,000 of the Mongol elite, trailing back to a land in which they were aliens, and where their deadweight presence ruined the traditional herding economy.

They never accepted their sudden demotion. Their descendants, crowned in Karakorum, went on saying they were the true rulers of China. They said it because they 'knew' a hidden 'truth': that the Ming were actually Mongols. The story, as summarized by Hok-Lam Chan, Associate Professor of Washington University, Seattle, in his *China and the Mongols*, went like this:

The queen of the last Yuan emperor, Toghon Temür, was already pregnant when she was captured and taken as a wife by the incoming Ming emperor in 1368. She said, 'If I give birth soon, they will certainly kill the child.' So she prayed to prolong her pregnancy, and her prayers were answered. She gave birth after twelve months, and the boy was accepted by the first Ming emperor as his heir. There was more: the Ming emperor had made Nanjing his capital, but one day the young Mongol/Ming prince met a man of 'an extraordinary bearing, with a swarthy face, dressed in black robes and riding a black horse', who told him to found a great city with four corners (after the four seasons), nine outer gates (after the planets), and other magical and religious attributes. 'In a golden place in the middle of the city,' the Black Rider said, 'set up a throne of jade, with nine interlaced dragons, and sitting on it become emperor yourself.' Thus did a 'Mongol' prince found modern Beijing, to which the Ming court soon moved.

It is all a legend, of course, with not a scrap of evidence to back it. But, as Hok-Lam Chan concludes, these stories, 'proving' that there was Mongol blood in the Ming emperors and a Mongol inspiration behind the rebuilding of the capital, gained strength in the decades either side of 1500 when Mongolia united again under a khan who claimed the mantle of Kublai, naming himself Dayan, from Da Yuan, Great Yuan, the name Kublai had chosen for his dynasty. The legends were being told and retold until well into the twentieth century.

Nonsense, yes; but there is a smattering of truth in the legends, for the legacy of the two conquerors, Genghis and Kublai, endured down the centuries, and still defines the context of today's geopolitics.

Although Kublai's Chinese territory reached way beyond China's traditional limits, and although successor dynasties claimed to be restoring old China, Kublai's additions dictated their agenda. The Ming adopted them without question. Yunnan, conquered by Kublai as a prince, remained Chinese. So did the Liao river basin in Manchuria, largely populated by Korean captives transplanted from their homeland by Mongol armies. Tibet, unified under Mongol rule, recognized the Ming as overlords, a position which the Ming asserted, if with varying degrees of success. As the Japanese scholar Hidehiro Okada argues, given the non-Chinese origins of these territories, 'the only possible justification of the Ming sovereignty over them was the claim that the Ming emperors were legitimate successors to the Mongol khans'.[1]

In bureaucracy, administration and military structure the Ming also owed a debt to the Mongols. Both civilians and the military, for example, were governed by the decimal system that Genghis had imposed on his new nation and Kublai had adopted for China. It was to lay claim to Mongolia itself that the Ming returned to Beijing. Indeed, as Okada concludes, 'The Ming Dynasty was in all its aspects a shrunken form of the Mongol Empire.'

Same thing with the Manchus when they took over in 1644. Again, no Manchu even thought of giving up territory acquired under Kublai. When the first Manchu emperor was crowned – even before seizing the Chinese throne – he proclaimed himself Vastly Gracious, Harmonious and Holy Khan-Emperor, laying claim to the imperial tradition originating under Genghis in order to legitimize his claim to the eastern half of the old Mongol

[1] Hidehiro Okada, 'China as a Successor State to the Mongol Empire', in Reuven Amitai-Preiss and David O. Morgan, eds, *The Mongol Empire and Its Legacy*.

empire. As Okada writes, the Manchu emperor straddled three worlds: Chinese (as emperor), Mongol (as successor to Genghis) and Tibetan (as patron of Buddhism).

And again with modern China. The far west – Gansu, Ningxia, Xinjiang – had Muslim populations that had more in common with the present-day 'stans' of Central Asia than with the Han regions of the east, but they were considered Chinese because Genghis had conquered Central Asia and Kublai had encouraged Muslim immigration. Western parts of Inner Mongolia had been Tangut territory, the kingdom of Xi Xia until conquered by Genghis and inherited by Kublai. True, his ornery cousin, Kaidu, had controlled a good deal of the west, but that did not make it any less Kublai's. It was on this basis that China regained from Russia areas almost lost in the nineteenth century. Today, it is Kublai's empire that is recalled by China's reach – ironically, minus Mongolia itself, which was allowed to opt for independence and to fall into the Soviet sphere at a time of weakness after the First World War.

It's Mongolia that has a special interest for me. Mongols are very nervous of the Chinese, whom they view as ex-imperial masters itching to pounce. Once I was in the southern Gobi at dusk, looking over immense expanses towards what I thought were clouds, but were not clouds. 'What's that?' I asked my Mongol travelling companion. The answer should have been: the snow-capped peaks of the Tien Shan. Instead he said: 'China. Very dangerous.' Mongols see how the Chinese have moved steadily north since the early twentieth century, beyond the Great Wall, beyond the Yellow River, up on to the Mongolian grasslands. Inner Mongolia is now more Chinese than Mongol. And in commercial terms, pressures on Mongolia itself increase yearly, for Mongolia has valuable resources, especially in the Gobi, that would find a natural outlet in China – with Chinese finance, Chinese transport, Chinese labour. To Chinese, this is as it should be, because, if they pause to think about the matter, which is not often, they would say, as one of my guides put it: Well, of course we know that Mongolia is *really* Chinese, isn't it?

There is, of course, an opposite view north of the Gobi: that China is really Mongolian. But demography rules, and 1,300 million may, in the end, trump two. If Mongolia ever becomes an economic colony of China (no-one speaks of a political takeover), China will shrug her ample shoulders and point out that Mongols have been members of the great family of China for centuries. Any growth in Chinese influence is merely a return to the status quo as established by Genghis, the founder of China's Yuan dynasty, and that dynasty's star, Kublai.

BIBLIOGRAPHY

These are the works that I found particularly useful. The choice is personal, and very selective. Almost all the references are in English. Even in English, they represent only a fraction of the material available to specialists. The best bibliographies for English readers are in Weatherford (English only), and Rossabi and Mote, which also include works in other western and non-western languages.

Abu-Lughod, Janet L., *Before European Hegemony: The World System* AD *1250–1350*. Oxford and New York: Oxford University Press, 1989.

Allsen, Thomas, *Culture and Conquest in Mongol Eurasia*. Cambridge: Cambridge University Press, 2001.

Amitai-Preiss, Reuven and Morgan, David O., eds, *The Mongol Empire and Its Legacy*. Leiden and Boston: Brill, 1999.

Atwood, Christopher, *Encyclopedia of Mongolia and the Mongol Empire*. New York: Facts on File, 2004.

Aung-Thwin, Michael, *Pagan: The Origins of Modern*

Burma. Honolulu: University of Hawaii Press, 1985.

Barthold, W., *Turkestan Down to the Mongol Invasion*. London: Luzac & Co., 1968.

Bartlett, W. B., *The Assassins: The Story of Medieval Islam's Secret Sect*. Stroud, Glos.: Sutton, 2001.

Bira, Sh., 'Mongolian Tenggerism and Modern Globalism: A Retrospective Outlook on Globalism', *Journal of the Royal Asiatic Society*, vol. 14, London, 2004.

Bira, Sh., 'The Mongolian Ideology of Tenggerism and Khubilai Khan', unpublished paper, 2005.

Bira, Sh., *Studies in Mongolian History, Culture and Historiography*. Ulaanbaatar: International Association for Mongol Studies, 2001, esp. 'Khubilai Khan and Phags-pa bla-ma'.

Biran, Michael, *Qaidu and the Rise of the Independent Mongol State in Central Asia*. Richmond, England: Curzon, 1998.

Boyle: see Juvaini.

Cahill, James, *Hills Beyond a River: Chinese Painting of the Yüan Dynasty 1279–1368*. New York: Weatherill, 1976.

Cannadine, David and Price, Simon, eds, *Rituals of Royalty*. Cambridge: Cambridge University Press, 1992.

Chan, Hok-Lam, *China and the Mongols: History and Legend under the Yüan and Ming*. Aldershot, Hants: Ashgate, 1999.

Chen, Paul Heng-chao, *Chinese Legal Tradition Under the Mongols*. Princeton: Princeton University Press, 1979.

Ch'ên Yüan, 'Western and Central Asians in China Under the Mongols', *Monumenta Serica Monograph*

XV, University of California, 1966.

Conlan, Thomas D. (trans. and interpretive essay), *In Little Need of Divine Intervention: Scrolls of the Mongol Invasions of Japan*. Ithaca, NY: Cornell University Press, 2001.

Crump, J. I., *Chinese Theatre in the Days of Kublai Khan*. Tucson: University of Arizona Press, 1980.

Daftary, Farhad, *The Ismā'īlīs: Their History and Doctrines*. Cambridge: Cambridge University Press, 1990.

Davis, Richard L., *Wind Against the Mountain: The Crisis of Politics and Culture in 13th-Century China*. Cambridge, Mass.: Harvard University Press, 1996.

Delgado, James P., 'Relics of the Kamikaze', *Archaeology*, vol. 56, no. 1 (Jan.–Feb. 2003).

Denney, Paul and Douglas, Julie, trebuchet research at www.artefacts.uk.com.

Eckert, Carter J., et al., *Korea Old and New: A History*. Seoul and Cambridge, Mass.: Ilchokak/Harvard University Press, 1990.

Farris, William Wayne, *Heavenly Warriors: The Evolution of Japan's Military, 500–1300*. Cambridge, Mass.: Harvard Council on East Asian Studies, 1992.

Franke, Herbert, 'Chia Ssu-tao (1213–1275): A "Bad Last Minister"?', in Arthur F. Wright and Denis Twitchett, eds, *Confucian Personalities*. Stanford: Stanford University Press, 1962.

Franke, Herbert, 'Siege and Defence of Towns in Medieval China', in Frank A. Kierman and John K. Fairbank, eds, *Chinese Ways in Warfare*. Cambridge, Mass.: Harvard University Press, 1974.

Franke, Herbert, *From Tribal Chieftain to Universal Emperor and God: The Legitimation of the Yüan*

Dynasty. Munich: Bayerische Akademie der Wissenschaft, 1978.

Franke, Herbert, *Studien und Texte zur Kriegsgeschichte der Südlichen Sungzeit* (esp. ch. 4: 'Hsiang-yang: Gelände und Befestigungen'). Wiesbaden: Harrassowitz, 1987.

Franke, Herbert, *China Under Mongol Rule*. Aldershot, Hants: Ashgate, 1994.

Franke, Herbert and Twitchett, Denis, eds, *The Cambridge History of China*, vol. 6: *Alien Regimes and Border States, 907–1368*. Cambridge: Cambridge University Press, 1994.

Gernet, Jacques, *A History of Chinese Civilization*, 2nd edn, trans. J. R. Foster and Charles Hartman. Cambridge: Cambridge University Press, 1996.

Goodman, Jim, *The Exploration of Yunnan*. Kunming: Yunnan People's Publishing House, 2000.

Grey Company, trebuchet website: www.iinet.net.au/~rmine/gctrebs.html.

Groeneveldt, W. P., 'The Expedition of the Mongols Against Java in 1293 AD', *China Review*, vol. 4 (1875–6).

Grousset, Réné, *The Empire of the Steppes*. New Brunswick, NJ: Rutgers University Press, 1970.

Harvey, G. E., *History of Burma*. London: Longmans, Green & Co., 1925.

Heissig, Walther, *The Religions of Mongolia*, trans. Geoffrey Samuel. London: Routledge, 1980.

Herrmann, Albert, *An Historical Atlas of China*. Edinburgh: Edinburgh University Press, 1966.

Hitti, Philip, *History of the Arabs*. Basingstoke: Macmillan, 2002.

Htin Aung, Maung, *A History of Burma*. New York and

London: Columbia University Press, 1967.

Jackson, Peter, *The Mission of Friar William of Rubruck*. London: Hakluyt Society, 1990.

Jagchid, Sechin and Bawden, C. R., 'Some Notes on the Horse-Policy of the Yüan Dynasty', *Central Asiatic Journal*, vol. 10 (1965).

Jagchid, Sechin and Hyer, Paul, *Mongolia's Culture and Society*. Boulder, Colo.: Westview, 1979.

Jay, Jennifer W., *A Change in Dynasties: Loyalism in 13th-Century China*. Washington DC: Centre for East Asian Studies, 1991.

Johnson, Dale R., 'Courtesans, Lovers, and "Gold Thread Pond" in Guan Hanqing's Music Dramas', *Journal of Song–Yuan Studies*, vol. 33 (2003).

Juvaini, Ata-Malik, *Genghis Khan: The History of the World Conqueror*, trans. and ed. J. A. Boyle. Manchester: Manchester University Press/UNESCO, 1958; 2nd edn 1997.

Karcher, Stephen, *Total I Ching: Myths for Change*. London: Time Warner, 2003.

Kates, G. N., 'A New Date for the Origins of the Forbidden City', *Harvard Journal of Asiatic Studies*, vol. 7 (1942–3).

KOSUWA (Kyushu and Osaka Society for Underwater Archaeology), website reports on the Takashima research into Kublai's lost fleet at www.h3.dion.ne.jp/~uwarchae/english.

Langlois, John D., ed., *China Under Mongol Rule*. Princeton: Princeton University Press, 1981.

Larner, John, *Marco Polo and the Discovery of the World*. New York and London: Yale University Press, 1999.

The Legacy Treasure of the Great Dynasty, catalogue of

Mongol–Yuan Exhibition, Arthur M. Sackler Museum, Beijing University, 2004.

Lewis, Bernard, *The Assassins: A Radical Sect in Islam*. London: Weidenfeld & Nicolson, 1967.

Li Chu-tsing, *The Autumn Colors on the Ch'iao and Hua Mountains – A Landscape by Chao Meng-fu*. New York: Artibus, New York University, 1964.

Lin Yutang, *Imperial Peking: Seven Centuries of China*. London: Elek, 1961.

Lindner, Rudi Paul, 'Nomadism, Horses and Huns', *Past and Present*, no. 92 (Aug. 1981).

Liu Bin, ed., *Atlas of China*. Beijing: China Cartographic Publishing House, 1989.

Liu Jung-en, trans. and ed., *Six Yüan Plays* (includes *The Injustice Done to Tou Ngo*, a.k.a. *The Injustice to Dou E*). London: Penguin, 1972.

McMullen, David, 'Bureaucrats and Cosmology: The Ritual Code of T'ang China', in Cannadine and Price, eds, *Rituals of Royalty*.

Man, John, *Genghis Khan: Life, Death and Resurrection*. London: Transworld, 2004.

Mansfield, Stephen, *China: Yunnan Province*. Chalfont St Peter, Bucks: Bradt Travel Guides, 2001.

Medley, Margaret, *Yüan Porcelain and Stoneware*. London: Faber, 1974.

Morgan, David, 'The Mongols in Syria, 1260–1300', in Peter Edbury, ed., *Crusade and Settlement*. Cardiff: University College of Wales, 1985.

Morgan, David, *The Mongols*. Oxford, UK and Malden, Mass.: Blackwell, 1986 (many reprints).

Mote, F. W., *Imperial China 900–1800*. Cambridge, Mass. and London: Harvard University Press, 1999.

Moule, A. C., *Quinsai with Other Notes on Marco*

Polo. Cambridge: Cambridge University Press, 1957.

Mozai, Takao, 'Kublai Khan's Lost Fleet', *National Geographic*, Nov. 1982.

Needham, Joseph, *Science and Civilisation in China*, vols 5 and 7 on military technology.

Nelson, Janet, 'The Lord's Anointed and the People's Choice: Carolingian Royal Ritual', in Cannadine and Price, eds, *Rituals of Royalty*.

Okada, Hidehiro, 'China as a Successor State to the Mongol Empire', in Amitai-Preiss and Morgan, eds, *The Mongol Empire and Its Legacy*.

Olbricht, Peter, *Das Postwesen in China unter der Mongolenherrschaft im 13. und 14. Jahrhundert*. Wiesbaden: Harrassowitz, 1954.

Peers, C. J., *Medieval Chinese Armies, 1260–1520*. Oxford: Osprey, 1992.

Peers, Chris, *Imperial Chinese Armies (2), 590–1260*. London: Osprey, 1996.

Petech, Luciano, 'Tibetan Relations with Sung China and with the Mongols', in Morris Rossabi, ed., *China Among Equals: The Middle Kingdom and its Neighbours, 10th–14th Centuries*. Berkeley, Los Angeles and London: University of California Press, 1983.

Polo, Marco, *The Travels of Marco Polo: The Complete Yule–Cordier Edition*: Henry Yule's 3rd (1903) annotated translation, with Henri Cordier's notes. New York: Dover, 1993. This is the edition I used. Ronald Latham's edition (translated and introduced by himself), *Marco Polo: The Travels* (Penguin, 1958, still in print) is more accessible. For other editions, see the bibliography in Larner.

Rachewiltz, Igor de, *Papal Envoys to the Great Khans*. London: Faber, 1971.

Rachewiltz, Igor de, trans. and commentary, *The Secret History of the Mongols: A Mongolian Epic Chronicle of the 13th Century.* Leiden and Boston: Brill, 2004.

Rachewiltz, Igor de, et al., *In the Service of the Khan: Eminent Personalities of the Early Mongol–Yüan Era (1200–1300).* Wiesbaden: Harrassowitz, 1993.

Rashid ad-Din, *The Successors of Genghis Khan*, trans. John Andrew Boyle. New York: Columbia University Press, 1971.

Ratchnevsky, Paul, *Genghis Khan: His Life and Legacy*, trans. and ed. Thomas Haining. Oxford, UK, and Cambridge, Mass.: Blackwell, 1991 (several reprints).

Rossabi, Morris, *Khubilai Khan: His Life and Times.* Berkeley, Los Angeles and London: University of California Press, 1988.

Rossabi, Morris, *Voyager from Xanadu: Rabban Sauma and the First Journey from China to the West.* Tokyo, London and New York: Kodansha, 1992.

Rossabi, Morris, ed., *China Among Equals: The Middle Kingdom and its Neighbours, 10th–14th Centuries.* Berkeley, Los Angeles and London: University of California Press, 1983.

Rouleau, Father Francis, SJ, 'The Yangchow Latin Tombstone as a Landmark of Medieval Christianity', *Harvard Journal of Asiatic Studies*, vol. 17, nos 3–4 (Dec. 1954).

Sansom, Sir George, *A History of Japan to 1334.* Folkestone, Kent: Dawson, 1958, 1978.

SarDesai, D. R., *Southeast Asia, Past and Present.* London: Macmillan, 1989.

Saunders, J. J., *A History of Medieval Islam.* London and New York: Routledge, 1965 (many reprints).

Saunders, J. J., *The History of the Mongol Conquests*. Philadelphia: University of Pennsylvania, 1971.

Saunders, J. J., *Muslims and Mongols: Essays on Medieval Asia*. Christchurch, NZ: Whitcoulls, University of Canterbury, 1977.

Shih, Chung-wen, *Injustice to Tou O*. Cambridge: Cambridge University Press, 1972.

Shih, Chung-wen, *The Golden Age of Chinese Drama: Yüan Tsa-chü*. Princeton: Princeton University Press, 1976.

Smith, John Masson, 'Ayn Jalut: Mamluk Success or Mongol Failure?', *Harvard Journal of Asiatic Studies*, vol. 44, no. 2 (Dec. 1984).

Stark, Freya, *The Valleys of the Assassins*. London: John Murray, 1934.

Steinhardt, Nancy, *Chinese Imperial City Planning*. Honolulu: University of Hawaii Press, 1990.

Tarling, Nicholas, ed., *The Cambridge History of Southeast Asia*. Cambridge: Cambridge University Press, 1999.

Temple, Robert, *The Genius of China*, intr. Joseph Needham. London: Prion, 1999 (a good introduction to Needham's massive work).

Thorau, Peter, 'The Battle of Ayn Jalut: A Re-examination', in Peter Edbury, ed., *Crusade and Settlement*. Cardiff: Cardiff Press, 1985.

Toms, Ron, website: www. trebuchet.com.

Turnbull, Stephen, *Siege Weapons of the Far East (1), 612–1300* and *(2) 960–1644*. Oxford: Osprey, 2001–2.

Vemming, Peter, trebuchet website at http://www.middelaldercentret.dk. See also his latest reconstruction in http://www.warwicksiege.com.

Wang Jiawei and Nyima Gyaincain, *The Historical Status of China's Tibet*. Beijing: China Intercontinental Press, 1997.

Wang Shifu, *The Romance of the Western Bower*, adapted by Xang Xuejing. Beijing: New World Press, 2000.

Weatherford, Jack, *Genghis Khan and the Making of the Modern World*. New York: Crown, 2004. (Includes the empire and Kublai Khan as well as Genghis.)

Wood, Frances, *Did Marco Polo Go to China?*. London: Secker & Warburg, 1995.

Wylie, Turrell V., 'The First Mongol Conquest of Tibet Reinterpreted', *Harvard Journal of Asiatic Studies*, vol. 37, no. 1 (1977).

Yamada, Nabaka, *Ghenko: The Mongol Invasion of Japan*. London: Smith, Elder & Co., 1916.

Yanagida, Sumitaka, *The Mongolian Invasion and Hakata* (in Japanese). Hakata Town, 2001.

Zu An, ed., *Beihai Park*. Beijing: China Pictorial, 1989.

INDEX

THE GREAT WALL
John Man

The Great Wall is the most famous of China's monuments.
Everyone has seen pictures of the line of stone snaking over
mountains. Millions every year take the five mile journey
from Beijing to climb its battlements. But what do we
really know about the Great Wall?

Many myths surround the wall. Many believe it is the only
man-made structure visible from space. Not true: it cannot
even be seen from earth orbit. Estimates of its length vary
from 1,500 to 5,000 miles. Even its name is deceptive – it is
not an *it*, a single entity, but many walls (hence the uncertain
length), most of which are not of stone, but of earth. In history,
the closer you look the less you see a single Great Wall,
but rather a series of walls erected at different times
and for different reasons.

But what is undoubtedly true about the Great Wall is that it
is a product of the most fascinating, and far-reaching, Chinese
history. Some parts were built by different states and originally
joined together in the 3rd century BC, to counter the threat from
nomadic barbarians from the north – a threat that was to be a
dark shadow on China's borders for almost 2,000 years.

In this riveting history John Man travels the length of the Great
Wall and through over two thousand years of history.
This wonder of the world is the perfect way into the remarkable
history of China, taking us from the country's tribal past, through
the war with the Mongols, right up to the modern day when the
Great Wall will once more be a powerful emblem of China
for the Beijing Olympics in 2008.

9780593055748

COMING IN JULY FROM BANTAM PRESS

BANTAM PRESS

GENGHIS KHAN:
Life, Death and Resurrection
John Man

'ABSORBING AND BEAUTIFULLY WRITTEN . . .
A THRILLING ACCOUNT'
Guardian

Genghis Khan is one of history's immortals: a leader of genius and
the founder of he world's greatest land empire – twice the size of
Rome's. His mysterious death in 1227 placed all at risk, so it was
kept a secret until his heirs had secured his conquests. Secrecy has
surrounded him ever since. His undiscovered grave, with its
imagined treasures, remains the subject of intrigue and speculation.

Today, Genghis is by turns scourge, hero and demi-god. To Muslims,
Russians and Europeans, he is a mass-murderer. Yet in his homeland,
Mongols revere him as the nation's father; Chinese honour him as
dynastic founder; and in both countries, worshippers seek his blessing.

This book is more than just a gripping account of Genghis' rise and
conquests. John Man uses first-hand experiences to reveal the khan's
enduring influence. He is the first writer to explore the hidden valley
where Genghis may have died, and one of the few westerners to climb
the scared mountain where he was probably buried.

The result is an enthralling account of the man himself and of
the passions that surround him today. For in legend, ritual and
controversy, Genghis lives on . . .

'A FIRST-RATE TRAVEL BOOK, NOT SO MUCH A LIFE OF THE
KHAN BUT A SEARCH FOR HIM . . . A RATTLING GOOD READ'
Independent

'A FINE, WELL-WRITTEN AND WELL-RESEARCHED BOOK'
Mail on Sunday

'FASCINATING . . . HISTORY DOESN'T COME MUCH MORE
ENTHRALLING THAN THIS'
Yorkshire Evening Post

0 553 81498 2

BANTAM BOOKS

ATTILA THE HUN
And the Fall of Rome
John Man

'SUPERB, AS COMPELLINGLY READABLE AS IT IS IMPRESSIVE
IN ITS SCHOLARSHIP . . . THE HUNS AND THEIR KING LIVE
AS NEVER BEFORE'
Simon Sebag Montefiore

Attila the Hun is a household name – a byword for barbarism and
violence – but to most of us the man himself, his world and his
place in history have remained elusive. Until now.

For a crucial twenty years in the early 5th century AD, Attila held
the fate of the Roman Empire and the future of Europe in his hands.
In numerous raids and three major campaigns he and his warriors
earned an undying reputation for savagery, and his empire
briefly rivalled that of Rome, reaching from the Rhine to the
Black Sea, the Baltic to the Balkans.

Attila's power derived from his astonishing character. He may have
been capricious, arrogant and ruthless, but he was brilliant enough to
win the loyalty of millions: his own people thought him semi-divine
while educated Westerners were proud to serve him. From his
base in the grasslands of Hungary, this 'scourge of God' so
very nearly dictated Europe's future . . .

Drawing on his extensive travels in the barbarian heartland and
his experience with the nomadic traditions of Central Asia,
John Man's riveting biography reveals the man behind the
enduring myth of Attila the Hun.

'RACY AND IMAGINATIVE . . . SYMPATHETICALLY AND
READABLY PUTS FLESH AND BONES ON ONE OF HISTORY'S
MOST TURBULENT CHARACTERS'
Sunday Telegraph

'METEORIC AND MOMENTOUS . . . FASCINATING READING'
Guardian

0 553 81658 6

BANTAM BOOKS

A SELECTED LIST OF NON-FICTION TITLES
AVAILABLE FROM BANTAM BOOKS